Baltimore Review

2012

Poems, stories, and creative nonfiction from the Winter 2012 and Spring 2012 online issues
baltimorereview.org

Founding and Senior Editor
Barbara Westwood Diehl

Senior Editor
Kathleen Hellen

Editors
Elise Burke
Nate Haken
Heather Harris
Lalita Noronha
Michael Salcman
Sam Schmidt
Joanne Cavanaugh Simpson
Dean Bartoli Smith
Jennifer Holden Ward
Todd Whaley

Webmaster

Matt Diehl

Cover Photos: Martha Cooper
Artist: Overunder (from Reno, NV)

ISSN 1092-5716

© 2012 The Baltimore Review

Editor's Note

We are pleased to present the poems, stories, and creative nonfiction of the contributors to our first two online issues: Winter 2012, our first online issue, published in January 2012, and Spring 2012, published in May 2012. In the future, our annual print issues will include the work from all quarterly issues.

We hope that you will enjoy the array of voices in these pages. There is music in the language here. There are stories you will remember for a long time.

About *The Baltimore Review*: The journal was founded by Barbara Westwood Diehl in 1996 as a publication of the Baltimore Writers' Alliance, publishing poems and short stories. The journal later became an independent nonprofit organization in 2004. Susan Muaddi Darraj led the journal from 2003 to 2010, expanding contributions to include creative nonfiction and interviews. In 2011, Barbara Westwood Diehl resumed leadership of the journal and now serves as Senior Editor with Kathleen Hellen.

In 1996, we began with a mission to showcase the best writing from the Baltimore area and beyond. Our mission remains just that. In our online format, we can now bring that fine writing to a wider audience, and more frequently. We can also explore new ways to bring you the world of writing, writers, and the writing life.

We thank Susan for her years of service, and we thank the many editors who have devoted time and energy to the journal over the years since that first issue. We are also thankful for the editors who have joined us for this new phase of the journal's life.

We also note the passing of two editors who worked with us for many years, Dick Green and Lynn Buck. Dick and Lynn reviewed countless paper stacks of stories and poems in the days before electronic submission systems, with great wit and wisdom. They were dear friends, and they are missed.

To our contributors, our editors, the Baltimore literary community, and the network of writers throughout the world—thank you for your vision.

Contact us at editor@baltimorereview.org

Contents

Winter 2012 Issue

Poems

James Walser	*Names for the Skies*	1
Edgar Silex	*Vision*	2
W. Todd Kaneko	*Reading Comprehension 12: The Crane Wife*	4
	Reading Comprehension 30: Peach Boy	5
Ned Balbo	*Dark Horse*	6
David Dodd Lee	*Replacement Parts for the Soul*	7
Angela Narciso Torres	*Waiting for My Father at the University Hospital Lab*	8
Paul Hostovsky	*Clutch Steal*	10
Tim Kahl	*Um Real*	12
Al Maginnes	*Against Relapse*	14
Dorianne Laux	*How long did I stand in the house of this body and stare at the road? – Mirabai*	16
	Letters in a Box	17

Stories

Catherine Parnell	*Morendo*	19
Gregory Wolos	*An Evening with Willie Freeze*	29
Josh Green	*Missing Athena*	41
Christopher Lowe	*Reform, Alabama*	55
Peter Kispert	*Hunting Season*	63
Nathan Gower	*Digging the Hole*	64
Ryan Millbern	*In a Room Made Up for Someone Else*	66
Wendy Oleson	*Man Skate*	76
Devin Murphy	*The Butterfly Man*	83
Ajay Vishwanathan	*Little Hands of Silk*	93
Catherine Thomas	*There Are Rules, Secret Little Rules*	104

Creative Nonfiction

Bram Takefman	*The American House*	119
Lockie Hunter	*The Witness of High Hats*	125
Colin Rafferty	*Digging In*	128
Stephen J. West	*The Drive from Morgantown to Baltimore*	131
Michelle Valois	*Human Resources*	133
Seth Sawyers	*Lettuce and Rabbits*	135

Contest

Emily Roller	*Improvement*	137
Jen Murvin Edwards	*Come In, Come In*	139
Heather Martin	*On Maimeó*	144
Linda Barnhart	*The New Victorians*	147

Spring 2012 Issue

Poems

Maureen Alsop and Josh Gottlieb-Miller	*IGP9448-1*	163
Jo Marie Darden-Obi	*Crème de Kathleen*	164
	Curtis	166
Mary Morris	*A Love Supreme*	168
Christina Cook	*Homing*	169
Steven Pelcman	*Between the Lost and the Forgotten*	170
Shira Hereld	*Six Months*	171
Harry Bauld	*Persimmons*	173
	On the Train After Leaving	174
Shiah IrgangLaden	*A Cold Migration*	175
Brandon Hartley	*The Day Before the End of the World*	176
Andrew Purcell	*Descent*	177
	Male Bonding	178
E.M. Schorb	*Death Row*	179

Stories

Luke Rolfes	*Straw Man*	181
Marc Hudson	*Habitable Space*	194
Michael Kimball	*There Isn't Anyone Expecting Me Here Tomorrow*	207
Jen Michalski	*God's Creatures*	215

Creative Nonfiction

Beth Lefebvre	*An Unwitting Accomplice*	219
Angela Morales	*Gunslinging*	227
William Arthur Delaney	*Rigor Mortis*	232

Contributors   235

Winter 2012

Names for the Skies

John Walser

Like my mother can say *Sweet Cicely, Doll's Eyes*
Sleepy Catchfly, Jack in the Pulpit
speaking in the pagan tongues of flowers.

What should I call the punch through blue
the honey pebbles of starting rain
the trajectory of crow caws
as they rush up dusk's grey ramps?

What can capture the agate morning horizon steps
the geode flaws in its soft shoulder
the celluloid flush of pigeon wings taking off
the coulter till of root and rot?

In an acorn squash light, a lethargy of moths
what single word, what single phrase
what this or that
what *Fireweed*, what *Quaker Ladies*
what *Wild Sweet William*
marks the purl of lint clouds disintegrating overhead?

Vision

Edgar Silex

I once helped build the eyes that watch the world
eyes that see through heaven's clouds
eyes that see you wandering in the dark
that watch you sleeping behind your walls
or wherever you may try to hide
I wrote the telemetric language of their sight
that gives them their intelligence
and I calculated all the costs of harnessing those eyes
to keep them focused on their tasks
through cold and dark their lives dependent on the sun
that shines upon the universe like an unblinking gaze
and though they mostly see the evil
and the tragedy befalling man and Earth
they also search the galaxies for distant promises
the earth for the riches to be found by mining deep within
for treasures that enrich the few
those eyes lock upon the eyes of storms
that sweep away those who cannot stand
against indifferent force and in the offices of life
in windowless and soundproof rooms
I tested those eyes against my own suspicious pair
sine-ing and cosine-ing equating and equivocating
and what I witnessed through those eyes
turned me against the god man envisions in himself
that gives him his belief that he can see through dark
see under the clouds under the earth
see into the distant origin of man and Earth
with eyes that really do not see that far at all

that turns the viewer into a savage god
who grows suffering into agony
who makes an industry of desperation
and sees only unclaimed dominions
and not the blue monastery the mother or the cradle
nor the emptiness abounding
and the only promise that I saw through those eyes
I once helped build to watch the world
was the promise of man's blindness

Reading Comprehension 12: The Crane Wife
_____

W. Todd Kaneko

It's never too early to remember she is gone, like that morning the fisherman must cook breakfast for himself—a sliver of eel on a nest of rice. He will wish his plate held something more elegant, like geese cloaked in the rushes or a house full of clean air for clean people. He spent the previous day on the river, casting his net alongside other men in search of fat trout or ingots of gold—something to remind him of how he once lived. He does not remember eyeing seagulls circling overhead, their selfish cries piercing the air like jagged beaks through placid waters. He does not remember the previous week, that loom covered in silk and feathers taunting him until he pitched it into the marsh to be consumed by cattails. It's never too late for old romance, for absent-minded men to capture earthbound birds longing for migration. He will not remember that exchange of talons for sewing needles, that sacrifice of flight for a threadbare mattress. He will pack his suitcase full of filament and bait. He will move to a new village in search of a house where he can forget about thunderstorms, broken wings, and that mysterious young woman with beautiful hands.

Question: What doesn't this fisherman remember?

a) There are no such things as feathers, only desire for nests.
b) A windowless room is no substitute for the sky.
c) There is no such thing as home.

Reading Comprehension 30: Peach Boy

W. Todd Kaneko

Every entrance is an exit, but when that woman discovers an infant in a strange piece of fruit, she does not wonder if there is a rumpled bit of blanket left in a distant crib, a hollow throat that chokes when a bough once laden with blossoms is reduced to kindling. Every exit is a spark, so when a magical boy strikes out to retrieve rubies hidden in faraway lands, his mother will smolder for years in the peach groves. He might wage war on witches and ogres, gather their babies and pitch them all into a bonfire. He might challenge the atom bomb to a contest of illumination. Every spark is a hope for flame, so when that boy fails to return home, the orchards will be bursting with new creatures: burned monkeys, wingless pheasants, dogs who sing sad songs in hoarse voices. Explain to that woman how her children are a bestiary for someone else's story, how mooncalves emerge squirming in edible places. Hope is a stone forsaken by long-extinct flora—it lies heavy in the palm like moonlight, delicate like an infant's skull. Watch her plant it in dry soil and linger to see what might sprout.

Question: What is a stone?

a) A jewel for the blind.
b) A pomegranate full of healthy animals.
c) A tiny shrine for the abandoned.
d) Nothing.

Dark Horse

Ned Balbo

This moonlit night we've come upon a horse—
his equine profile looms above barbed wire,
so close we might have touched him accidentally
as we pass along this country road
on foot, our flashlights small moons flicking off.
We don't want to startle him: he's still,
and we can't see his eyes—is he asleep,
awake and watching us, or in the grip
of dread? He might be dangerous at night.
By day, he's chestnut-brown, but now, he's shadow,
eyes invisible, mane moonlight-tinged,
the hills behind him dim, vertiginous
with all the history his kind have known
entwined with ours, each day and every darkness.

Replacement Parts for the Soul

David Dodd Lee

It wasn't that late: cattle stampeding in the
water of the mirror, the lower half's reflection of sunset,

the moon a U magnet, trees sinking under the
swamp grasses, an audience of two, one large knuckle along the

ridge of the spine, the loosening of plates
and bolts and braces . . . The framed glass made

a sort of white noise as each steel piece
emerged from the mud—slender rods, shields with

rivets, whole bone replacements—while on the wide
bed hidden deep in one corner of the indoor river her nipples

floated pinkly on the dark absorbent water, the smell of
crushed lilies on her thighs. I like it when I have cuts

on both arms, like the sun sinking down into blood,
the hands together, the stinging all the way there, the heartbeat a window.

Waiting for My Father at the University Hospital Lab

Angela Narciso Torres

On his desk, coiled against a fragment
of uterine wall, the fetus floated
in a mason jar, pale thumb raised
to its voiceless straw of neck.
Shaken from moth-balled sleep,
my father's lab coat—starched, pressed,
lily-white—sloped across his shoulders
behind the Underwood. A blank
sheet waited for letters to pound
through carbon: malignant, benign,
malignant, malignant, benign.

Pipette-thin, barely nine,
I crossed the doorway. No sound
but the shuffle of patent shoes on tile.
Clicking against the microscope,
his ice-cube lenses magnified
that other universe—berry-stained

cells congealed into rocks, ringlets,
ferns unfurled, moon craters.
Curled amidst books and paper,
I became infinitesimal, a tight fist
of fire and constellations, no larger
than a dust mote on the camera lens

he polished with a scrap of chamois
before peering into the deep
rivers of a heart pinned open.

Clutch Steal

Paul Hostovsky

"This John Havlicek, he is Czech,"
says my father who is Czech
and doesn't speak English all that well
and doesn't know what a lay-up is, or a free-throw,
or a pick. We are sitting on the paisley couch,
watching the Celtics play the 76ers. It's 1965.
I hate to tell him, I tell him
as I steal the bag of potato chips from him,
but John Havlicek isn't Czech.
He's from Ohio. Born and raised. My father
was visiting someone in Belgium
when the Nazis invaded Czechoslovakia—
someone who set a pick for him, someone
who saw it all coming—and he escaped
to Paris, then to Lisbon, then to Oslo,
then to New York. Always one step ahead.
He was lucky. He was more than lucky.
He was—what's the word in English?—
charmed. And he lived. He lived, unlike his own
father, and mother, and brothers and sisters—his entire
team. All lost by the time that nightmare
was over. Twenty years later, he's sitting with me
on a paisley couch in a house in New Jersey,
watching the Celtics play the 76ers,
the announcer's impossible English sprinkled
with Havliceks: "Havlicek for two." "Havlicek

from the corner." "Havlicek under the boards."
And then John Havlicek steals the ball—
a clutch steal in the closing seconds of that game,
clinching the Eastern Conference Championship
and immortalizing Havlicek forever. My father
steals the potato chips back, and says, "I am
liking this John Havlicek. He is maybe
from Ohio. But he is Czech. And he is charmed."

Um Real

Tim Kahl

When money stands still, it is no longer money
    - Georg Simmel

Stranger, you flutter on the face of this bill,
hummingbird from the high mind of the Banco Central,
whose opinion is a force of nature.
It produces the buzzing praças and the percentage
that prompts a currency trader's leap of faith.
It cycles through the opportunity fields.
Its pulse is taken by the surgeon at the faults,
where the seismic patterns make
everyone panic to stay ahead of the wave.
When you stand still, you become unreal,
the mystery play of a well-traveled
professional, a secret stranger.
Stranger, you inspire the unwilling and
the unable. You are the necessary atom.
When I first saw your face, your tiny wings
beating at a stock ticker's pace,
I could sense you were bringing something
new with you, something beautiful and
invisible. All my life I have heard the thrum
but couldn't imagine how you moved,
how you might enter my life and my religion
of the solid return. The roar of trade is rude,
and you never stay long enough for me

to hear the tales of your voyages, off to add
another eighth note to the foreign chatter.
You vibrate and hum and interrupt,
but, stranger, you can't buy silence anymore.

Against Relapse

Al Maginnes

Drunk at ten in the morning, said
    the man at the table behind us,
as though it was something unusual,
    as though he had never swayed
at the starting gate of an aching new day,
    seeing only chalky gray flat
before him, his blood too weighted
    to move and tasting the need
to light it up or shut it down.
    It's clear he never thought it was
a good idea to dance in the office
    of his ex-wife's lawyer or to sing
"Blue Moon of Kentucky" on a bus
    filled with people going to work
and busy with cell phones, briefcases
    and coffee cups. He has forgotten
he could have been me or anyone
    thirsty and confused enough
to need the day's possibilities reduced
    to one. Some afternoons I play
hide and seek with my daughter
    in an old graveyard or inside
the labyrinth of a used book store,
    hoping she will find as I have
a love for quiet places. But I don't
    want her to go for days
as I did speaking to no one
    but bored store clerks who wanted me

to shut up and take my vodka
    home to its orange juice, the blinds
already pulled on the day.
    Yesterday, driving to work after
dropping her at school, I saw
    two men I might have been,
one falling in slow motion,
    the other bending to help him up,
the pathway treacherous, the day
    narrow and endless before them.

How long did I stand in the house of this body and stare at the road? – Mirabai

---

Dorianne Laux

How long did that turbulent week last, those
seven star-strung nights I stood under the Pleiades
in winter, season of my birth, my body young yet,
still a flock of gulls, the ocean at my feet,
froth on fire with green luminescent creatures.
I had no mirrors then, and so could not see
my own lit beauty, the tiny lanterns of my cells
swarming like bees. Even the gristle in me burned
hydrogen bright, golden as I was, every window of me
open, every door. I've watched the road and waited
as the hours passed, as the wallpaper curled
and slipped from the plaster and the furniture
settled in the dust, the dresses in my closet
unlaced by white moths. Now I see her
as my sister who will not come back, her face
a clock inside a box, the lid nailed shut.
All that shapely radiance hidden inside
the softly receding years. Though sometimes
remnants of her reappear in candlelight,
in firelight, smolder behind a wing of gray
uncombed hair fallen over one blue eye.

Letters in a box

Dorianne Laux

Your letters are packed
in an anonymous brown box,
the blurred pictures we took
not suspecting you were, even then,
becoming a ghost.
Our love was massive, a continent
set like a table on the backs
of four elephants. We lived there foolishly,
squandering the days we didn't know
were scarce, standing on the wooden bridge,
already the hook in your collar, soon to be
hoisted up, already the bulbs
buried in your chest that would bloom
like the lilies on your grave. Our days
were standard: a phone call,
a hurried kiss, a netted bag of oranges
that burst, the bruised globes rolling
between our bare feet.
We didn't know to ask the favor
of mercy, a few more
unmarshalled mornings
to wake to the sounds of construction,
nails and hammers, drills and saws,
the neighbor's dog and his abandoned bark.
Commonplace. Would we have touched
one another differently? Said anything other
than what we whispered into
each other's mouths, our lips

closing over the words, intercepting
our voices: yours, that has all these years
been silent, and mine still trapped
in the cage of your body that floats
ungirdled, beneath the earth.

Morendo

Catherine Parnell

My fifty-year old brother collects money from people who park their cars in chain-linked cement lots scattered around a neon city in a dry desert. Las Vegas, city of sin, where they once used camels as pack animals. My brother Jonnie looks like a camel—jowly, droopy, saggy and dusty. He's got a hump, too. You can't see the hump; it's an invisible burden. I know it's there because I have one too. It's so heavy I should be crawling on my knees. One of these days I'll unpack it, lighten my load, surprise my hard backbone with release. Jonnie—his hump is permanent. Not a thing in the world can change that.

I remember when Jonnie was a blond, blue-eyed boy. Not a freckle on his sad white skin. He walked like he'd been shackled, arms longer than his torso so he shuffled around with his hands shoved under his armpits. When his hands weren't stuck there, they were in his mouth. An entire fist. As he grew older he learned to suck one finger at a time, very methodically, until each finger and both thumbs were shredded and bloody. He wore a bright red baseball hat, each year a new one, until his head got too big for any hat at all.

In the parking lot booth in Las Vegas, his fingers shake when he takes the dollar bills and he never looks anyone in the eye. He pulls his hair out so he looks like he has mange. His teeth are all cracked and broken because, since he can't afford cigarettes, he sucks on nails he steals from construction sites. Sometime he forgets and chews the screw-shanks, as if by eating steel he'll become Superman, his hero.

How do I know this? I go out West once or twice a year to visit, but Jonnie and I don't talk much. I just watch. If I could say something it might be, *We aren't so different.*

I can't risk it though. Jonnie'd just call me names. *Daddy's Girl. Little Apple. Gwen the Wren.* Dad wanted to name me Roxanne, but my mother said absolutely not. My father said in my next life I was sure to come back as Roxie, he could just see it. Not like your brother, he'd say. He'll come back as a potted plant.

When we were kids, our father beat Jonnie for getting bad grades. He stuck my brother's head in the toilet when he didn't make the softball team. He threw him against the garage wall for bringing home a stray dog, which my father shot with his service revolver. *Rabies*, he said.

My mother said my brother cried so much as a baby she wanted to give him to the postman, that each day when the mail came she hid in the shower until she was sure the postman had gone to the next house.

What was I like as a baby? I asked.

Adorable, she said. *Perfect.*

~

Hood rats. That's what they are, those girls who cluster around cars in parking lots. Midnight blue. Asphalt black. Slick butterscotch. Anything but white. Anything but good. They claim bad. They want bad. They want boys bad and they get bad boys. And that's the way they like it. That's what they say. *I fucked your friend and I'll fuck you, too.* Unzip those flies. Lift those crotch-cut skirts. Rip off the hoodies. Peel away the skinny cotton shirts. Get greasy. Because hood rats, they don't like clean. They want you to know where they've been.

My brother let them into the lot, even though I told him not to. He thought the hood rats were his friends. Jasmine, T-Cola, Zara, Angelique, Brittany and G'less. *Big Daddy got big money?* They rapped on the booth, danced around the cars to a scritch-scratch song. G'less bent down, lured my brother out of the booth. *Big Daddy come out and play?*

Hood rat attack. They beat my brother, left him for dead, took the cash from the till.

Now all his teeth are gone.

~

In the University Medical Center in Las Vegas (now Jonnie and I have both been to *university*) my brother meets a guy who tells him life is good in the mountains in California. Things grow there. They can grow things. *What things?* I ask.

Jonnie doesn't know. He says they will be farmers. He and Tony will grow things, and Jonnie will sell them at the market.

Jonnie, I say as I cradle the phone. *This doesn't sound good.*

I can take care of myself, he says, but we both know he's lying. He's on the other side of the country, and I hear the sound of a door slamming in his voice.

I have a kid, I say. *I've learned a few things. Like how not to get suckered.*

Tony's my friend, he says, as if to say I am not. I ask Jonnie why he called me.

The hospital social worker made me, he replies. *I told her you wouldn't care, but she looked you up on the Internet and everything.*

God bless cyberspace. I wonder what the social worker found – my faculty page or my Facebook page.

Let me talk to her, I say.

She tells me she can't discuss my brother's case without his permission.

Fuck you, I mutter. *He's right there. You want it signed in blood?* What I leave unsaid: Then why are you dragging me into this now? To make me feel bad? OK, I feel bad. Now what?

I'm afraid I can't help you, she says. *Talk to your brother. Get his permission.*

I'm on it, I say. But Jonnie hangs up. I am guilty, guilty, guilty. I have betrayed my brother; I have not walked through the valley of the shadows beside him. Throw me down the ravine where the animals will pick me clean. Maybe I will blow my brains out. They have not served me well.

But I resist this urge because I know that some people are born homeless, and that is a fact. I cannot change this. What difference does one person make? I have witnessed too much and been blind-sided by my mother, who, the night before she died, said: *You? I don't worry about you. I know you'll take care of Jonnie.*

Now how am I supposed to do that? I asked.

You'll know what to do, she said. *God gave you strength. Use it.*

I shake my head at the thought of this, her misplaced faith. She might have worried about me. Just a little bit, because I am just as lost as Jonnie, but I have money. A wedge of green.

~

The year after the hood rat attack shoots by like a rubber band and snaps in my face. A year lost to time. No word from Jonnie for three-hundred and sixty-five days. I do not know if this is a good thing or a bad thing. In the end, I will find it was a bad thing. But with Jonnie a good thing and a bad thing are the same thing.

After, after, after. After exactly what? Using the strength my mother thought I had, which is not so strong anymore, I bridge time and space. After the fact (I am big on facts), I piece things together. I start from the corner edge and work in. Don't look for four corners, I tell myself. Nothing squares where Jonnie goes.

During the forever-gone year Jonnie and his new friend head to an old campsite in northern California. Police warn hikers to steer clear of it. The homeless gather there in the spring, rob lost trailblazers. Sometimes a group raids a nearby campsite; they come back with cans of food and bags of chips. Once Jonnie and Tony tried to bring back a bottle of vodka but they drank it all and spent the night next to a stream.

Tony hates Mexicans. He tells my brother he killed a Mexican and took his pickup. *Like who's going notice one dead Mexican*, Tony says. Later, much later, too much later, when my brother tells me this I ask him, *Who would notice one dead homeless guy?*

You would, he says. *Wouldn't you?*

My brother, my other half, the half that hit the road not taken, and hit it hard. What a road. He stopped for incarceration, yielded to false affection, threw himself under the bus I was on. I sent him money when he popped up. I tracked him down when I could, when he called. Sometimes years went by and I didn't hear from him. Just when I began to wonder where he'd been buried, just when I made a little alter out of what I saved from his childhood—a gray Matchbox Chevy, a pale blue rattle with a yellow duck on it—Jonnie appeared as if summoned by genies. Or maybe my mother shoved him back onto my road. She can do things from the grave she could never do in life.

So, it is on day three-hundred and sixty-six, a day after the anniversary of the hood rat attack, that a postcard arrives from California. A redwood. Petrified. On the back, in beautiful cursive, my brother has written, *I like farming*.

Jonnie's back on my radar. My feet hurt from his trudging, but I can't be sure it isn't my imagination – or my job. On my feet all day teaching. On my ass all night, hunched over my laptop, spilling my guts to cyberspace.

Two months later, another postcard arrives. *We're growing things*.

That fall, my brother harvests the crops with Tony, who sends him seven miles down the mountain to meet a guy who will buy the stuff. Like a mule, my brother goes. He's standing in front of the general store when he passes out from dehydration and malnourishment. He falls so hard he breaks his cheekbone and five fingers. The crop? Jonnie can't remember what happened to it. For five days or maybe it was only one he wanders around town begging, a bone sticking out at the first knuckle, his cuts suppurating. The local sheriff picks him up, dumps him in the hospital. By then Jonnie is hallucinating about Tony and guns and killing. *I'm dead*, he wails. *He's going to kill me*.

Tony is the least of his problems. Jonnie's liver is failing.

Like a bird I will fly cross-country to see my brother.

~

Twenty years ago.

Our parents are dead, long dead, and Jonnie finds me. I'm in the phone book, and Jonnie can read. He knows I'd never leave Boston, even though I don't want to run into people who used to know us. I hide in my new life—wife, mom, teacher. I look for kids like Jonnie and I find them all over the place. I teach them. It's penance. It's not enough.

In the three days Jonnie has lived with my family he has been good. He showers every day and brushes his teeth, even scratches at the scum on his tongue with the bristles of the brush. I buy him deodorant, but he uses the entire can the first day. I discover he has not sprayed his body; he has sprayed his clothes.

We buy new clothes.

The second day I find him in the kitchen. He has opened every box and can, looking for something that tastes good.

I pour milk over cereal and he eats. He watches my daughter smear oatmeal and strawberries over her face with her little spoon, and he does the same.

They laugh.

This might work, I think. My husband stands behind Zoe, kissing the top of her head. Jonnie's eyes go bone mad and black. He will steal love by destroying the loved, but I am trying to believe he is better than the boy who ground my forehead in driveway gravel, the boy who stuck a steak knife in my shoulder by mistake. He was aiming for my heart.

The third day we go to the zoo. I let Jonnie push Zoe's stroller. The monkeys on hot rocks, dipping their paws into cool water. The impossibly graceful giraffes. The putty-dusted elephants. We stop at the lion's den. *Roar!* I say to Zoe as I lick her mother of pearl ear. She laughs.

Jonnie lifts Zoe out of the stroller and holds her over the pit. A lazy lioness looks up, ears flicking. Fresh meat.

Never scream around Jonnie. It makes him really mad.

Jonnie, I say. *Let's get ice cream. Your favorite, ok?*

Ice cream? he replies. *Can I have chocolate?*

Only if you let me hold Zoe.

Who wants your stupid baby anyway? He turns around, hands her to a complete stranger, who hands her to my husband. And Jonnie clomps like a horse (*Neigh! Neigh!*) to the ice cream cart.

You promised chocolate, he yells, because it's ok for him to yell. I buy two scoops on a waffle cone for him. Jonnie doesn't like it when people break promises.

That night I read bunny stories to Zoe while Jonnie stands under the window, blowing cigarette smoke through the screen. *Good Night, Zoe,* I say, and I kiss the tip of her nose. When her long lashes flicker and she sleeps, I go to Jonnie.

That's one bratty girl, he says. *Someone should hit her.* He grabs my arm and grinds his hot cigarette into my wrist. I don't flinch.

Jonnie, I say. *It's wrong to hurt people.*

He shakes. *You're going to send me away.* The burn on my wrist blisters. *The fat parrot at the zoo said you would.*

Jonnie talks to birds and they talk back. And why wouldn't they? He's one of them. Hollow bones and beady eyes, his talons gripping an electric wire, watching the world below. He tugs my hair, not hard, but hard enough. *Talk like a parrot*, he says.

Gwennie loves Jonnie, I say. He grins. I grin. It's like the day when he let me have a lick from his ice cream cone. We're related.

The next day I pack his bags and my husband walks him to the car. We drive him to the nearest psych ward where he spends ten days. After that he disappears, long enough for me to understand that Jonnie and I will always be playing hide n'seek. Which is why I try so hard now. *All-y all-y in come free.* I do not like California, I do not want to go to California, but that's not the point. Jonnie is the point.

Perhaps this effort will make my mother happy. Then again, she's dead, so how will I ever know?

~

My husband thinks he's clever when he says my father liked to beat women, small children and dogs. I let my husband think what he wants, but I don't think my father liked it at all. My father had a plan and then woke up on the breaking wheel. Poor guy. I know how he felt; I understand the necessity of hurting someone before they hurt you. That was my father's gift. And my mother, what did she leave? The lesson that it was better to absorb the hurt than pass it on. It worked for her, until it didn't.

So when Zoe asks me about my parents I tell her my mother was a saint and my father was a sinner. It's a parable, I say. She looks at me with disgust, the sort of angry incomprehension best suited to twenty-year olds, and asks, *Did they even love each other?*

As a matter of fact, I say, *they did. They had a hot relationship.* That shuts Zoe up. Sex talk is off limits.

But Zoe's not finished with me. Her inch-long red hair sticks straight up like bloody needles, and she scuffs the hardwood kitchen floor with her biker boot. *Can I come to California with you? I want to meet your brother.*

This is a new request. It's not like asking for the salt and pepper, or maybe it is. Zoe has grown up without relatives. They are all dead except Jonnie, and Zoe has been about as interested in him as she is in hand-painted china.

My daughter doesn't know Jonnie tried to feed her to the lions when she was a baby. When I tell her she clicks her tongue stud against her teeth. I see that years of dental work have paid off. *Awesome,* she says.

Jonnie's not like other people, I say.

You're not like other people, she says. She even grins a little bit. And it's that grin, that sweet little smirk, that rips me to pieces. She looks just like Jonnie in red. So I ask, *You really want to meet him?*

Yes, she says slowly. *He's my uncle.*

I never thought about it that way.

~

I'm thinking about uncles (Uncle Wiggily comes to mind) as I walk down the hospital corridor to Jonnie's room. I'm alone because I'm alone. Zoe hates flying, so she backed out. She says she'll ride her 2010 Ducati Multistrada 1200 S Sport to California. *A hog.* I guess we're all on the road now.

Hospitals in California seem so much cheerier than hospitals in Boston. It must be all that sun. I stop at the nurse's station and introduce myself, and the nurse looks at me as if I rip wings off flies. I want to explain, but what's the point? She's wearing pink scrubs. In my experience, people who wear pink are bleeding hearts, which is why I wear black and blue. Life is one long jazz riff, or maybe it's punk cabaret. I count up the times I've been truly happy. I don't run out of fingers.

I poke my head in Jonnie's room. *Hey,* I say. *I brought ice cream.*

He lifts his head and smiles. He's got teeth—how did that happen? Angry red patches like Rorschach blots dot his bald head. His rickety arms reach out for the carton of Ben & Jerry's. *Chocolate?* he asks.

You bet, I say.

You bet, he sings. *You better watch out. I'm really sick and I might give it to you.*

I hand him the ice cream and a spoon. Just as he's about to dig in, he looks out the window. *I've been talking to the birds*, he says.

And?

They said if you don't take me then Dad will.

Dad's dead.

That's what he wants us to think. Jonnie narrows his eyes and throws the ice cream at the window. The nurse comes in and gives him a shot, while I clean up the ice cream. I dump the mess in a kidney-shaped bedpan. When I sit down in the chair next to his bed, he stares at me. He looks like an eighty-year old man, folded badly into his flesh. His eyes are so sunken you could float a toy boat in his sockets. And then his eyes close.

I lean over and kiss his sallow cheek. He stinks. His eyes flutter and he reaches for my neck. I let him close his hand around my throat, but the medication kicks in and his hand drops hard against the bed's metal rail.

Maybe he'll die in his sleep.

A day later he does.

So Zoe will never meet her uncle, unless you count her walk-on as lion bait. She will never know what she missed unless I tell her.

And I won't because there's nothing to say.

~

But the strange thing is I do miss him. Not the him he became, but the him he should have been. He is the shadow that's fallen across my heart, my stomach, my lungs, my colon. Collectively, they go on strike, leaving me gasping, ticking, and leaking everywhere. My gauges are off. I drive down familiar roads, but I don't know if I should turn left or right.

Statues spring to life and jump in front of me, and I slam on the brakes. All the houses look like the house we grew up in. School buses are full of us.

Sorrow is absurdly common.

I go to the attic, rummage around for our tenderly composed baby books. I open six boxes before I find what I am looking for, and even then I have to dig through a pile of kitchen towels, my brown and white Steiff doggie, Jonnie's sucked-on twisted Teddy Bear, a stack of report cards, art projects smashed beyond recognition, and an old glass baby bottle. And then, the baby books: *I'm a Girl! I'm a Boy!* I consider this: the hours our mother spent on them, the effort she made to chronicle our little lives. Well then, let the story be told.

I open *I'm a Girl!* You can take a lot of pictures in five years. So, yes, I am five years older than my dead brother. I look at one page at a time. Just look. There I am with my dolls. My hair is tied up in pigtails with striped ribbons at the ends. That's me holding a kiddie stethoscope to my chest. I'm wearing one of my dad's long-sleeve white shirts. In another photo I'm sitting in the tub, my hair styled in a soapy topknot. And there I am rocking an empty cradle while my obviously pregnant mother looks on. My starched and frilly dress sticks up in the air as I bend over the cradle, which has a duck on the small headboard.

Here is what I never told Jonnie. I asked for a brother.

Here is something else I never told my brother, and that's what my father, his fist in the air, said to me: *You asked for it.*

From outside I hear the shriek of a bluejay.

I lick my index finger and touch the upper right-hand corner of another page in the scrapbook, which is, all of a sudden, so heavy I struggle to hold it. The whorled, wet tip of my finger leaves a spot on the paper.

If I don't turn the page I will never come to the part where my brother is born.

An Evening with Willie Freeze

Gregory Wolos

The Cubmaster introduces our guest speaker as George White Eagle. I don't recognize the name, but his face is familiar—it's a twist of rawhide, eyes hooded to a slit under bruise-purple lids. You'd think they were shut completely, except a gleam sneaks out now and then that reminds me of the husky dog we had when I was a kid. Wolfy slept with his eyes half open, and the dead look in them made me shiver, like he was watching us from some evil world. George White Eagle's black hair is tugged back into an inch of ponytail. New blue jeans cinch his waist, and his flannel shirt, rolled up at the sleeves, bags at the chest because he hunches.

"Mr. White Eagle is going to tell us some Indian lore and play his flute for us," the Cubmaster says. His face is ham red, as if his yellow neckerchief is too tight. "So let's quiet down, kids, okay?"

The scouts are sugared up on soda pop and cupcakes, unconcerned about whatever is happening on stage. They shout and bang folding chairs and play keep away with stolen caps or sneakers. The Cubmaster raises his hand and calls, "Akela." A ten count passes, and he repeats: "Akela!" The kids sag to the tiled floor in front of the cafeteria stage as if their bones have dissolved. Danny and I have been sitting for five minutes—sugar is not part of my nephew's diet. He rocks slowly, careful to stay on a black tile. He's fixed his attention on a heel mark on the white tile in front of him. The other kids keep their distance. Danny attends this school too, but he's in special classes. He doesn't meet eyes.

With all the kids and dads on the floor, the Cubmaster leads a recitation of their oath. Only Danny and I and Mr. White Eagle abstain.

The cub scout follows Akela.
The cub scout helps the pack go.
The pack helps the cub scout grow.
The cub scout gives good will.

After the oath, the chattering starts again. The adults don't help—two dads near me discuss creosote buildup in chimneys while one of their boys, his cheeks smudgy with chocolate, chokes his freckled pal.

My sister Tara thinks scouting is a good idea for her son. Her boss at the Walmart made it all the way to Eagle. As I see it, Danny will never be management material. Tara calls his autism "mild Asperger's." He's not a head banger yet—Tara doesn't need to hide his red curls under a helmet—but doctors warn that it's a possibility down the road.

Often at pack meetings a father will sidle over during refreshments, usually dragging his son, who'll be smirking around at his friends. As Danny presses against me, swaying to his own rhythm, the dad will say, "How's the boy—how ya doin', son?" Danny won't answer. Maybe he rocks harder. Maybe he makes a keening sound. To fill the awkward moment, I ask my default question: "So who's this Akela, anyway?" The dad will smile without answering. "We'll see you later," he'll nod, and shift away, while his son zips off like a released fish.

Tonight, I touch my nephew's shoulder, and he flinches. I think I hear him humming, and I slide my hand from his shoulder to his back, but I don't feel the purr I expect— only the ridge of his spine and the ladder of his ribs. The sound comes from the stage: Mr. White Eagle is chanting. The hubbub in the room subsides until everyone except my sister's son is staring at Mr. White Eagle.

"Respect," he whispers. His purple lids are squeezed shut, as if we're something he doesn't want to see. "My people use a special, holy word: *Blah-dee-blah.*" The syllables melt together. "It is a tradition that passes from fathers to sons. Say it with me: *Blah-dee-blah.*" We try. We watch each other's lips. "*Blah-dee-blah*" Mr. White Eagle repeats, and we catch on. "*Blah-dee-blah.*" Our chorus echoes through us, as if we're in church. Danny's mouth is shut, and he's still staring at the heel mark.

"It is with respect we treat our elders, our parents, our guests, each other," Mr. White Eagle says. The Cubmaster bows. These are the values we hope to instill in our boys. Several dads nod, too. I'm still trying to figure out where I know George White Eagle from.

Respect hasn't been part of the formula with a lot of our Pack's guests: the young veteran of the Iraq war lost the kids to giggle fits when he couldn't keep from swearing and quit his speech in the middle; the professional football player who'd never made it off the Oakland Raiders taxi squad only took questions. He said "yes" or "no" to a few, then stationed himself at a table where he signed autographs for two dollars each. After twenty minutes he stood and asked, "Who do I see about my fifty dollars?"

But Mr. White Eagle commands the kids' attention. He blows three long, sad notes into his wooden flute. We hear wide open plains and forests full of wildlife. "These are mourning songs," Mr. White Eagle tells us. "Songs of loss. Songs of death. Loss is part of the great circle of life, boys. Life begins with creation. Sex is creation. The mating of creatures. Of your mother and father. We have respect for sex—*Blah-de-Blah.*" Our "*Blah-de-Blah*" is automatic, but "sex" has some fathers frowning. The Cubmaster's got a glazed look; his ears and neck are crimson.

"I'm going to tell you a story about respect." Mr. White Eagle speaks in a slow, measured beat, with his head still and his eyes closed like a blind man's. "It's an important story. It's about my people, the Creek. And America." I expect something about the world on the back of a big turtle, about brave warriors.

"Not too long ago, I was driving on a long stretch of Interstate 10," he begins, "just into Arizona from New Mexico, on my way to visit some people in Ohio. My car was borrowed from a friend in Bakersfield. The highway stretched far and wide in front of me, with great mountains in the distance. I was smoking— a cigarette—something you shouldn't do, boys. But when my people smoke, we're mourning our losses." Several adult heads bob, most likely the smokers. "It was a bright afternoon. No one else was on the road. Then, in my rearview mirror I saw a car, a state trooper, closing in quickly, and I said a prayer of welcoming. The trooper's lights started flashing, and I said another prayer to speed him safely to whatever emergency called him. When he pulled up beside me, he looked at me. I nodded at him through my open window, and when I smiled, my cigarette fell out of my mouth. I couldn't see his eyes behind his mirrored glasses, but I saw his lips curl with hatred. He pointed to the side of the road, and I pulled over."

Mr. White Eagle has been speaking in a prayerful monotone. From time to time there's a glint from between his shut lids, as if there are jewels hidden behind them. He continues his story: he's asked for his license and for the registration of the vehicle his Bakersfield friend apparently failed to renew; he's ordered to wait with his hands on the hood of the car while the trooper searches it; finally, he's handed citations for littering (the fallen cigarette) and the lapsed registration, and the trooper races off, lights still flashing.

"Do you see?" Mr. White Eagle asks the boys and their dads. "Shame—it sucks the warmth from the sun and the sparkle from the lakes; it steals the sweet scent from the pines. Do you see? It's this—" and he presents his profile: his hatchet nose, his high cheekbones and crag of a brow, the stump of the pony tail he waggled between his thumb and forefinger. There's a hush. Then Mr. White Eagle turns toward us and opens his eyes fully wide for the first time, and we gasp. His eyes have no whites—they're silvery irises set in absolute black—eyes that belonged only in nightmares. And I remember where I'd seen Mr. White Eagle before.

He's nearly whispering now. "What that officer showed was the ugliest thing in the world: prejudice. Against me. Against my people, for nothing more than a ponytail, and for skin a few shades too dark." He doesn't mention his eyes. He doesn't have to. "No respect. *Blah-dee-blah.*"

I'd seen him about a year ago, at the first and only AA meeting I'd ever attended. That's when Tara and my now ex-girlfriend, Janie, got together and "intervened," as they called it. For Tara the few joints a week I smoked, the six pack or so that helped quench my dry mouth and round off my buzz, made me a doubtful risk around her son. "You've got to be a better role model for him," she said, knowing how much I depended on his company.

Janie's reason for wanting me sober was more complicated; it was another aspect of the situation that forced me to move out of the rented bungalow we shared, the one on the river bank where there used to be an amusement park almost a hundred years ago. I've seen old photographs of a midway and a carrousel, and a ferris wheel at night all lit up and reflected in the black river. I can match up the shoreline to my fishing spots. I liked to tell Janie when we were in bed that that the wind rustling the leaves outside our window was the ghosts of happy people laughing. I moved out because Janie was pregnant—not by me, though I wish that would have been possible. Janie had the best one-time job I'd ever heard of—she was a surrogate. The fertilized egg of a rich woman had been implanted in her womb; she didn't know who she was bearing the baby for, only that she was to be paid a small fortune when the kid was born—exactly how much it wasn't my business to know yet, she said. She also received a monthly sum to eat properly, and a nurse visited once a week to check on the progress of her pregnancy.

Janie is beautiful and ambitious—she has a college degree, and when she was picked to be a surrogate, you'd have thought she won the lottery and bags of gold would soon be dropped off at our door.

"You can't stay here," she told me. "They think I'm single. I signed something. You'll have to get an apartment, and I'll visit you there. And if I am going to visit, you'll have to change your habits. There'll be no smoking or drinking around this baby. He's going to be my down-payment on life."

I should have noticed that she said "my down-payment" and not "our down-payment." But I promised both Janie and Tara I'd go to an AA meeting, and I quit smoking and drinking. When Janie started swelling, I talked to the baby in her belly, which she let slip was a boy. Janie would sneak over to my tidy little apartment every weekend, at first, but she visited less and less frequently the more and more pregnant she got. She stopped letting me touch her. It wasn't that she wasn't horny any more—she said she was "superstitious" about my fingers and tongue so close to "the portal," which would be the rich child she was carrying's access to the world. Sometimes I thought Janie was afraid I would contaminate the unborn kid with my ignorance—as if she had just enough class for him, but I'd never be in the same league.

When her nine months were nearly up—it was just after the night of that one and only AA meeting where I saw Mr. White Eagle— I suggested that we could deliver the kid ourselves, then take off with him and start our own family somewhere far away—a tropical island or a village in the Brazilian rain forest. I thought it was a funny idea to have to kidnap something inside of you. I never saw her again after that night. I don't know where or on which day she had the baby, and when I returned to the bungalow on the site of the old amusement park, there wasn't a scrap to indicate she'd ever lived there, let alone a note.

But while I waited in the dim fluorescence of the Methodist church's meeting room for that AA meeting to begin, I'd thought I was opening a new chapter on Janie's and my life, not closing the final one. Maybe two dozen folks, mostly men, sat in three rows of folding chairs. Despite the ban on tobacco, the room reeked from clothing steeped in smoke. The people in charge were welcoming, but there wasn't much chit-chat. Everyone was too intent on publically nursing a private woe. I thought I'd be required to share my story, and I decided I'd tell the assembly about the testicular cancer that left me single-balled and sterile. I'd reveal that I'd never be able to father a child of my own, and that the heart-wrenching disappointment had driven me to anesthetize my sorrows in drugs and drink. The truth is, I'd never had cancer, just a sperm count approaching zero—I'd been tested periodically because I'd grown up in a tract house my folks bought that was built on a nuclear waste dumping ground. That situation involved some mismanaged lawsuits, and if anyone in my family reaped a penny from it, I never knew. But a cancer story would draw more sympathy than a lawsuit, I concluded. I imagined the eyes of these hardened substance abusers filling with tears at my tale of woe.

Tara and I don't talk about it, but she grew up over the same nuclear waste I did, and maybe her irradiated eggs caused Danny's problems. Her husband left after the weight of Danny's turning out to be the kind of kid he is cracked marital ice that was already thin. Tara and Tim didn't have it in themselves to deal with the situation as a team, which is why I'm scooched up next to my nephew at this scout meeting while Mr. White Eagle has resumed sounding melancholy notes on his flute. When I look at him I can't believe I didn't recognize him immediately from the Methodist church basement.

He sat in the first row, and when he popped up to tell about his tribulations, he made no effort to dim the effect of his frightful eyes: they were like dimes floating in black ink.

"I have been a conman and a terrible human being," he began. His tale was set "in another city" where he had custody of a little girl, a toddler "not really my daughter." To make his very long story short, somehow he managed to scam the congregation of a church into believing that this child entrusted to his care was dying of "something like leukemia." He'd thrown himself on the mercy of the big-hearted congregants. "The good people organized a fundraiser," he told us, and netted a "blessed" profit in the thousands from the gullible church folk before skipping town.

"I have paid my debt for that and other offences," he said, by which he meant he did prison time, "and as a confirmation of that payment I inked my eyes." I shivered. I hadn't known it was possible to tattoo your eyeballs. "These eyes are my public admission of the midnight thoughts that always lurk inside. They warn everyone I meet, 'Trust me if you dare.' Being seen as I am is part of my daily battle."

Anonymous no longer, here he is, "George White Eagle," toodling his flute and yammering about *Blah-dee-blah* to a pack of Cub Scouts for the sake, I assume, of fifty dollars. How, I wonder, had the scout leaders found him? How had Mr. White Eagle advertised himself?

I'm fidgety, and at a loss as to what to do with my knowledge. Is there a statute of limitations on anonymity? What if Mr. White Eagle's got a bigger scam in mind than just that fifty? "You okay?" I ask Danny, mostly to calm myself down, and my nephew doesn't respond, but the father next to me shushes me and gives me a look like I've just violated *Blah-dee-blah*. I raise an eyebrow at the shusher and cock my head toward Mr. White Eagle, but the dad misses the signal. His plump son's mouth hangs open as if the nonsense Mr. White Eagle is feeding him is better than a cream-filled donut.

What I should do is get up and take my information about Mr. White Eagle to the Cubmaster. He stands at the back of the room, smiling at the stage; but if I leave Danny, I'm afraid he'll start howling, like he did when I left him on a movie line with a nice old lady so I could get the wallet I'd left in the car.

Mr. White Eagle has stopped playing and addresses us again. His silver and black eyes gleam. There's a beat in the pit of my stomach like a tom-tom.

"*Blah-dee-blah*," Mr. White Eagle intones.

"*Blah-dee-blah*," almost everyone replies. Danny makes his own sound.

"Boys," our guest says, "you make my heart glow. Your ways, the ways of scouting, are the ways of my people. And there are two things we must value as much as *Blah-dee-blah*: Truth and Vigilance."

Heads nod, though I'm sure few of the boys know what "vigilance" means. This is the real deal, dads are telling themselves, this is why we signed our boys up for scouting. Not to tie knots. Not to carve race cars out of blocks of pine. Not to earn badges for taking out the trash. But to grab hold of those old virtues, Truth and Vigilance. Virtue, I think, and that's when I decide that it's up to me to unmask Mr. White Eagle. I'm panting, and the hand I rest on Danny's knee is damp.

"And so," our guest continues, "I offer you myself as a lesson in Truth and Vigilance." He bows deeply. I brace myself—there's the kind of hush that Danny often fills with a wail. But his breathing is regular, and for a moment I understand the relief of fitting in. Who would it hurt to let the whole thing slide? But then Mr. White Eagle smiles—for the first time this evening—and the way his face twists beneath those eyes hits me like a blow to my manhood. I'm being disrespected—no *Blah-dee-blah*.

I remember the first father-son Cub Scout project Danny and I undertook. Tara had dropped Danny off on a Saturday morning at the bungalow I'd re-occupied after Janie's desertion. He sat at my kitchen table with a milk mustache while I whittled away at a Pinewood Derby car with a steak knife, the closest thing I owned to a tool. The magic marker for Danny to color the raw wood had dried up, so I gave him a Bic pen, and he slashed stripes along one side of the car, again and again and again, hundreds of them, then said, "TV," and I said, "Okay." We brought the car to Derby night, where other scouts displayed glossy, aerodynamic racers they seemed to be handling for the first time. Their dads swapped details about weight distribution and wheel bases, decals and metallic paint. Compared to the others, our car looked like it had been gnawed into shape by squirrels. I caught one father looking at it and muttering to another with a shake of his head, "You'd have thought . . ." The other dad shook his head too, staring at our scarred chunk of wood. The first dad repeated, knowing I was in earshot, "You'd have just thought." I turned to my nephew, who clutched our car to his chest like it was a gold ingot. "Who the heck is Akela, Danny?" I demanded. "Why can't anybody tell me that?"

So I have no choice. Mr. White Eagle must be exposed. But I'm still waiting for a sign that the moment is right when he beats me to his own unmasking.

"Truth," he says. "The truth is, I am not who you think. There is more to George White Eagle than meets the eye. I was baptized George DiBello, but I have gone by many other names. I have been William Smith. In prison they called me Willie Freeze." His words seem to echo from a pit that's opened beneath us. The blood has drained from the Cubmaster's face. "Truth: I was not born a Creek Indian. I am of Italian and Greek descent." He grins, and his eyes flash. "And now you think I have deceived you. That's good—you're being vigilant. There are those who will tell you lies, boys—you will meet such people as you journey through life."

Confusion reigns—dads look to the Cubmaster and to each other for some kind of reassurance, but there's none to be had, and as the boys feel their fathers' grips loosen, their eyes round with fear. It's frightening and exhilarating at the same time. It's a feeling I wish I could get credit for creating.

"But even now I have fooled you," Mr. Whoever says. He waggles a finger. "Truth and Vigilance— I became a Creek in prison. My cellmate was Creek, and after an intimate ceremony, we became blood brothers. He assured me I have full tribal rights. Then I had my eyes inked—I gave up their whites. And now, the blackness is a symbol. As I look out at you, my darkness is behind me. So, learn this lesson, just as I learned the lessons of my adopted people, the Creek— don't trust what you see. Don't cast judgments until you know the whole Truth. That trooper who pulled me over? He was wrong about who he thought I was—but he was also right, do you see? But in the biggest way of all, *Blah-dee-blah*, he was wrong."

Silence. There's too much to digest to understand it all. But the Cubscout oath prevails: *"The cub scout shows good will."* A unified opinion settles like a golden cloud on Mr. Dibello-Smith-White Eagle's audience: *The subject was Truth. No one has been deceived. Good people chose this speaker. We will all sleep well tonight.*

"Thank you, boys, fathers, Cubmaster." Our guest is reluctant to leave the stage. I'm waiting for one more *"Blah-dee-blah"* when I feel Danny seething next to me. He's rocking on his haunches, forward and back. His lips part.

"Boo," Danny says, the sound a burst bubble that only I hear, because everyone else, all the dads and their kids, have begun to clap— louder and louder, applause that grows bolder as it justifies itself. Danny tilts his head back, and his jaws seem to unhinge. "Boo!" he bleats. "Boo, Boo, Boo!"

"Shh, quiet!" the dad behind me growls, and "Hey" and "Quiet" and "Shh" erupt around us. "Get him out!" another dad nearby hisses, because Danny won't shut up—"Boo-boo-boo-boo-boo—" he rattles like a machine gun. Outrage swells, and in a second I'm on my feet, and I pull Danny up, too. He's looking at the floor, and he stumbles stiffly after me as I lead him out the emergency exit that takes us into the parking lot and the night. "Boo-boo-boo-boo-boo," he's muttering. I haven't once told him to knock it off. Behind us I hear the Cubmaster's enthusiastic voice, muffled, then more applause. Did he just thank the speaker—had he apologized for my nephew and me? I take Danny into the darkness, onto the playing field stretching beyond the parking lot, walking him almost all the way to the trees at the far end. It's a cool evening, and it feels good to move. After a while Danny stops booing.

"Look at the stars," I say, catching my breath. I drape my arm over his slight shoulders. He doesn't say a word, but he lifts his eyes. "There's the Big Dipper," I say, "and the Milky Way." I haven't really found them, but I know they're up there somewhere. Danny's staring up— at the stars or the spaces between them. I plan to stay out on the field until the parking lot empties. Then I feel Danny freeze—he senses before I do that we've been followed across the field.

"The Seven Sisters," a voice whispers. It belongs to the man I first saw at AA. He points at the heavens as he circles around us until he blocks our way. "The Creek tell a story about them." His back is to the trees. There's an odor from him like incense. He lowers his gaze and I can feel its blackness spreading over us, thicker than the night. "You booed me," he says, addressing me, not Danny. "Do I know you?"

The truth is, maybe I did boo him. Maybe Danny got the idea from me. I don't say anything for a few seconds. Up close he's not very tall, almost a head shorter than I am. His grin is tight, hiding his teeth. "We're just tired," I say. "It was a long night."

"There's something wrong with your boy," he says matter-of-factly. *There's something wrong with your eyes*, I want to say, but hold my tongue.

"He's my sister's kid." The moment I say it, I feel bad. "I can't have my own," I add, but it's too late. I have never before in my life hit another human being, but I'm feeling the instinct for it. My arm tingles and my hand closes into a fist. The man holds his flute like a club, as if it's heavier than anyone would think, and I assess how much it might hurt to block a swing with my forearm. Then I ask him, "Who's Akela? You should be able to tell me that."

"Akela? It's another name for the Great Spirit. Shawnee, I think."

"Wrong," I say. "It's Hindi. It's *Indian*-Indian, not Native American. From Kipling's *Jungle Book*. Akela is the lone wolf—the lone wolf who leads the pack." A lot of truths can be found on the Internet.

"I'm a hypnotherapist. And a homeopathic doctor," he says. "Maybe there's something I can do for the boy. For you, too." I twitch as he reaches into his jeans pocket, but he pulls out a card. I relax my hand to accept it. "Give me a call. We can work something out. No charge for session one." He looks at Danny, whose gaze has fallen from the starry sky to the turf. "*Blah-dee-Blah*," the Creek adoptee says. He salutes us with his instrument and turns toward the trees. I see now that there's a path through them to a lit street not more than fifty yards beyond, and he's striding toward it. "Boo," he throws back over his shoulder, followed by a laugh that turns into a smoker's wheeze.

By now my sister will be wondering where we are. I might have to tell her we're done with scouting, and I'm trying to think of how to break the news. Maybe I don't have to say anything; maybe on Tuesday nights Danny and I could just do something else, like bowling or a movie. What we won't do yet is visit Dr. DiBello—that's the name on his card. The parking lot looks empty now, but I no longer care. The school's big classroom windows are bright yellow, and we can see the late-shift custodians moving around. I palm Danny's back and guide him forward.

"Akela" I say.

"Boo," my nephew says, his eyes on the night-blue turf he kicks at with each step.

Missing Athena

Josh Green

"Did you know," asks Joe in seat 17 C, "that penguins can swim thirty miles per hour?"

Hank Obelisk doesn't know how to respond. Of course he didn't know that. Or perhaps he could've guessed, having seen that special on Antarctica before dozing off the other night, the half-smoked joint a tarry nub in his fingertips, his Crown Royal drained. On television the penguins seemed awfully stupid. Hank had wondered why some massive, glacier-prowling shark didn't rip them all apart, a chummy stew of penguin meat in the icy abyss. Too quick for sharks, the penguins, he concluded. Then he passed out again on the couch.

Before replying to his son, Hank looks out the cabin window. There's a thick haze over Georgia, a smoggy dome above the black-green carpet of rolling hills and pines—down where his wife must be, somewhere. From twenty thousand feet the topography bears contrast to the checkerboard Midwest, back where the land's cut in sections he could easily search and catalogue. From this altitude he knows the Southern forest is a hopeless expanse.

The kid pulls Hank's sleeve, exhibiting his impatience with a piercing whine. Hank crushes his empty soda can and smiles, his teeth big and white as mini-marshmallows.

"The world record for fast swimming was set by a swordfish," Hank quietly fibs. Joe, a precocious seven-year-old and only child, stores each word as undisputable fact. "One near Cuba went a hundred-fifty."

"When?"

"This one time."

"*Dang*," Joe says, satisfied. "That's like Corvette fast."

It warms Hank's heart to see his son decked out in Chicago Cubs gear. The soft blues and reds are friendly shades in Hank's eyes, the colors of his own childhood bedroom, a cramped space bedecked with aerial shots of Wrigley Field. He'd move his son back to where they'd just left, the Chicago suburb of Glen Ellyn, if it weren't for the apocalyptic winters. His family visits up there never last long enough, and returning to Atlanta has become painful for him, a procession ending in the stark realities of single-parenting. After a few days, the convivial rhythms of the South weave back into Hank, and his longing for home dissolves. In moving to Georgia, he'd spoiled himself with temperate climes, and now his son wears the same thin skin. The boy has never seen the Lake frozen and probably never will. Hank would hate to taint his notion of the northern beach, to paint gray the emerald crescents of Lincoln Park summers. He thinks it best to leave good memories alone.

"Dad," the boy says. "Is this going to be a bad landing like last time?"

"To be honest, that's highly doubtful." Hank suppresses laughter and then guilt for wanting to laugh. "Don't worry so much."

The boy tucks his book of sea-animal pictures in a carry-on backpack. He burns his father with the quizzical stare that tells Hank he'd better be on his game.

"About the landing," Joe says. "How do you know? Did they teach that in the academy?"

"No," Hank says. "Firemen know jack about planes."

"Then *how?*"

"Because our last three landings were bad." Hank opens his hands like airplane wings, yaws them. "The law of averages is in our favor."

"The *what?*"

"Just trust me," Hank says, palming the boy's shoulder. "This'll be like landing in a giant tub of butter."

The fasten seatbelts sign clicks on: *bong*. The middle seat is unoccupied, so between Hank and Joe lies a pile of travel accoutrements: bottled water, Skittles, peanuts, taffy, a *Sports Illustrated*, and three twisted action figures. The boy's getting so big his knees bend fully over the airline seat, his calf muscles growing like balloons above his skinny ankles. Hank marvels at the simplest things his son does. The way he turns book pages, smiles back, bumps fists in greeting, laughs at fairly complex jokes. Nothing pleases Hank like seeing the boy learn.

"I'm afraid this time," Joe says. "It's like I don't trust the pilot."

"I told you, there's nothing to—"

"I know, but how would *you* know?" the boy says. "You said you never flew a plane. We're way up in the sky."

"I know how to survive things," Hank says. "I know when we're safe, when there's no need to worry. This is one of those times."

Hank shuffles the magazine around and looks across the aisle to the lone woman in the row. By habit he examines her hands, two sun-bronzed swans, elegant and cappuccino. No ring. He wants to smack himself for looking.

"Look, big man, I've heard of this pilot, heard great things," he says, leaning over Joe to maximize his authority. "He's so good they call him the Air King, or something like that."

"*Liar*," the boy snaps. "You lie. You make things up so much."

"Don't talk to me like that."

"I'm worried," Joe says. "I don't know why. I don't know why this time and not other times."

"It's okay," Hank says. "When we get to the condo, we're off to the pool. I'll let you do backflips."

"It's not okay."

"Breathe, buddy," he says. "Put your seat up. Breathe in and out. This is a natural reaction."

"No," Joe says, "not natural."

The boy can be stubborn, pigheaded even, crunching his forehead into little ravines to telegraph his displeasure. Hank knows the attitude isn't from him, and he can't recall Joe's mother acting this way. As a child, Hank was easygoing to a fault, borderline indifferent—hardly a budding emergency responder. The last time he saw his own father, Earl was behind the wheel of a Lincoln Continental, the lone passenger a blind neighbor named Scratchy. Southward the men bolted toward Gary, Indiana, the bookie and the blind man. Not exactly cowboys and sunsets.

Joe clenches his armrest, kicks his sandals off. Nearby passengers slyly watch. Hank unclips his seatbelt, clears the middle seat, and hops over. He holds Joe.

"They call this claustrophobic stress," Hank says. "You're reacting to prior experiences, and we all do this in one way or another. Just remember that not all landings are bad."

"Stop it."

"You might not think much of me right now, but I know what I'm doing," Hank says. "Sit still."

"Please," the boy says. "Don't touch me."

~

Hank met his wife in a barbershop called Johnson's, a few blocks from his firehouse in Glenn Ellyn. She was in town canvassing the area for a marketing firm with aspirations of branching out of the South, and she was lost.

At first she was a curvy silhouette, her cat eyes lost in backlight. Johnson's dirty windows stood behind her, behind that kids running in the street, and beyond it all a picturesque baroque hotel. She asked for directions to Briar Street. The old pervert Johnson asked for her name.

"Athena," she said, pulling the latter half into syrupy drawl. "Like the town in Georgia, or almost."

"No," Johnson smiled. "Like the goddess."

Another barber had just finished Hank's trim and lined up his neckline with a razor. Had Athena walked in twenty minutes prior, with his sideburns and temples like bushy hives, she would have left alone. She would have lived. But Hank could feel his swagger coming on, a hot rush of confidence.

"I'll point her there," he told the guys. "I know Briar Street. Let me pay for this haircut, miss, and I'll get you on your way."

They stepped into the street. A lake breeze pushed clammy air across Chicago's suburbs, gulls whistling overhead. Athena's lipstick was mauve, not red, a dead-on match to the pumps she wore. That impressed Hank. Everything about her was refined, a contrast to the sports-pub floozies he'd been dealing with. Athena's ears were hidden under shimmering, curlicue locks, and Hank worried the ears were humongous, like his. He worried about his worrying. They walked to Briar Street and chatted, mostly about baseball. He took a chance and asked her to dinner. She blushed like a flattered child and said okay, what the hell.

The next night, over linguini in the Gold Coast, Athena had swept her hair in a ponytail, confirming that her ears were borderline perfect, Hank thought, like tiny conch shells from the Keys. She'd be in town only three days. He felt rushed. Over dessert, he slipped her his business card, proud to have his fire company's emblem in her dainty hand.

"It doesn't turn you off, what I do?" he said.

She poked her tiramisu.

"The long hours?" he said. "The dangerousness?"

She sipped cabernet and swayed to a slow violin. The lights dimmed and the room—quaint, shadowy, and dripping with velvet—took on an underwater quality. Hank worried he was out of his league.

"Tell me," she said, "are all women crazy for big-city firefighters?"

He liked the question, found it easy to deflect. "My only dates lately have been with five-alarm warehouse blazes."

She didn't laugh. He worried she was examining his response, combing it for proof that he was a lothario, perhaps his whole firefighting story a shtick.

"I grew up on the Georgia-Florida line, where dad was a volunteer," she said. "He didn't know a damn thing about fighting fires. I'd imagine you're as professional as they come." She nibbled the dessert, a dusting of cocoa powder around her lips. "I have a question."

"Okay." He filled his mouth with wine and swallowed fast.

"You won't get mad?"

"Shoot."

"With all due respect, what kind of name is Hank *Obelisk*?" she said, napkin to her lips. "I've never heard such a funny last name."

He exhaled without meaning to. "My great-grandfather translated it from something unspeakable," he said. "Not in a bad way, but something not ready for English. He came here from Russia, an engineer fascinated by elevated trains. Believe it or not, 'obelisk' was the first English word he'd learned, other than the essentials. Of all the damn ugly words in the language—"

"But I like it."

~

At ten thousand feet the stewardesses have vanished. Hank presses the overhead HELP button twice but nobody seems capable of responding, the descent so extreme. He keeps cool for his son's sake. He hopes his composure will shine favorably on the woman in the next row. She wears a pantsuit that from ten feet away looks like seersucker. He shakes his head, expelling thoughts of her at a time like this.

"We'll be laughing about this in an hour," he tells Joe. "You'll see how silly it was, and we'll stuff ourselves with pizza. Think about the pizza."

Joe breathes himself dizzy. He fiddles with an action figure, a grimacing soldier in desert fatigues. He downs the last of his bottled water.

"Did mom ever have this problem?" Joe says.

Hank leans the opposite way, toward the window, watching the plane pull a steep bank around the city, a great bird changing its mind. He sees the canopy and hills. A few carved gaps for shopping centers and major business districts, but otherwise a green abyss, a global cashmere sweater.

"No," says Hank. "Your mother is a cool lady. Wherever she is, she's being cool there."

"Did she like to fly?"

"She *loves* to fly," he says. "What'd I tell you about talking in past-tense?"

"Sorry," Joe says. "It just kind of seems right."

"Right?" Hank says. "You mean appropriate?"

"Yeah," Joe says. "Doesn't two years kind of make it okay?"

Hank crosses his arms in his best authoritative pose, his grade-school principal. "You're not as smart as you think sometimes. You should learn when to bite your tongue."

"Dad," Joe says, "I'm going to puke."

~

Seven hundred miles, an hour and twenty minutes in the air, the distance between cities was bearable. The first winter, Hank and Athena racked up hundreds in cell-phone overages to compensate. The second, Hank hoisted a white flag on his bunk at the station, declaring himself southward bound. The boys threw him a party befitting his captain rank, and by Christmas he was gone.

The day before he drove down, she called him at home to say her period hadn't come. "Three weeks late," she said. "I have a test stick in my hand that reads positive. It's the third positive since *yesterday*."

Hank dropped the phone and nearly buckled at the knees, the realities of adulthood draping over him like a plastic sack. He told her issues like pregnancy are best discussed in person, though he knew frighteningly little about what he said. When he hung up, he poured a gin with lime wedges, and well past midnight was still writhing in bed.

At daybreak he gave up on sleep and started the Ryder. He brewed a thermos of black coffee, pushed his keys in the drop box, and roared away. He saluted the Drake Hotel and the soaring Amoco Building as daylight unveiled them, whooping as the truck spun fresh snow down Lake Shore Drive.

~

Joe heaves in the airline vomit bag as if inflating a raft. Hank runs his nails over the boy's head, taps his fingertips lightly on his back. The passengers who sneak glances are met with disdainful stares from Hank. To think his sick boy is that interesting pisses him off.

"Doing good, buddy," he says, purposefully loud. "Nobody's watching."

Joe got sick like this a few nights after his mother's abduction, in the first frantic days when Hank couldn't bear to stay home. They slept at an extended stay hotel beside the interstate with hookers roaming the garden suites. Oddly, Joe would wear nothing but his father's clothing, and when running to the bathroom his shirt trailed like a parachute. The nausea resulted from constant microwave pizzas, soda, and Twinkies—a clueless father's specialty.

"All done?" Hank says now. "You've put a hurting on that bag."

"How much longer?"

"We're almost there," he says. "I can see our place now."

"*What?*"

"Okay, that's exaggerating . . . but we're close."

"*Uhhh.*"

Hank tucks the bag under his seat, hopeful the sandaled feet he saw beneath him earlier aren't still there. The boy cranes his neck to see out the cabin window. Without the baby fat his jawbone is sharp, Hank notices, the cheekbones high, eyebrows straight and persuasive like his mother's. He offers the boy a stick of gum. Joe declines and scoops sweat from his eyes.

~

Athena liked to put the formula in a bowl in front of the baby, let him dip in his hands and catch the runoff with his mouth, a primitive feeding method that struck her as hilarious, her husband not so much. It made a mess of their 1940s bungalow, filling the kitchen with sour fumes.

"He looks like an animal or something, eating like that," Hank said. "Like a sea otter."

The couple relied on one car, a clunky Toyota Corolla, no small feat in a city of sparse public transit. When people worried aloud that the car was dangerous, Hank shot back: "Our mortgage rate made me do it." He'd been hired at Station 14, though lower on the totem pole than he liked, and his work was five miles away; the MARTA train stop was seven blocks. It went without saying that Athena would do the walking, even when she had to work late, which in winter meant a dark walk home.

"It's my thinking time," she'd say, optimistic even when she hated to be. "Good for clearing the lobes."

When Hank's schedule allowed a weekend off, they'd spend it making love. Long bouts all over the house—often the kitchen, sometimes the hallway, once the screened porch. They broke a barstool and ripped a swag curtain.

"This," Hank said one afternoon, "is the pinnacle of living."

"That," his wife teased, "was cheesy."

Athena got promoted to regional manager. They celebrated with champagne, a candlelit dinner of grilled salmon and steamed asparagus on the porch. She was tipsy two sips in. Along with the position came managerial tasks, longer hours editing press material written by her underlings, other menial headaches.

"If it comes down to it," she suggested, "there's no shame in being a stay-at-home dad these days."

"Not in five million years."

The longer Athena worked, the darker her walk home. She walked faster, developing blisters, scabs. She took shortcuts down Boulevard without telling her husband.

~

The plane rattles through a low patch of clouds, and all eighty passengers gasp. Two genteel ladies in business class demand drinks, but the crew politely declines. Joe chews on his fingers.

"Flight crew," the pilot cracks, "prepare for landing."

Joe drains the last of his water and quietly belches. Hank points out rooftops visible between the trees. The nearness to earth eases the boy's tense face.

"Mushrooms," Joe says. "Or barbeque chicken pizza, with pineapple."

"You bet."

The afternoon sun heats the cabin, fills it with a cantaloupe hue. The woman in the next row draws down her plastic blind, and Hank mimics her, trying to catch her attention while avoiding Joe's. He hates to draw comparisons, especially physical ones, but she has wonderful hands.

~

Joe turned five, entered public school, and Athena got blunt. She asked her husband one morning to leave the fire department, to find something with steady hours. She complained that her feet felt arthritic, and she wanted a consistent ride. Hank kicked his feet onto a flea-market ottoman and tossed his newspaper aside.

"It's more than a car you'll be buying, and we don't have cash in these walls," he said. "How much is parking downtown, by the month?"

"I have no idea."

"Hundreds," Hank said. "I heard it's hundreds."

"That's exaggerated."

"Listen," he said. "There's going to be overtime in the next few months. I'll work every minute of it. We'll get you a car. In the meantime, if you want to use the Toyota, I'll take the train, end of story."

"That's not sensible," she said. "I can wait."

"You're sure?"

She kept walking.

Two weeks before Thanksgiving, the babysitter rang Hank at the station. The call itself was unusual, but Jackie, the sitter, had troubled him with trivial inquiries at work before. Only this time Jackie was angry, perturbed that Athena had worked late without calling. Nearly eight o'clock and not a text, email, nothing. Hank knew she wasn't working late. His gut told him something was gravely amiss.

Hank entered what families of the missing call a cacophony of negative thinking, an otherworldly knowing that the cosmos is somehow off-kilter. He hung up the phone and told his lieutenant someone would need to cover for him because he felt ill. He left without hearing definite approval.

En route home, he called Athena's cell phone, then her office. A janitor said it was a ghost town, nobody there but him. Hank tried the cell phone again. Straight to voicemail: "Hi, y'all!"

On Freedom Parkway the streetlights hung in gauzy yellow mist. Hank glimpsed his home's clapboard exterior, and it occurred to him his wife might never be there again. The thought struck him as bizarre. He stopped at the Boulevard light, a truck and two taxis preventing the final right turn.

Crossing Boulevard, he saw it, and his mind went ballistic, a thousand directions at once. Athena's ladybug umbrella—caught between a bus-stop vestibule and a garbage can—rolled in the night breeze.

"Drug gangs!" Hank told the responding officer. "They're holding her for ransom. I've heard the stories. They work the Quick-Mart and that pizza shop farther down, work it in shifts. They roll drunks and rob people for groceries. There's no time—"

"Have a seat, sir," said the cop, a thick-wristed Hispanic man with strands of white in his sideburns. "Let's start with a timeline."

"Her cell phone," Hank said. "I'm calling it right now. I know how these things work. Trace the call by how it pings off cell-phone towers. I'm calling her, right now."

"Put the phone down," the cop said. "You don't want to alarm anyone, if something did happen. But I'm sure she's just hung up somewhere, or lost."

Hank walked the officer to his porch, away from Joe, who sat on the couch, awed by his frantic father. Hank thought it strange his son didn't cry.

"Don't ask me how I know this," Hank said on the porch, "but she's in a bad way. I know you handle these cases a lot, but I'm begging you to go after this, with everything you can expend, tonight."

"About that timeline," said the cop.

"*Fuck* the timeline," Hank said.

The cop grabbed him by the wrists. "Shut up," he said. "C'mon, brother, *think*."

"I'm giving you leads," Hank said, shrugging him off, "and you're standing there."

"Think logically," the cop said.

"Watch the boy," Hank said. "I'll walk these blocks myself, you worthless son of a bitch."

The cop radioed for an investigator and watched Hank vanish, a wet vest and two militant arms swallowed by the shadows of Glenn Iris Drive.

~

Joe bites his lip as the landing gear spreads. He sits on his hands and squirms, tucks his head between his knees. The wheels touch gently, their connection with sun-baked asphalt barely noticeable, a shallow pothole on a country road.

"I told you," Hank smiles. "Hot butter."

They taxi slowly across innumerable lanes and Joe unbuckles prematurely.

"Can we keep the barfing a secret?" Joe asks.

Hank winks and puts his forefinger across puckered lips.

~

The disappearance made waves with regional media for several weeks. The newspapers grew particularly excited when a team of horseback searchers from Texas descended on the Old Fourth Ward, a band of cowboys on the urban frontier. The umbrella was the eerie touch that editors pine for, and Athena's eventual life-insurance payout lent the story an unfounded layer of mystery.

Hank, once cleared by police, became something of a folk hero, a decorated firefighter whose want of answers outshone his inability to fund a private investigation. His screw-the-police subversion won him favor with hipsters and college kids. The ones Hank took the time to meet would channel him baggies of high-grade weed, which he said aided his sleeping.

"Keep it coming," Hank told one kid with sleeves of skull tattoos. "They don't have the balls to drug-test me."

On local TV broadcasts, and once on the radio, Hank decried the efforts of police—"Quotas! The PD's got one thing on their minds, and that's arrest quotas!"— which, of course, prompted his termination from the fire department. Political science students at the downtown college picketed city hall for three days.

Donations in blank envelopes made their way to Hank's porch, and hardly a street post in the Old Forth Ward was bereft of a reward poster. Neighborhoods came together to cull traces of the career woman who went to work and never came home.

But there was nothing left of Athena.

The investigation stalled and the case was quietly shelved. Hank sold the home to her family, a joint purchase between several sympathizing aunts and uncles. He got fifty thousand over market value and poured forty into newspaper ads. Not a single tipster called.

"People don't care about the vanished after a year," Hank said on the last television broadcast he was invited to. "I take issue with the attention span of police and the city at large. I take issue with the public's forgetfulness in general."

Hank bought a cookie-cutter condo in the sky, a home off the street. In the tiny living room stood a telescope; on the balcony hung expensive binoculars. Hank would invite Joe to the balcony after homework, when the smoke had cleared. Together they'd watch the day conclude.

"Look at that sunset," Hank said one evening. "It's like red sheets, ripped off the city and pulled out west."

Joe cocked his head, his eyes in philosophical squint. "I bet mom liked sunsets."

"*Likes*," said Hank. "She likes them."

~

At the gate, a stewardess speeds through her final, uninspired spiel. Businessmen activate cell phones. Hank tilts back his head, enjoys the overhead fan one last time before the heat. He stands up and gathers their bags.

Hank thinks of the progressions they've made. For the first time in a year, he can sleep without too much dope, and Joe can now tolerate pitch-dark rooms. It shames Hank to feel any sense of recovery, but a guy has a life to live, two mouths to feed. A self-pity hibernation of booze and smoke is no option.

The woman in the other row pulls a purple snakeskin bag from the overhead compartment. She flashes curious eyes at Hank; he gives her a dismissive nod and turns around to help his son. He pulls the backpack straps over the boy's chest and pats his head, corrects the alignment of his Cubs hat. He knows there will be a time for women with cappuccino hands, but now is not that time.

Reform, Alabama

Christopher Lowe

When I catch up to the dogs, I realize it's Pearl that's treed the raccoon. The blue-ticks are baying, jumping here and there, showing their asses they're so excited about the coon, but Pearl's just standing there, a fleck of white curving out from under her lip, telling the creature in the tree that she ain't messing around.

The coon's looking for a way out, but Pearl's got him up a half-dead oak right in the middle of the field, off away from the other trees. There's nowhere for him to go but down, and he's getting frantic, his claws grating at the bark. I can hear the scrabble above the noise of the blue-ticks, and my flashlight finds him trying hard to get up to a higher branch.

"Aw'right, now," I say to the dogs, raising the twelve gauge. "No need for all that."

~

Was a time, Warren would be out hunting with me, walking alongside, his daddy's .22 pistol shoved into his waistband. We'd started going out when we were just boys. Then, still too young to be given shotguns, we used the old .22 to shoot squirrels and crows. If what we killed was edible, his Mee-maw would fry it up. She always cleaned the animals for us, soaked the meat in melted butter, sprinkled little flecks of rosemary from her garden into the skillet as they cooked. After we'd eaten, she left us to clean the mess. We scrubbed the old cast-iron under scalding water and left it to dry in the oven. The entrails went into the weeds at the far end of their property. Some afternoons, full of the gamey meat, I'd lay out in the high grass and drowse while Warren used an old roofing hammer to tack the skins to the side of their shed. When I asked him why he did that, why he papered the old wood that way, he said he wanted everyone who came by to know what kind of man he was. That even at seven, he was a hunter.

~

Back at my daddy's, I give Pearl the kidneys. She swallows them down without much chewing, and I think about gifting her some of the entrails, but I decide against it, tell her to get on back to the porch. In their pen, the three hounds lick their chops, saliva dripping and drooling, but I don't toss them anything. "Only give 'em what they earned," Daddy told me when I was five, going out with him for the first time. "A dog gets what he ain't earned going to end up lazy, won't tree much of nothing, squirrel nor coon."

When I've finished cleaning the thing, got it on ice for my daddy to take down to Walt's for stuffing, I head up the porch, pet Pearl as I move by. In the kitchen, Daddy looks up from his cup of coffee.

"What time you go out?"

"Quarter to three," I say, and he whistles through his teeth. I pour myself a cup of the coffee.

"You get you one?"

I nod. "Pearl got it."

The old man frowns. "Thought I told you not to take that dog hunting."

"She likes it. And she treed that coon before any of your hounds."

He shakes his head. "Don't make a damn. She ain't a hunting dog. She's a porch dog, maybe a yard dog, but she ain't made to be out in them woods."

"She's my dog. And she does just fine out in the woods."

"You taking your dog with you back to Wyeth? You going to take care of her in that dormitory? Or are you leaving her here for me to feed and water and look after like I been doing?"

I feel heat rising in my face, bringing pain back to my cold-numbed cheeks. "I can't take her with me. They don't allow pets."

"Then don't sass me. And don't take that dog hunting."

"Yessir."

He takes a gulp of the coffee, and I do the same. It's acrid, burned from sitting in his old metal pot, but I take another sip. "What time's the service?"

"Eleven," I say.

"What you doing till then?"

I shrug, swallow some more of the coffee.

"You going back right after?"

"I got an exam Monday. Got to get back and study." I think about Carrie, about how she's probably still in bed in her apartment, the one her father pays the note on. I think about how if I'd of woke up next to her, under that down comforter, I'd not have had the get-up-and-go to hunt on a morning like this. Instead, I woke up on the old cot in my room, my back stiff from the metal bar.

"You be back for Christmas," he says.

"Yessir."

"And you can leave that attitude in Wyeth when you come. Your granny ain't coming to town to see you with your nose up in the air."

"Yessir."

I begin to walk out of the room, thinking that I'll go on and shower, change into the suit I brought with me, the one Carrie bought me last year for her sorority's formal. Before I'm out the door, he says, "Your grades in line?"

He hasn't ever asked about my grades, hasn't paid much attention to school nor classes nor how I fare in them. "I'm doing all right."

"Keep it that way. You lose that scholarship, they won't have much interest in keeping you around, you'll be back here, bothering with the dogs and getting underfoot."

"Yessir," I say.

~

I found Pearl when I was thirteen. Me and Warren had wandered off down the tracks, over toward Millport and Kennedy, and she'd come sniffling up to me, just a puppy. Then, she'd been all blond, looked like a little of pit-bull and a little of shepherd and a little of everything else besides. None of the pieces of her matched. Legs were already muscled, chest broad, like you see with bull-dogs, but her head was dainty, lacking that flat plane, those laid back ears. Her body seemed too long, a by-product of basset hound I reckoned, and her tail curved up like a beagle, though she never had that warble you get with them. Her eyes and ears were all German Shepherd.

She came up to me there on the tracks, and I fed her a bit of the white bread I was carrying in my pocket. Warren said we ought to tie her to a tree, throw rocks at her, but I told him no, and we moved on. She followed us over to Millport and back again, laying herself down on the porch when I got back. My daddy took one look at her and told me to get that damned mutt the hell away from his house. Told me we was a blue-tick family, always had been, and weren't no way in hell we was keeping some goofy-ass Heinz 57.

After a while though, he got sort of used to her, let me name her. We'd been reading Steinbeck over at the middle school and I was starting to figure that sometimes reading wasn't so bad a thing, and around that same time, Warren found half an old pearl necklace buried out back of his place. We'd been digging out there for weeks, hoping to find the rest of it, so I figure I just had pearls on the mind.

"Ain't no kind of name for a dog," Daddy said. He preferred the tried and true names: Buford, Otis, Guy, Buck, Arleen, Doris.

"It's my dog," I told him.

"Name her what you want," he said. "Don't make it a good idea."

"Ain't got to be a good idea," I said, and he'd smacked me a good one, and we didn't talk much about her name from then on.

~

The sun's come up a bit, letting just a hint of warm into the crisp air, and I head down to the railroad tracks, Pearl following along like she used to do.

Weeds are growing tall on the tracks now that they aren't used anymore. I walk plank-to-plank, and Pearl keeps to my heels, snorting through the grass in my wake. Moisture is coating the shiny black shoes, and I can feel it soaking through the bottom of my pant legs and socks, but I figure nobody'll be paying much attention to my legs. The air, sharp in my chest, brings little flecks of tears to my eyes. I blink them away, wipe at them with the sleeve of my jacket. Pearl whines once, looks up at me, and I tell her all right, motion down the trestle, down to the ground below us.

She barely gets off the little slope before she sets to, dripping runny turds that steam up, the hard smell reaching me even from this distance. When she's done, she begins to move back up the slope, back to the tracks where I'm waiting, but mid-way up, she hears something, her ears sticking up at that German Shepherd tilt, and before I can stop her, she's off through the brush, heading for the tree line.

All this land is posted, and it's dangerous this time of year to wander off the tracks. Go too far in the woods, you're liable to get a ass full of buckshot from some dipshit in from Birmingham for a weekend's hunting. I call to Pearl, but she doesn't slow down, and before I can really think too much on it, I'm moving toward her, trying hard to keep up, though my shoes stick in the shallow mud.

She leads me a quarter mile before I catch up to her. She's caught the scent of something, and she doesn't want to let it go, no matter how I pull at her collar. When I wrench her backwards, she looks up at me with anxious eyes, her fur bristling high against the cold. I think of my father, of his warning not to take her in the woods.

I let loose her collar. As soon as she's free, she sticks her nose to the ground and moves forward again. I follow, listening close for the skitter of an animal, but the field's quiet.

~

When my daddy called to let me know about Warren, I was lying naked next to Carrie, sweat drying, a high, feral scent coming up from our bodies. I answered the phone without thinking about it. If I'd taken a second, I'd have seen the caller ID, said, "I'll call him back later," but instinct kicked in and I answered without looking at the screen. Carrie rolled away from me, closed her eyes, and my daddy said, without greeting, "Your buddy went and got himself shot."

Since then, the details have come out a little at a time. He'd gone to the Kroger's, blood laced through with the meth he brewed in a trailer on his grandfather's land. He had the old .22, but it was unloaded. In better moments, I tell myself that he didn't want to harm anybody, but I know he probably just forgot to put the bullets in.

It was his uncle shot him, from behind the register with a Smith & Wesson he kept for such purposes. I don't know if he recognized Warren before he pulled the trigger. I figure he must have. Though Warren was wearing a mask, I think it'd be hard to mistake the rail-thin figure, the jittering hands, the dull eyes.

"Funeral's Saturday," Daddy told me on the phone.

"I'll try to come." I looked at Carrie, who was already asleep. "I may not make it."

I heard a wet sound, spit being shot through teeth. "They skip out of funerals much over there in Wyeth?"

"No sir. It ain't got a thing to do with Wyeth."

Before he hung up, he sighed, said, "Boy, it's got ever thing in the world to do with Wyeth."

~

After a minute, Pearl stops, buries her nose in a patch of weeds. I reach down into the thick tangle of green, figuring I'll feel the quick movement of a field mouse, but instead, my hand grazes something smooth and cold rippling across the surface of the mud. I jerk my hand away, grab Pearl by the collar to haul her back, but it's too late, the thing's latched onto her leg, it's fangs sunk in deep, and she's got her head down on it, gnawing into its scaled hide.

I hear the hard snap of the snake's back being broken, and I try to pull Pearl's jaws free of it, but she stays locked on. The fangs are still dug into the meat of her leg, and I try to pull that loose too, but Pearl just whines, so I let it be.

I sit down in the mud next to her. She'll be gone before I can carry her back to my daddy's and even if we make it in time, what then? No money for a vet. I put a hand on her head, rub the bristle of fur, imagine what my daddy'll say when I tell him. "Shouldn't of been out in them damn woods no way. She was a porch dog, and if you'd listened to me, she'd still be alive."

I massage the muscle behind her jaw, trying to coax her loose, but it stays knotted tight, holding the dead thing. A little blood is dripping out of her mouth.

I look down at my watch. I've only thirty minutes to hike back to the house, drive down to the funeral home in Reform. I couldn't make it in time, even if I didn't have Pearl to carry, so instead of trying to do something, I just sit, one hand in the mud beside me, one hand on Pearl, smoothing back her fur, coaxing her hackles down. I give myself a moment of guilt, tell myself that if I'd ignored my daddy, if I'd stayed in Wyeth, with Carrie, this wouldn't of happened. But that kind of thought doesn't do any good, so I just sit and pet Pearl some more. She's not whining, and I wonder if she's gone numb, if the poison has worked its way deep enough for that. I wonder too, if the meth coursing through Warren's system kept him from feeling the sharp pain of the gunshots. One in the arm, two in the chest, dead in five minutes. When he walked in the door, did he think himself a real criminal? Did he imagine loaded guns and empty bank vaults?

I lean down, look Pearl in the eyes. They are sharp as ever, comprehending. I say, "Aw'right now, girl," and I massage her jaw a little more. She finally releases, choosing loyalty over instinct. I take the tie off, use it to wipe at the blood dripping from her mouth. I let myself believe that this is the way to go. A wide field, the hand of someone you love gentle on your neck, the sharp iron tang of victory on your tongue. Sometimes, I think, it's okay to pretend we are that which we are not.

"Get it, Pearl!" I nudge the body with the toe of my shoe, make it shift a little in the grass. She looks down at the snake, starts growling. Her hackles are up, and the growl is growing stronger, and I want the fight to resume, want the poison to do its work while Pearl gets after the snake. "Sic 'em!" She stands on her three good legs, her wounded paw wavering an inch above the ground. I nudge the snake again, and she lowers her head toward it, flashes tooth, and I bump it once more, make it rustle the grass. As she lunges toward the snake, I run a hand along her side, feel the heave of inhalation. I say, "Get that motherfucker!"

Hunting Season

Peter Kispert

You tried catching one there on the lip of forest, snaring it between the shoulder and snout, wading in a drift of damp meadow: a Tuesday. The line had been set, fifty yards south, and you sat—spine curved like the bend of a bow, tracing the cardinal, ebbing wind as it combed the bluestem grass. An oily groan, from your left. One, maybe two hundred yards past the oaks. You examined prospective culprits: the strict vermilion of raspberry bushes, silent in the slight cinnamon of fall. A gun, cold against your palm. Noise returned: the formal, gullet pinch of a mating call. You began to notice the backlit horizon, a black train pulling further away from you into a stretch of forest autumn had not yet stolen. Air rolled to fog. Your line pulled forward. For a moment, you understood: the seismic neutrality of your presence, the bullet's path as it lodged in the bear's peachy skin, the orchard hours away, picked clean in the wake of blackberry season.

Digging the Hole

Nathan Gower

Where are you? Evie asks. We lie in bed, staring away from each other. This is our habit. This is our life.

The first time Evie and I slept together was an accident. I fell into her in the midst of our collective drunken stupor the way a tottering child might fall into his first busted lip. We rolled, felt, hurt, and screamed our way into the next five years where our world became different than yours, different than anyone's. We blossomed like tiger lilies, our flowers bursting from a single overnight rain, so much love, so much color that we knew we'd have to die too soon.

On one of the happy nights we drove my Explorer to the middle of an empty field. We took a fifth of Jack and swigged from the bottle, never even thought about the ruts the tires dug into private land. The liquor ate our insides the way that it will, and Evie said she wanted to have my baby, a boy if I could swing it. She let her clay-red hair slip over her eyes, just let it play on her face like it didn't even tickle. I would have traded everything I owned to be the one she'd let tuck it behind her ear. It's magical to think we conceived that night. We probably didn't, but we tell each other we did.

Matthew Alexander had gray eyes and perfect waves of black hair, so perfect that Evie says she ordered him from a catalogue. She felt lonely and happy when she tucked him close to her breast, as he cried hoarsely through the night--not even a cry at all, but air escaping from his lungs the best it could, as if it already knew what was coming. Evie was a whirlwind in those days. She looked like the painting that hung on our bedroom wall: an Indian woman twisting out of her skin, her soul flying blue across an orange-red sky.

Doctors changed their minds a lot, but it didn't help in the end. We drank a lot after the fact, one burn on top of another. Now, we stay up all night staring away from each other, wondering who will blow up first. I can't ask her what she thinks about on these lonely nights. I'll never know for sure, but I think we're haunted by the same image: the size of the hole in the ground - three times as big as his shoebox-sized body-- like if they kept digging, maybe, just maybe, he would have had more time to grow into it.

Where are you? she asks again. Our silence thumps in my eardrums like a beating heart.

In a Room Made Up for Someone Else

Ryan Millbern

Bill picks me up at the Riviera Motel in his blue Astro van and I climb into the front seat, nod to the four Mexican guys in the back—Miguel, Emilio, Rodrigo and Pat—and we take the interstate an hour into the city. We stop at the Shell gas station on our way out of Galvin and Bill buys six 20-ounce coffees and we drink the coffee and smoke our cigarettes with the windows down and the already humid air rushing in to fill the van. Bill and I are the only two on our crew who can speak English, but most mornings we don't talk. We listen to classic rock on Q95 and watch the fields on either side of the interstate rush past us in a green-brown blur.

During the first few weeks of the job it felt good to be awake and moving 80 miles an hour toward a full day of work, beating the sun to the city. I had always lived on the other side of dawn, crawling into bed at the same gray hour that I wake in now, my head singing with a night's worth of booze. A year ago this hour felt like dying. It's starting to feel that way again. We're halfway through a 60-day hotel job in downtown Indianapolis. We've been working 12 hours a day, seven days a week, furnishing the 1,650 rooms of the hotel one-by-one with beds, end tables, armoires, ironing boards, televisions and telephones, filling up the empty spaces where people much richer than us will one day spend the night.

Bill runs these cash jobs all the time. He brings me in whenever the work is too much for him and his Mexicans, and for that I am grateful. He pays me 12 dollars an hour in cash and he gives the Mexicans 10, which, according to Bill, is "still a lot for Mexicans."

My first job with Bill was four years ago. We cleaned the machines at the Clayton Bottling plant in Galvin. We'd roll in during an off shift when the factory was dark and silent, lit only along the perimeter of the manufacturing floor by small yellow lights, and we'd crawl into the dead machines and blow them out with air hoses, wipe down the accumulated grime with thin rags. I'd get home just as the sun was coming up; cash in my pocket, my body covered in grease and stinking like cleaning chemicals.

And then one morning a lot like this morning, I walked out of the factory, bought a fifth of Canadian Mist at CVS, got drunk before noon and broke into an old woman's house. She lived a couple of blocks away from the Riviera Motel. When I was out of work, I'd walk the surrounding blocks just to fill the hours and I'd see her, a petite older woman, trimming the hedges or sitting alone on the front porch drinking iced tea.

When I let myself in the front door she was in the backyard, bending over her dried out garden, picking cherry tomatoes and dropping them in a five-gallon bucket one at a time. As I sorted through her purse in the kitchen, I could hear the hollow plops of the tomatoes hitting the bottom of the bucket through her open window. Her license said her name was Judith; that she was 79 years old, 5 foot 1, 140 pounds. I pocketed her wallet and a turquoise bracelet and then found her bedroom on the first floor and scooped up a pair of pearl earrings.

I could have gone out through the front door unnoticed, but I stopped in the entryway. I wanted Judith to see me. I walked back through the kitchen and out the back door and stood on her back porch, watching her pick the tomatoes. I stood there silent and sweating in the sun for five minutes until she finally turned around. When she saw me she gasped, a terrible sound that was more terrible because she was old and lived alone, and probably rarely exercised her voice. My blood slammed against the inside of my skin, and even through my drunkenness I felt dangerously alive, living at the edge of my heartbeat. She dropped the tomatoes and raised a trembling hand to her face. Her whole body shook and she started to take a step backward into her garden. Her foot got tangled in the tomato plants and she collapsed backward, her sun hat tipping back off her head, then her short legs were up in the air and she was down, the dust and insects jumping out of the garden all around her. Then she was very still.

I ran, holding the pockets of my overalls, clutching everything I stole from her so it wouldn't spill out onto the sidewalk, and I didn't stop until I was safely inside my room at the Riviera Motel.

I tell Bill a lot about my life—the drinking and the sober stretches and the fistfights and how this job at the hotel could be the opportunity I ride into sobriety—but I've never told him about Judith.

~

We get to the hotel right before seven and pile out of the van and into the loading docks at the back of the building where a row of semi-truck trailers, separated from their rigs, wait to be unloaded. "They're still here boys," Bill says, nodding to the trailers. He says this every morning. He kills the engine and holds onto the belt of his jean shorts as he steps down out of the van.

We split into pairs, Miguel and myself, Bill and Rodrigo, Emilio and Pat. I find a metal cart against the back entrance to the hotel and drag it to the edge of the loading dock and step out into the trailer bed. We pack the carts with boxes of unassembled furniture and drag them to the freight elevator, and I use my key to unlock it. We pause to wrap our boots in plastic. "Put your boot condoms on, boys," Bill says. We start the day on the South End of the 16th floor. There are 33 floors altogether, 50 rooms on each floor.

Every room in this tower shares the exact same layout, drawn up by interior designers on blueprints specifying to the inch the spaces between everything: the bed and the end table, the computer desk and the wall-mounted television, the end of the couch and the door. During the first week, Miguel and I had to refer to the blueprint for the exact measurements, but now we know the numbers by heart: 55 inches from the closet to the armoire, 36 inches to the bed, another 70 to the desk, 37 more to the window. We work quickly and rarely talk. The only sounds are the swishing of our plastic-wrapped boots on the plush carpet.

Until the rooms are furnished, I imagine that they are not so different than my room at the Riviera Motel in Galvin, which I rent for 75 dollars a week because my uncle knows the manager. With the 12-hour days and the two-hour round-trip commute, I'm only there to sleep and shower and sometimes watch the news. When I first moved in and was out of work I would sit on my bed with the television on mute and listen to the people on either side of me through the thin walls. Sometimes I was rewarded with the muffled sounds of two people meeting over their lunch break to fuck and I would masturbate to the sound of them, my head pressed back into the headboard, both straining to hear and also bracing myself for climax. Other times I would light a cigarette and smoke and listen to the people move around and try to imagine what they were like.

One couple, Janet and Ted, had stopped in Galvin to explore the handful of antique shops at the edge of town. "Fireside Antiques is supposed to have the best glass collection around," he'd said, and I imagined him peering at a tri-fold brochure over the top of his glasses. Janet would have been standing in front of the mirror, drawing on her eyebrows. I wanted to whisper to them through the wall; to tell them that I knew Barry, the owner of Fireside. But I said nothing. They had each other and their love for antiques and I had them to listen to, for a night.

~

Bill brings a two-pound tub of peanut butter and a loaf of bread for our lunch. We each grab four slices of bread and a plastic knife from the box and make the sandwiches on our laps. We rinse our coffee cups out in the bathroom off the lobby and fill them with water from the faucet and eat our peanut butter sandwiches and drink our water in the shade of the awning along the front sidewalk. Miguel shows me a picture of a young girl, his daughter. She is chubby and shirtless, two fat braids framing her moon face.

I smile. "Very pretty," I say.

He gestures toward the picture and points at me.

"I don't have any kids," I say, but he doesn't understand. I point at the picture and then point to myself and shake my head.

I heard somewhere that Mexicans give their kids Coca Cola in their bottles. I want to ask Miguel if this is true but I don't. It seems like too much work. I finish my sandwich and stand up, stretch and light a cigarette.

Two young women in suits walk past us. One talks excitedly, using her hands. The other walks with her head down, nodding. Both women are slender; they look like athletes. Their suits fit well. They carry expensive handbags. One wears over-sized white sunglasses.

We see women like them every day in the city, walking and talking, always moving quickly in expensive shoes, gazing up at the hotel's blue glass façade. They don't see us; we are part of the landscape. They'll be the ones turning down the sheets on the beds we're positioning in those rooms, climbing under the covers after a long day of meetings and client dinners and empty conversations. I want to be there with them, although I'm not sure what I'd say.

I used to talk a lot when I drank. I had so much to say and people who would listen. I told them about running from the cops through the woods of Sullivan County after a busted house party, hiding high up in the guts of the Yountsville Covered Bridge until the sun came up. I told them about the summer I spent roofing houses in Carrington Hills, the rich subdivision outside of Galvin, and how our crew could see down into Amanda Simmons' backyard, where she sunbathed naked every afternoon. I told them about Bill and the jobs he runs and I would regret it most times, fearful that they might seek him out and rob me of work.

But more than the stories I remember the scene inside the Green Street Tavern: bottles backlit against a mirror, the white noise of the bar; the sound of other conversations I wanted to be a part of. I remember the feeling of sinking into myself, my brain inching down my spine, submerged with each drink until I was looking at the room through a hole in my chest.

~

After lunch we ride the elevator back to the 16th floor and open the door on to another empty room, and I realize that the days are all the same: the 20-ounce coffee, the first cigarette, the drive over, the rooms stretching out on either side of the narrow hallway before me, above me and below me, all of them empty and waiting to be filled. And the filling of those rooms becomes my morning and my terrible afternoon, and my afternoon becomes my evening eating fast food on the drive home. And then there is the same long night in another room made up for someone else.

Standing in Room 1648, staring at an unassembled nightstand, it becomes clear to me that I can't live the way I should. There are too many hours in the day, too many days. I wait until Miguel breaks to use the bathroom and, with five hours left on my shift, I leave without saying goodbye. I take the freight elevator down and then out the front door, duck into a gap in the orange mesh construction fence. I stand in the street, hugging the mesh. Cars pass by a foot away to my left and I can feel the hot air of their wake, the sheer force of their movement. I wait for a break in the traffic, and then I walk toward the center of the city.

~

I feel small in the late-afternoon shadows from the bank towers and hotels. I want to stop in every building, in every room and office and restaurant, and see how the people live there. In Galvin I am too big for the town, for the room at the Riviera, for the van with the fucking Mexicans and Bill's handful of tired phrases and sad stabs at conversation. I'm too big even for this day. I want it to become two and then three.

I enter a sports bar called Champions and sit at the bar and order a draft from a bartender wearing a referee's shirt. I drink half of the beer in one series of hard swallows and sit breathing heavy, sweat standing out on my skin. I smell sour, and I can smell the sweat on my hands and feel it everywhere on my skin. The restaurant is fairly empty, the bar deserted. Two guys in polo shirts and khaki pants watch SportsCenter highlights at a table in the corner and drink cokes. It is cool in the air conditioning and I enjoy the cold beer. I finish the beer and tip the bartender.

My phone rings. It's Bill. I hold the vibrating phone in my hand for a moment and then place it on the bar and walk out into the sunshine.

~

I stop and drink in each bar I come to until it's after midnight and I'm drunk, sitting at a dirty plastic table on an outdoor patio by myself. I stare at the twisted black wick of a tiki torch and sip a Budweiser. A woman sits down, lowers her white purse off her shoulder and onto the table.

"Is anyone sitting here?" she asks, gesturing toward the table with what looks like gin and tonic in a small plastic cup.

I shake my head.

She's short and pale with bleach-blonde, almost white hair. Fiftyish and rail thin, her shoulder bones test her skin beneath her pink tank top. Her teeth are crooked. She has a silver bracelet on one wrist. Her knuckles are arthritic knots.

"You need a fresh beer?" she asks.

"Sure."

"I'll get you another."

She motions for the waitress and orders a beer and a gin and tonic.

"It's been forever since a woman bought me a drink," I say.

"I don't believe that."

"It's true."

We sit in silence for a moment while she lights a cigarette. "I'm Beth," she says, extending her hand.

"Jack. I want to warn you, I threw away six months of sobriety earlier this evening."

"I'm sorry to hear that."

"Yeah," I say. "I don't know if I'm sorry yet or not. Right now, not so much."

"You probably will be in the morning," she says.

"You're right. There's a good chance I'll lose my job."

"Why?"

"Walked off this afternoon."

"Why did you do that?"

"I don't know," I say, except I do know. I know everything: the number of cells in my blood, the number of stars in the sky, the number of inches between the bed and the end table, the number of days in a life, the shape of Miguel's daughter's face, ways in and out of consciousness, how to jump ship, how to take someone's breath, how to ruin a good thing, how to start something, how to seduce a woman. I know how to listen through thin walls and how hard a heart can beat. Most of all, I know that I don't want to be alone.

"It looks like I found you in crisis," she says.

"Isn't that the best way to find a stranger in a bar?"

"It depends on what you want to happen."

"I want everything to happen," I say. "I've been waiting for a long time for something to happen."

"You couldn't have been waiting too long," Beth says. "How old are you, 30?"

"32."

"You haven't been waiting long enough," she says. She takes a drink. "Aren't you going to ask how old I am?"

"No," I say. "I don't really care."

"I like you," she says.

We finish our drinks and order another round and then another. She tells me that she was married once, that two miscarriages had been too much for them to handle. She works as an administrative assistant to the floor manager of a cell phone packaging plant. She might be able to get me a job. I tell her about the drinking and about living in a hotel, but I don't tell her about breaking into the old woman's house. After an hour we know as much about each other as we will ever need to know.

She is kind and getting drunk and suddenly everything seems possible. I imagine a new life with Beth in the city. I could work in the warehouse of the cell phone packaging plant on the south side, second shift. When I got off work we could go to the bars downtown together, follow the veins of the city directly into its heart every night. We could stand in crowds on weekend afternoons and listen to the sound of the living all around us.

The waitress signals last call and we order a final round, finish the drinks, exit the patio and walk into the deserted street. The city is dead.

"I have something I want to show you," I say.

"OK," she answers.

I take her by the hand. We pass a one-armed homeless man and his dirty beagle sitting on the sidewalk outside of a movie theater. We pass the doorways of other bars and the sound inside spills out into the street, but we don't stop in any of them. We move toward the hotel.

We slip in through the rip in the orange mesh fence and circle back to the loading docks and stand there, breathing heavy and looking at each other. I jam a dirty thumb in her mouth because I've always wanted to do this to a woman and, after walking off the job and meeting Beth, I feel like I can do anything. She just closes her eyes and rolls her tongue over the thumb and we stand there on the loading dock platform, with her sucking my thumb in the dark.

I guide her to the freight elevator, unlock it and we take it up to Floor 16. In the elevator we kiss hard and it happens: My heart kicks blood into my brain, and the blood is moving everywhere: into my lips and my fingers and my crotch, everything an extension of my heart. I taste my own thumb in her mouth and a day's worth of cigarettes and every word she ever said to her husband and her dad and her boyfriends, and all of it is passing between us, the history of our mouths, as we ride the elevator into the sky.

The elevator bell sounds and we stop kissing and I'm suddenly aware of the possibility that there could be someone else in the hotel. More than likely it will be Rhett, the security guard in the lobby, watching our ascent on a tiny television. I wonder how long will it take him to reach us.

We step off the elevator and I start to jog, and all the while Beth is strangely silent, following me blindly through the dark hallway. We open the door to room 1648. It is furnished and waiting for us. I shut the door behind us and lock it, flip on the light in the entryway. I tell her to undress. She does everything I say.

She moves toward the bed while she undresses and the numbers are running through my head: 55 inches from the closet to the armoire, 36 inches to the bed, another 70 to the desk, 37 more to the window.

Then we are naked, kissing and moving through the room. I turn her to face the window so we can look out on the lights of the city and then we are both lost in it, so much so that we're not sure if there's a pounding at the door, or if it's our hearts in our ears or our bodies against one another or the sound two things make when they find each other in the dark.

Man Skate

Wendy Oleson

From the outside the roller rink looked like the warehouse where my father had stocked office supplies before he left my mother and me. But inside the rink pulsed muscle and meat, sugar and syrup, a maze of what ifs like I'd never seen. It smelled of sweaty socks and licorice whips and nighttime. The air was as cool inside as out, and I was surprised by the twirling lights, the taffy and cotton candy, the quarter play Pac Man, Asteroid, and Mario Bros next to a machine dispensing a rubber ball for a nickel.

The colored lights of the rink reminded me of the rock we'd cracked open in Mrs. Rothby's science class. She never said there would be another world inside, so when she unscrewed the vise, I fell in love with her and the network of crystals she held up to her chest. A geode over Mrs. Rothby's heart, the flickering of deep purple jewels: I wanted her to take me home and tuck me into bed with the sheets pulled up to my chin.

But it was Uncle Roy who held my hand at the skate rental counter. I had a fresh scrape on my left palm from a skateboarding fall, so I turned and gave him my right. It was the two of us, Roy taking me on my first trip to the roller rink. I remember getting boy's skates because I had a wide foot. Uncle Roy brought his own skates: black boots with neon wheels. My rentals, size four, were a dirty Naugahyde —not quite vinyl, not quite animal—with pumpkin orange wheels. Chocolate brown laces. I looked at Uncle Roy squatting in his tight acid jeans, lacing me up as I sat on a large, carpeted stool shaped like a mushroom. These mushrooms were everywhere, along with more kids than I'd ever seen: bigger kids, better kids, kids flashing glittered wrist bands and heavy metal t-shirts. The boys, I watched the boys pull off their high tops, shed sweatshirts to reveal tanks and flesh—biceps, triceps—I wanted to touch the skin over those muscles. I wanted it to be silly putty so I could leave fingerprints.

The rink played the same song we'd heard in Uncle Roy's car. Poison, they were his favorite band. Uncle Roy had freckles along his temples and forehead that never made it to his nose. He began to lace me up even though I asked to do it myself. I saw my father a couple times a year then, and he let me do everything myself. But Uncle Roy insisted helping me into the skates, his cupped palm against my arch, then his fingers running up my heel like a shoehorn. He had dry lips. He'd laced me up too tight and had to wrap the extra length of the laces around my ankle before tying them in one bow, then another. The skates pressed on the round bone on the inside of my ankles.

"You're ready, Erin." He grinned up at me like I was the most fabulous person he'd ever seen. "You're gonna blaze a trail."

He got up to sit next to me. I had to watch him put on his own skates, and I think he took extra time fooling with eyelets, re-lacing, because he liked feeling my eyes on him.

Roy was my mother's younger brother. He was a secretary at the dairy plant. The first time we were truly alone together (my mother busy taking her final nursing exam), he'd brought me to the plant's "dairy museum," where I saw the evolution of pasteurization equipment and photographs of a life-sized Holstein sculpted in butter. At the end of the tour I drank a pint of chocolate milk; Roy tipped the corner of his into mine. "Cheers," he'd said.

Uncle Roy and Grandma had encouraged my mother to attend nursing school after my father left. Mom got a job at a nursing home while she worked toward her degree. After school I'd take the city bus to the home to watch television with the residents who liked westerns and *I Love Lucy*. I could barely see the TV because a blind, retarded woman sat right in front of it. The old people felt sorry for her—she still had creamy-smooth skin—so they let her press her palms to the screen.

Government cuts took my mother's job at the home, so she settled for the night shift at a hospital. I stayed at Grandma's, then with Uncle Roy. My mother tried to make it so we had dinner together. We ate from a can, but she always heated it on the stove. I loved her, and I knew she was good because one day I asked her about the commercials with the starving black kids and their huge stomachs. Give seventy-two cents a day, the TV said. Less than the cost of one cup of coffee. My mother told me those kids' bellies weren't fat. Bad bacteria produced gas that blew up their stomachs like balloons. She said it was very painful; one day when we had a little money she would call the number. I'd already asked Uncle Roy that same question. He didn't know why starving kids were fat, just that the flies on their faces made him want to puke.

~

"Don't be afraid to grab me if you lose your balance," Uncle Roy said. I wasn't afraid, and I wouldn't fall. In gym class I was the best: the first girl picked for teams and second-best of all the fourth graders for chin ups—seventeen. We stood at the edge of the rink, where carpet met wood, waiting for an opening in the stream of skaters. A breeze found my face as people whooshed by. That air smelled different, a little like fruit punch. Boys held girls' hands.

"Should we do it?" he asked.

We stepped onto the rink. He grabbed at my hand but missed and held my fingers. I didn't want to look like a baby. There were some other kids with dads holding their hands, but they looked like toddlers in glorified Fischer Price skates. That wasn't me.

I pulled my hand away.

Uncle Roy grabbed for it again, but I kept it out of reach until he gave up.

Roller-skating wasn't any harder than skateboarding. I had the neighbor kid's old Santa Cruz and sometimes rode it down Grandma's driveway. She told me I'd break my neck. I loved her, but she was all cigarette smoke and hype. She promised to crack my head open if I didn't wear the jumpers my mother sewed me. There wasn't anything better than the couple times a year I saw my dad, because he pulled the dresses out of my overnight bag and laughed at them. Flowers? Rosebuds? We'd make gagging noises together, then go to the hardware store to buy screws and drill-bits.

There was a DJ booth built into the far wall. Inside a man wearing a camouflage jacket spoke into a microphone. He said things like: "Here's a song for city folk," and "If you know how to live it up on Friday night, this is for you." He didn't annoy me, but I kept thinking that if I had a microphone, I'd say something that mattered: why the starving kids' stomachs looked fat or that it's stupid to make people wear dresses.

I was skating better—I even managed to vary my speed—but Roy stayed next to me. He probably didn't have many friends if he'd volunteered to baby-sit. He wasn't cool, so I pretended he wasn't right there, smelling a little like onions. I thought about who I'd like to be skating with, whose hand I would want to hold. Mrs. Rothby's. But she wore fancy shoes with heels, and I couldn't imagine her in skates. I surveyed the skaters around me, eventually spotting a cute girl. She looked about thirteen and wore a ponytail with a pink ribbon. Girls needed pretty things. Colored spots of light revolved around the rink, blurring the walls blue, red, and green. They stained the skaters too. My girl turned purple—her blouse and skin—then yellow, orange. I skated just behind her. Her boyfriend wore a baseball cap for Detroit. I had that hat. But Grandma didn't like me to wear it.

When the DJ announced the Man Skate, I felt a crawling in my stomach. To think of it now, it was like those seconds when you're scratching a lottery ticket—when the first two boxes show ten thousand dollars, and you only have to match a third. It's that rush of excitement that sours as soon as the third box gets scratched.

What was a Man Skate? It sounded reptilian. Even though the composition of the rink was changing—it looked like just the girls were getting off—I stayed my course, kept skating.

"Wait over there." Roy shoved me toward the mushrooms. "You can't skate."

I wasn't stupid, but I wanted to know why. I tied for second most chin-ups. At recess I raced with the boys. "I'm better than him." I pointed at a skinny kid on the rink waving to someone by the mushrooms.

"Here," Uncle Roy wormed his hand into his jeans' pocket. "Buy some candy." He gave me a wad of paper money.

Since my allowance came in quarters, the dollars distracted me. I cupped the bills and went to the mushrooms to count the money. Most of the mushrooms were full by now. Girls. They giggled together and grabbed each other's hands. I stood at the edge of a forest, the smells and sounds thick and unfamiliar. They weren't paying attention to me, but I felt as conspicuous as the buzzing neon over the snack bar.

The men still hadn't started to skate; the sound system had malfunctioned, and the camouflage guy messed with it. I found a partially-open mushroom with a view of the rink. I didn't notice at first, but my girl sat opposite, legs crossed. A head taller than me, she had her hand in her ponytail, was brushing it with her fingers. She wasn't as pretty from the front; her mouth was crooked and hungry, like my old goldfish, Bob. But her eyes were nice. I couldn't tell the color because she sort of squinted, like she really wanted to see stuff. I opened my hand to count the money. It had seemed like more, but the bills were crunchy and mangled, bulkier that way: three dollars.

Still, the roller rink was mine with three dollars: sixty bouncy balls, twelve arcade game credits, and cotton candy or pop wouldn't cost more than a dollar: three pops. I was about to walk to the snack counter when I noticed my girl looking at me. I wore brown corduroy pants—I didn't complain about those—but my shirt had a white doily bit at the collar. She looked at me like she didn't know why I had a doily around my neck. I didn't know, except that if I tried to rip it out, Grandma would rant about cracking my head.

I thought to shrug at my girl to show her I was cool, but the music for the Man Skate began. She turned to watch the rink. My eyes followed. I found Uncle Roy in the mass of skaters; he looked like a Poindexter—too tall and thin to be any good at skating.

Uncle Roy skated near the front of the pack like it was a race. My girl's boyfriend strained to keep up. Red and blue lights spun like police warnings. The bills in my hand dampened with sweat. I wanted my chin-length hair to blow back; I wanted to pump my arms and cross my legs one over another around the rink's curves; I wanted my veins to stand out from my forearms and neck like they did on my dad when he worked on the roof. My girl would see me and wonder how I could skate so fast without falling. I would wave and keep my balance. I'd even describe the Man Skate to Dad: the speed and lights, the loudest music I'd ever heard. I would tell him I was out there skating, the fastest of all.

It lasted for a couple songs, enough time for the dads to impress their kids and the boys to impress their girls. I clenched my jaw the whole time.

"Last time I was here a guy broke his arm." My heart raced at the surprise—my girl had spoken to me! Now I saw she had braces, and they made her mouth hungrier even though they made it full.

"Really?" I said, scratching my chin like Dad did.

"Yeah, I'd never want to go out there." She shook her head as she got up; her ponytail swayed.

"I would," I said.

She stopped. She hadn't expected me to say anything. She'd started the conversation out of boredom, and I told her I wanted to Man Skate. She stood there looking down at me. Her eyes really looked, squinted like she was figuring something out. Then she smiled with her lips together. A smile that closed off her face. It seemed like it would be hard to smile like that with so much metal on your teeth.

She returned to the rink, but I stayed on the mushroom. She'd peeled something away from me. And though I hadn't begun to understand what I'd lost, I knew to be thankful for the darkness and noise of the rink, for its thick, musty smell; I hoped it would hide me if I kept still.

~

When Uncle Roy found me at the mushroom, he was breathing hard. Sweat held his t-shirt to his skin and soaked the hair at the nape of s neck. He asked if I'd spent the money. I lied. I thought about what I could do with those three dollars. Last time I visited my dad he had his eye on a circular saw. But that was too expensive.

I didn't want to skate anymore, but Roy pulled me back to the rink. We slipped into the flow though I hardly moved my legs. Sometimes I stopped skating completely, let him drag me around the corners. As Roy's hands began to sweat, the salt made the scrape on my palm sting.

The DJ announced a song for "People who like to dance," even one for "People who have dreams." I thought I saw my girl playing Pac Man in the distance, but by the time Roy wanted to leave, she wasn't there.

I sat on the mushroom; Uncle Roy crouched below. He was trying to get my skate off, but I didn't want him to. He struggled, determined to do it even though he hadn't properly loosened the laces. My foot was wedged inside. The more he pulled, I pushed. Then, I thought I saw my girl watching; adrenalin pumped through me. Roy swore now: Jesus and shit. His fair skin pulsed a sick pink. He let go. Without his resistance, my leg swung through his face. The toe of my skate bashed his nose, and the wheels rolled over his eyes. I felt it through my whole body. He brought his hand to his face; blood flowed. "I can do it myself," I said. And I did, while he went to the snack bar to get napkins.

No one seemed to notice what had happened. I looked for my girl. Had she witnessed my glory? As I unlaced my other skate, I squinted to see her. She was gone.

Uncle Roy returned, the napkins a bloody blossom under his nose. He glared at me as we returned my skates. My skates with the pumpkin wheels and chocolate brown laces. Just walking through the parking lot I felt like I was still rolling; my legs were not my legs anymore. It was time to get into his car again, his smelly Buick, clunky as a battleship, with cigarette burns on the dash. Uncle Roy leaned over to fasten my seatbelt, then tugged to make sure it was taut. The car soon filled with his sweaty onion smell. He turned on the radio, but I didn't know the song.

The Butterfly Man

Devin Murphy

Conway Catholic Elementary School is the last of seven school visits Wayne has in the central part of the state. The building is a four-story rectangle with the blinds drawn differently in each classroom. He sits in his van and watches the first hazy gray-blue of morning working its way up over the parking lot. Soon after the sun is up, a steady stream of teachers' cars fills the parking lot. Then the school buses come. He waits for it to finally be nine and imagines being in South America again.

He shuts his eyes on the schoolyard and is in a remote pocket of Venezuelan jungle two days travel by boat down the Orinoco River. His hired guide shuttles him along the shore and helps string a giant net made across a small tributary. When it's fully spread, the fibers are so fine it looks like a damp spider web framing the light. He explores the banks for the day and returns to find the net fluttering orange and black with hundreds of Monarch butterflies. The guide rows the boat beneath the net as he carefully removes each butterfly, cupping it in his hands, slowly loosening his grip and letting it fly off if it isn't worth keeping. It's the perfect specimens that slow time, make the air around him visible as a fog bank.

A short blast of the school's bell brings him back. He pulls the van up to the front doors and walks inside to check in with the principal's office. After checking in, he brings his cases in one at a time to the school's library on the fourth floor where he'll meet the students. On his first trip, the hallway is full of boys marching down the hall. Wayne tucks the case in his arms tighter against his chest as he watches them pass. Their school shoes slip over the dust on the tile floors. Laces and sleeves trail behind them from sneakers and gym clothes held under their arms.

They smell like a shifting animal, and their smell with the bleach in the hall makes him tighten his grip on the case and shut his eyes.

~

"Can I help you, sir?" Opening his eyes he sees a middle-aged woman wearing a maroon dress standing in front of him. "Yes, please. I forgot which way the library was," he says.

"Just down the hall." She points over her shoulder. "Connor," she says to the last boy in the crowd that just passed, "walk this man down to the library, please." The boy spins around and looks up at Wayne with a flushed face and stands there waiting for him to start walking.

"Well, go on then," the woman says to Connor.

"What do you have in that box?" Connor asks as they walk down the hall.

"Can you keep a secret?"

"Yeah," the boy says, pushing back the doors to the small library. There are a dozen folding tables set up in a half circle against the windows. Inside the circle are rows of small folding chairs. "Wow, what's all this for?" Connor asks.

"Hello there," an older woman with an argyle cardigan says, "You must be Mr. Denny."

"I am, but you can call me Wayne," he says to the librarian.

"You may set the room up any way you'd like." She looks at the boy waiting next to him and says, "Thank you, Connor. You can go back to your classroom now." Connor looks up and Wayne feels the boy's gaze searching for a promised secret. He looks closer at the boy to see how the hair just over his ear is streaked back in dark fingers from a poor attempt at combing it. The boy's shirt hangs off his shoulders, and the fine line of his collar bones stick out through the cotton. Wayne turns from him just as he feels the urge to run his finger over those bones.

"Inside the box, Connor," Wayne says, seeing how curious the boy is, "I've got proof of how much magic there is in the world. But keep that to yourself for now."

~

Wayne hauls each of his cases up the stairs and places them on the tables in the library. Each of the cases has a silk slip to protect the mahogany wood and glass windowpanes from being scratched. He uses Windex on each windowpane to remove fingerprints, then drapes the slips over the cases so he can reveal them one by one.

A woman in a yellow cotton dress with an auburn ponytail leads a group of children into the library, and the kids begin filling the seats.

"Okay, kids, listen up front here," the librarian says, trying to get the attention of the first group of students. "Today we have a special guest for you." The woman looks at Wayne with her stern, tired face when she finishes talking, and he walks in front of the rows of chairs. This part he does from habit, knowing the mystery of the covered cases behind him already has the kids' attention.

"Hello, everyone, my name is Wayne, and I'm The Butterfly Man," he tells them. Then he describes what such a life entails—traveling all over the world in search of butterflies so he can bring them back and share them with school kids. He lets them know how special these insects are, worth protecting, and how he's trained his eyes to the slightest twitch and lift of moths in the jungle.

"Some of you may have seen something like these in your neighborhood," he says pulling back the silk slip from the first case, and holding it up for them to see. Inside the red mahogany case he made are Monarchs, varying stages of caterpillars, yellow butterflies the size of quarters, and several moths, all with wings fanned out and pinned for preservation into the cork. With this, the children are already leaning towards him. The kids in the back rows are moving their heads around for a better view.

"Now these are amazing insects, and I'm going to tell you all about them and some other insects I've found all over the world, such as this one." He pulls a sheet off a smaller box and holds it up. Inside, there's only one butterfly pinned to the cork with its wings stretched out—a Queen Alexandra's Birdwing, the size of a dinner plate and the color of cobalt chips in the sun.

Looking at the kids' faces, he knows he has them all now. Their eyes are wide. They are all silent. He holds a pair of binoculars up to his eyes and scans the library, then swings his net over their heads for effect. "The world's out there for you," he tells them, "and you'll be amazed at some of the things you find."

He takes off another slip and lifts a new case. "Not all of them are beautiful." He holds up a case of large cockroaches, beetles, and spiders splayed out on the cork. The thin pins through their body cavities make some of the kids squeal.

A red-haired girl in the front can't sit still after looking at the odd bugs and spiders, "Did you have to touch all of those?" she asks.

"Most of them I used my net for, but I had to touch them all eventually."

"How long did it take you to catch all those bugs?" someone calls out.

"Oh, I've been at this for almost twenty years," he tells them, "which is a lot longer than you've been alive."

"Do you go out looking for one bug at a time, or do you just catch what you find?" another asks.

"That's a good question," he tells the kids. "I go to a place where I hope to find certain insects but I'm always surprised by what I find."

The children keep asking questions after he finishes telling them about the caterpillars and butterflies.

"Do you fly from school to school?" the redheaded girl asks.

"In my private jet, you mean? I'm afraid the butterfly business isn't that good. I have a van I travel in with a portion of my collection."

In truth, it has been twenty years of constant motion, always searching for something and finding something completely different. Once he had his van towed and impounded in Reno, Nevada. His life's work sat behind a chain-link fence surrounded by stolen Buicks and rusting pickup trucks that would go to scrap before ever getting claimed.

He gives the same talk for two more classes in the morning and takes a break for lunch, which he eats in the library.

The library windows facing west look down on the parking lot and playground where a class is having recess. He watches the children playing below as if he is stalking them with a gigantic butterfly net. He sees himself lower the long boom of his net so the clear white webbing on the basket lowers over one of the boys. The boy, indistinct now in the mesh and sunlight, is pushing out against the encasement. There are only sections of him forcing through the net. First, the side of a small face, the ear and part of the nose. Then there's a small hand, fingers spread out and flat until the fingertips bend outward and claw for freedom.

~

He watches the sixth graders, who are the last group of the day, file into the chairs. From the back of the line Connor hurries around his classmates and gets a chair in front of Wayne. "I didn't tell anyone," Connor whispers.

"That's good. Let's get the rest of your class seated and I'll show you what I've got."

He holds up cases of bugs and tells the sixth graders about all the little things in the ground, things that know the cool damp earth and how good it is to be buried. He shows them the smaller and intricate side of life, the tiny larva that run the world in trillions. Larva, cracking open into small proofs of god, and that there is no god, the great dilemma lying in all things ugly and slimy and thoraxed, wound in cocoons, trembling with possibility. That's the real appeal for him, the envy of the ability to wrap up until you come out something new and better, stunning and pure.

The teacher is in the back of the room when he finishes talking and the kids come up for a closer look at his collection. Connor stands next to him, leaning over the cases.

"What's this one called?" Connor asks.

"That's a Western Pigmy Blue," he tells him as he looks up and sees the teacher thumbing through the books on the back shelf.

"And this one?"

"That's a Violet Marpho."

"These are really great. That big one you showed us," Connor says, pointing to the small case that holds the Queen Alexandra's Birdwing, the largest butterfly in the world, "this one here. This is my favorite. Where'd you get him?"

"I got that in Papua New Guinea." Each butterfly represents a different trip, a corner of the world, where, for one moment, Wayne found something that he wanted, held close, and then preserved. He kneels down next to Connor, with several other kids standing around him and working their way down the tables, looking at the cases. He tosses out the insects' Latin names as well. "Can you spell Ornithoptera Alexandrae?" he jokes with the boy. Connor's white polo shirt is untucked in the back. It hangs just over his waistline. Wayne puts his hand on Connor's back and continues pointing out the bugs. He touches the boy's spine and feels the width between the shoulder blades, the spot where he'd pin-stick him to a corkboard for display. The glass window of the case just under his chest is covered in small fingerprints, smudge marks shining dully in the fluorescent lighting. He'd put his own fingers over the greasy spots several times over the years, those being the only human touch he'd been able to find.

Connor grips both hands on the side of the case and leans over to see the details of each butterfly. His shirt lifts in the back, and seeing that, Wayne drops his hand further down, hooking the shirt away from the boy's back by the hem with his thumb and slips his fingers underneath.

This is the first time he has touched anyone beyond a handshake in what feels like his whole life. The boy's skin makes Wayne feel like he's falling into a hole. He feels the downy hairs at the base of the Connor's back, and for a moment, before he feels the boy's discomfort, he felt like he could see all the air in the library—it was clear but he still saw it, like it was a rolling fog bank. He breathed in and for a brief moment felt whole and alive.

Connor glances up from the case. He looks confused, and the look sickens Wayne.

"Excuse me, Mr. Denny!" the librarian says behind him. Her face is cold, wrinkled severely, and knowing. He can't bring himself to move his hand which is still up the back of the boy's shirt. Connor's look and the old woman's voice have frozen him.

"Mr. Franklin," she says, looking towards the young teacher in the back of the room, "You'd better take your class to get ready for the busses."

Wayne feels Connor's shirt slip over the back of his hand as the boy walks away from him, but his hand stays where it is, like he's waving goodbye or taking an oath.

"This is highly inappropriate! Most inappropriate. You need to come with me." The librarian demands Wayne follow her down the stairs to the principal's office, without saying a word.

"We can't let people be touchy-feely with students, Mr. Denny," the librarian hisses at him before they walk into the school's main office.

Touchy-feely. The word runs through Wayne's head and pings off an exposed nerve. "Touchy-feely" would go out on some email and it would travel faster than he ever could. The phrase would get forwarded to the booking agents, and the schools' guest lecture programmers, and that phrase would be the end of his bookings. They'd all cancel. *Touchy-feely*. The phrase would stain his skin so that people could see it all over him.

~

The librarian tells him to have a seat in foyer as she marches inside. There's an announcement about buses being ready, and from his chair he watches the kids empty out the main doors. He wonders where they'll all go, how some will go home, or to a friend's home, to parks, or clubs, or to games. They run out the doors like a pod of locusts emerging from the earth, and watching them he feels like a monster working its way out of a tight embryonic sac, and he realizes that not all insects make it out of their casings.

Wayne thinks of those fingerprint smudges from children excited about what he had to say, forgetting themselves and leaning into the mystery he'd found for them. That's the only good thing he does with his life, and the feeling that it's all been ruined by one graze of his fingertips pounds through his chest. For all his love of butterflies, the feeling of being a bat blooms inside of him—flittering through the dark, pulling back just at the moment of contact with the world by some instinctual twitch before ever touching anything solid.

The librarian walks out with a short older man with two tufts of gray hair on the sides of his head. "Mr. Denny, this is our Principal, Mr. Marcheson," the librarian says, then leaves the room.

"Why don't you come in my office, Mr. Denny," the principal says, and quickly sits at his desk. "Look, this is a bit awkward." His fingers were playing invisible piano keys against the top of his desk.

Wayne sits in front of Mr. Marcheson and feels an odd sense of relief at being caught just in time, just before some dormant want dragged him inward to who he may really be.

"I'm sorry about all this," Mr. Marcheson says. "I think our librarian means well, but she has a dark imagination."

Wayne isn't sure he heard what the principal has said. He looks at him closely and realizes how embarrassed the man is.

"I see," Wayne says. "I was showing the boy how I find the right place to mount my insects into their casings. So, I can see how she misunderstood." The words seem to come from someone else. They just come out smooth and easy—almost understanding.

"There you have it," the principal says, standing up as if to clap his hands and be done with the whole matter. "I knew it was just a misunderstanding. I really am sorry. I mean, we really loved having you here today. I can't imagine a better break in the routine for our students." Mr. Marcheson wipes the palms of his hands on his pant legs as he stands in front of Wayne.

Wayne walks to the door with the principal next to him. "Oh, and now that you're here, I might as well give you this, and save some postage." Mr. Marcheson turns back towards his desk and grabs a school district paycheck envelope with Wayne's name on it. "You're welcome back any time Mr. Denney, and please forgive us for this mix up."

Wayne goes to the library to gather his collection. The school is empty now, and not even the librarian is in the room. He stands in front of the tables, looking at the cases. He learned how to steam and bend wood, getting the mahogany sideboards wrapped into ninety degree angles to form squares. He took great care in making each of his butterfly cases, buying real cork and laying it out on the inside, then sanding the inner lip of wood which would hold the glass window once he fitted it with hinges.

Then he looks at the smudge marks on the glass cases and feels deeply ill.

Touchy Feely. He promised himself years ago to never cross a line—never touch anyone, and it had become a habit—not touching anyone—something he no longer had to think about until today when he went far enough to be too far.

He walks around the room opening the small brass latches on each case, lifting the glass up so there's nothing covering his collection. He pulls a Dung Beetle out of the cork by the pin and spins the pin in front of his face. The dark bug orbits on its metal axis. The details of its legs alone are intricate beyond anything he can comprehend. He takes the pin out and places the beetle softly into a silk slip. He knows how gentle you have to be to touch a butterfly, so he's careful pulling the pins of all of them, even though they now feel deeply tainted. He pulls pins until his entire collection is hanging Waltzing Matilda style in the slip over his shoulder.

He opens one of the large east-facing windows that pull back like a mailbox lid. Warm air comes into the air-conditioned room. He looks at the surrounding houses beyond the school's playground and watches trees shift with the breeze. Those sedate homes make him think of all the roadside meals he's eaten alone. On the sidewalk he sees Connor and an older boy that looks just like him.

He lifts the silk bag gently to the lip of the open window, and shakes the contents into the air.

Rare butterflies drift over the street. Their brittle wings scrape apart on the coarse pavement when they touch. The fine flakes lift and fall with the breeze. Some stick in the grass below, and others clutter over a sewer grate and sink in. He watches a Calico cat dart out from a front porch and pinch its teeth into the body of an African Butterfly, carrying it to the doorstep of its own home, where it has probably left bits of mice and birds before. Tonight, it will leave one fully spread and preserved Swallowtail Butterfly's wing, bright blue with yellow rings working their way outward from the middle like a large eye staring into a light at nighttime.

Little Hands of Silk

Ajay Vishwanathan

"See them wriggle? And raise their heads?" asks Pandu, a silver chain shimmering in sweat around his neck, its oval glass pendant flickering and going dim on his bare chest. Though not as tall as my father, Pandu towers over me.

I cannot see clearly in the poorly lit factory shed but nod. In a large wicker basket, scattered among mulberry leaves, the silkworms look like tiny white trains dipping in and out of green tunnels. There are so many and they chomp so hard that it sounds like a flurry of raindrops.

"Get closer," he says, pushing my head forward with his bulky hand. The worms smell terrible, like the errant cricket ball that I often fish out from the gutter. Two boys, also bare-chested, hunkered over their own baskets, titter in a dim corner. "Now, Giri, search for ones that aren't moving. There's one right there." I nod again.

"Those are the dead ones. You search for them and pull them out before the bastards kill the others," continues Pandu. I wonder how the dead worms could do that to live ones but decide not to ask him. I don't want him or the two boys to think I am stupid. "Get going now," he says, and walks over to the boys whose faces suddenly scrunch up in focus.

He stares into their baskets, then yells. Dragging the smaller of the two boys by the ear, Pandu pulls him to the ground, then whips out his belt and whacks the boy repeatedly on his back and legs. The boy doesn't resist. Grabbing a handful of worms from the basket, Pandu flings them in the boy's face. His friend continues to work on his basket. "The next dead worm you miss, I'll shove down your throat," he says, making a grabbing gesture with his hand, tongue sticking out.

Pandu then slings the belt over his shoulder as if it were a large snake, and storms out, his head almost touching the top of the doorway.

The two boys look at each other and then at me, the smaller one rubbing his left ear. I look down into my basket, my head reeling. My own father is short-tempered but has never raised his hand to me, which Mother says is rare. There are a couple of worms in the right corner that don't move. I pick them up, and inspect them before setting them aside, their curled bodies feeling like soft dough. The idea of feeding the worms generously to reap more silk from them is fascinating. My basket is the smallest one, I realize, perhaps meant for trainees like me.

"You can get sick from touching them, you know," says the bigger boy, wide-eyed. "Dhina almost died."

"He had high fever for three days," chimes in the smaller boy, still stroking his ear.

"Does Pandu know?" I ask.

The bigger boy grimaces. "Of course he does. He doesn't care. He just needs the job done. A real demon, that Pandu. He only smiles at the big boss. Everyone else around here is vermin to him."

I figure by "big boss," he means the factory owner. Through the doorway I see Pandu at a distance, bending down and chatting with a woman in a lemon green sari. He is smiling, but she doesn't look like his big boss. Later, I hear someone refer to her as Jothi.

Pandu didn't look as big two days ago when he stood next to Father, going over the financial details of my employment. I wonder who would win if Father and he got into a fight. I've heard stories from Mother, of Father in his younger days, overwhelming grown men double his size in wrestling rings.

Last night, I heard Mother and Father murmuring late into the small hours, Mother weeping at one point. I wondered if it was about me walking all the way here to the town of Rangeri to work, instead of going to school. I picked up a few words: Moneylender. Deposit. Rains. Uncle Srini. For a few months.

I know Father wants me to get an education and then move to the city to work, just like Uncle Srini who always visits us in clean shirts carrying large suitcases. He chooses to stay in a motel in town. Mother told me Uncle Srini is frightened of snakes lurking in corners. But I suspect it is because our roof always leaks, water constantly dripping into old plastic containers, and because our bathroom is small and dank.

Time seems to pass slowly in the small wooden shed. I miss school, the open windows, the Peepal tree outside, the constant chatter and giggling, the loud toll of its bell. And my teacher, Master Ram, the look on his face when he gave me a small silver coin, impressed by my performance in the surprise quiz. Keep it, he had said, patting my back, Whatever you do, continue to work hard. I wondered if he gave similar coins to other students.

Then for the next few weeks, I stared at the coin, running my fingers over the engraved lines of Saraswati, the Goddess of Learning. I'd always wanted to ask Master Ram if there was any other meaning to giving me the coin. Before coming here to work this morning, I buried it behind my house.

Pandu doesn't return to check on us. I learn that the bigger boy's name is Chaami, and the smaller one, who pointed to many fingernail marks on his arms, is Ganga. At ten, Chaami is a year older than me, while Ganga is eight. Chaami and I, we discover, live in adjacent villages, his on the way to mine. Just before sunset, Chaami tells Jothi that we're done for the day, and she comes in to check on our baskets. "I heard that you dropped out of school," she says to me, her eyes surprisingly warm, and pretty. I don't respond.

~

As we walk back home, I realize that Chaami likes to talk, and wander. He escapes into little alleys through sunflower fields and returns with funny-looking pieces of wood, sends unsuspecting goats scurrying, and stops to stare at ant hills before decapitating them with his slipper.

Chaami tells me that he lives with his brother who is more than ten years older than him. They've been together since his parents died. Chaami hardly remembers them.

"You know, Ganga lives in the factory," he says. "I'm happy to be going home."

"In the factory?"

"Yes, in one of the shelters there."

"Why can't he go home?"

"He cannot. His home is several miles away. Every month his father comes to collect his wages, but hardly spends time with Ganga. I heard he remarried after Ganga's mother died. He's only interested in the money."

Perhaps my parents were talking last night about what they owed the moneylender. In the past month, he has already visited us twice. I know Mother sold her golden bangles last year. She has been sick lately, shadows under her eyes dark and deep, like abandoned wells. I think of Ganga's mother, and then my own again.

"Ganga talks often about his aunt Leela," says Chaami. "He even has a crumpled sheet of paper somewhere with her address in the city. He wishes he could go to her."

"You mean, run away from the factory?"

"Yes. It's not easy. He tried it once, got lost and almost died. Someone brought him back, and Pandu punished Ganga for trying to escape. The next day, I noticed *beedi* burns all over his chest." Chaami shudders.

I don't mention anything about my work to Father and Mother that night. They don't ask me anything, which I find strange, as if they are afraid of what I might say. I fall asleep thinking of Ganga, imagining the dark figure of Pandu chasing the boy around a tiny room, smoke spewing from his mouth, a *beedi* between his fingers.

~

I don't see Ganga for the next few days. Chaami tells me he has seen Jothi hugging and kissing Pandu in one of the sheds. We giggle. Three new boys join us, fingers bandaged in white cloth as if they are guarding them from the worms. They keep to themselves, their hands weaving in and out of the baskets, like humming birds.

Chaami tells me Pandu and his people might have moved Ganga to another shed, the dreaded hot water area.

"Or maybe he's in the mulberry fields," says Chaami, a hopeful smile on his face. I know what those fields mean to him; it's where kids pluck fresh mulberry leaves the whole day, bag them, and hurl them into bullock carts that haul the bags into the factory. Chaami thinks that is the best place to work in the factory: to be running around in the open green, stopping once in a while to stare at the blue skies and to wave at flying airplanes. He would rather be in the blazing heat of the sun outside than sit all day soaking in sweaty coops.

In the afternoon, Ganga comes into our shed. I'm happy to see him. He walks to me, and asks that I follow him. "Jothi told me to call you," he says.

He takes me to another shed, much bigger, a few meters away. "I heard they plan to get many more boys here," says Ganga.

I see Jothi standing in one corner of this two-window room that smells like rotten wood. She nods at me. The calmness in her face seems strange in this factory. A few dozen youngsters are standing over steaming metal containers that hold hot liquid with something white floating in them. Ganga takes his place next to one such vessel. Scattered plentifully throughout the room are wooden reels that are taller than the boys, some of whom have their fingers in the water.

Jothi motions me to take the empty spot next to Ganga and walks toward me. Water boils in a container in front of me. Jothi bends down and grabs a bamboo basket full of oval balls that look like tiny eggs.

"You throw these cocoons in the water and let them sit for a while, until the silk coating starts coming off," she says, flicking a couple into the hissing liquid, and turns to Ganga. "Why don't you show him?"

Ganga, I quickly recognize, doesn't talk much. He thrusts his hand in the hot water, his face expressionless, while my eyes widen in surprise, and starts moving his fingers as if searching for something. "The white coating, you keep touching it, feeling it," he says, "until they are soft and ready."

"Isn't that water hot?"

"It is. But I don't feel anything." Ganga pulls his left hand out and shows it to me. I notice dark purple blisters below his knuckles and tiny bubbles with fiery rings of red skin around them. "You get used to it."

I don't respond, but stare at the damage to his tiny hand.

"Do we have to use bare hands?"

"Yes. Fingers work best. They say we need to pull them out at the right time. Tools damage the silk."

I continue staring.

"Try it," he says. I shake my head. "Try it," he says again. "Or someone will force you to."

I look around the room. Boys, not older than six or seven, going by their size, stand like little soldiers with their tender hands groping underwater, some wincing, some unmoved. My gaze shifts outside one of the windows where Pandu and Jothi are talking, standing next to bins full of cocoons that look like unstrung jasmine flowers. He seems angry, his hand gesturing in front of her face. Next to the fair-skinned Jothi, Pandu looks dark, like a silhouette.

She spits on his face. He strikes her with his right hand, undoing her hair that was tied in a bun. She tries to hit back but he catches her wrist and pulls her away. They move out of view.

"Come on, Giri, do it. Or I'll get into trouble." Ganga grabs my right hand and plunges it into the boiling liquid. I scream, my voice cracking, withdraw my hand, and whimper to myself as all eyes turn to me. A burning sensation seeps into my skin, and spreads to my arm. I look down. The back of my hand is red. Pandu, with his lumbering, lopsided gait, walks in through the door, expression grim. His eyes fall on me.

"Do it," mumbles Ganga. I poke my hand back into the water, and feel the sting again. It drags on my fingers like leeches, and then subsides. I wonder if it is just numbness or if my skin has dissolved to the bottom of the vessel. One of the cocoons feels softer than the others. I pull it out and ask Ganga if it is ready. There is a dull quiver in my fingers. He strokes the soft silk and nods yes.

I sense Pandu's eyes still on me. Ganga gets the attention of the boy in front of me who turns around, grabs the cocoon from my hand, and inspects the loose fabric. Unfurling it expertly, he pulls out the brown worm trapped inside and chucks it into a bucket nearby. He then drags the silk threads like a sock over an oval, wooden board, and allows them to dry. The flexibility of the fabric surprises me.

We work into the afternoon. The dead worms in the bucket, brown and slimy, fill up fast. We're interrupted by a stranger who rushes into the room and herds us outside through the back door. "Be back in an hour," he commands. We roll out like marbles from a tilted pail. Rumors float that uninvited inspectors have arrived.

~

Ganga and I squat near the edge of a mulberry field, the gentle breeze and nodding treetops providing relief from the insides of factory sheds. My eyes linger first on my right hand now burning in the naked sunshine, little bubbles breaking out below the knuckles, then move to my unscathed left hand that reminds me of times I have left behind.

"Hurts, right?" asks Ganga. I nod. "The bubbles get large and water comes out. Hurts till the skin becomes dry and peels off. Then it happens again. You will soon stop staring."

"How long have you been here?"

"Since I was five."

"I heard you tried to escape."

Ganga shrugs. In the distance a bullock cart full of mulberry leaves, appearing like a strange animal with a funny hump, pulls up near the factory entrance.

"They did bad things to you for that, right?" I ask.

"They do nothing good here."

"Would you try it again?"

"Not the way I did. We're in the middle of nowhere." Ganga looks up at the horizon. In the clear sky two birds chase each other, a broken chain of mountains in the background.

"My aunt's in the city," he says. "I know where she lives. Wish I could go to her."

"Why doesn't she come and get you?"

Ganga shrugs. "She's probably afraid of my father. He can do horrible things. But I know she likes me."

I look down at my scalded hand again and imagine Mother holding it on her lap, whispering in my ear, telling me it will be fine, her gentle voice gliding through my body like a caress. And Father snarling, his fists jammed in his pockets, harsh angles of his face stiffening. He gets quite upset when someone hurts me.

The bullock cart driver, a sprightly, turbaned man in white shirt and shorts, gets off and hustles into one of the sheds.

"That's Heera," says Ganga. "Comes once a week, takes a bathroom break at the factory, chats with Jothi and a few boys. He always wears white."

"From here he looks like my father, short and stocky," I say.

"He will now drive the cart to the nearby train station where he sells the leaves."

Soon, Pandu and his cronies come out and call us back into our shed. I hear someone yell, "Hhrrr . . . rarrr. Rarrr." I turn around and see Heera urging his two brown bulls around the bend, the two-wheeled cart lurching and moaning. Even his voice sounds like Father's. I watch him till he goes out of sight, then enter the shed.

~

Chaami is quieter today as we walk back home. He hardly even glances at the lamb that jumps at us from the bushes, or asks me about my hand, even as I keep wringing it in pain. When I finally ask him what the matter is, he tells me that his brother's getting married. And that he has decided that Chaami should live in the factory.

"He didn't even ask me," says Chaami, his voice thin, wistful. I put my arm over his shoulder, and he does the same. We walk together like joined twins.

I don't talk about my scalded hand. But I want to show it to Mother, and whine about how it burns, and how difficult it will be for me now to hold a cricket bat and launch the ball high over the fence, my friends watching in awe, and about how I wish I could join them in school again.

I enter my house and find Mother crying, crouched next to a pot of stew. The moneylender, wearing thick glasses and pearl necklaces, his stomach sticking out like a misshapen watermelon, hovers over her, talking loudly and waving a stick. Father is sitting in one corner, head bowed. The moneylender looks at me and gestures with his large hands. "Here comes your savior," he says, and walks by me, lips curling in scorn, and out through the door.

For long moments, we sit in silence after he leaves, shadows dulling in failing light.

"Amma," I say, and show Mother my hand, slowly bringing it to eye level, scars now dark and ugly. She stares at it, covers it with her palm and looks away, as if she doesn't want to know the blisters exist. I wince in pain. She takes a deep breath, lets go of my hand, and leans back against the wall.

Father gets up and walks in my direction, his gait hesitant. Bending forward he peers at my hand without touching it, then shakes his head, looks at Mother, and walks back to where he was sitting.

"Go and wash yourself," says Mother. "I have *sambar* for you. You'll feel fine after dinner."

~

Sleep doesn't come easily to me. I smell the cool oil that Mother applied on my scars before lying silently next to Father. With words dead, even the door creaking at the hinges seems loud. Whatever I think of makes me bitter, even thoughts that once made me happy. I think of Master Ram, remember the birds singing on the Peepal tree outside my school, remember Father telling me to become like Uncle Srini.

~

In three days, Chaami joins us in the hot water area. I'm happy and sorry at the same time. He will feel worse here, but at least all three of us can be together. His brother is getting married tomorrow, but Chaami's been thinking of life in the factory, life without long walks through fields and past muddy runnels, life in constant fear of unfriendly shadows.

"I'll especially miss diving into those mounds of hay by the road," says Chaami. "And playing hide and seek in them."

Ganga smiles. I smile, then become quiet, listening to new thoughts unfolding in my mind. I look around the room.

"Heera will come tomorrow as usual," I whisper. "How long would it take to sneak out the back, run to his cart, and hide in those mounds of leaves?"

"Through the back?" asks Chaami, turning to look.

"Less than a minute," says Ganga. "But if the other boys notice, they will create a scene."

"Leave that to me. I'll distract the boys."

"And you?"

"I'll join you later. Maybe you could come here one day with Aunt Leela and take me."

I look out the window at the dirt road where Heera would park his cart, and feel my heart thump faster. Cloud shadows float over open grounds and across the bright trees swathed in sunshine. Someone grazes my elbow, and I sense a presence behind me. Turning my head, I see Jothi glaring at us.

"You three have been working or telling each other stories?"

We stay silent. "Stop murmuring, or else I'll send you to different parts of the room," she says, and walks off.

My hands are in the scalding water but they feel nothing. I wonder briefly if Jothi heard us.

~

Morning rains make everything around look a shade darker. Little ghosts of mist wobble on dirt. The three of us work in silence, occasionally peering out the window. Jothi is in a red sari today, the brightest I've seen her wear. She's talking to a cleaning lady who nods silently, and points to the open window. Perhaps Jothi wants it cleaned. Perhaps she will draw the shutters, and make it impossible for us to see Heera pulling in. The cleaner leaves the room, but doesn't return.

Pandu doesn't come in the whole morning, which passes slowly. My eyes are tired, for I hardly slept last night, thinking about today, about the precious coin that Master Ram gave me. I dug it up this morning and dropped it in my pocket.

Now I place the coin in Ganga's hand. "Take it," I say. "Keep it with you, somewhere safe." He looks at me with surprise. He knows the story behind the coin. I have told him many times.

Past noon, we see Heera round the corner, wheels creaking. We look at each other. Heera is in a blue shirt today. He takes longer than usual to dismount.

"Now, wait till no one is looking in your direction," I say, and walk to the front of the room. On reaching the front door, I pretend to slump to the ground, making sure I hit the wall and make some noise. Someone yells. I feel footsteps running in my direction, and the buzz turning into clamor, and commotion. Minutes pass before someone pours water on my face. I open my eyes, crinkle my face and act dazed.

Strong hands lift me to my feet and someone asks me if I'm okay. I nod yes and pat down my dirty shirt. I walk gingerly to my spot, and see that Ganga and Chaami have gone. And that no one else has noticed. I see Jothi standing at the spot where I had fallen, her eyes fixed on me.

I wait till she turns away, then look toward the window. And catch the back of Heera's bullock cart staggering away from the factory.

I imagine my two friends whispering to each other under the blanket of leaves, giggling, relieved, excited to be heading towards a free world where they can run barefoot, scrambling after frightened frogs, and catching raindrops in their mouth.

I wish I was with them on that cart.

Then, I think of inconsolable Mother, and helpless Father holding her hands.

The cart disappears from view and I feel the familiar bite of the water on my hands. From the corner of my eye, I catch the redness of Jothi's sari beside me.

"You feel better now?" she asks. I nod, and look into her eyes.

She places her hand on my back. "Tomorrow I'll try to move you to the mulberry fields."

There Are Rules, Secret Little Rules

Catherine Thomas

Sometimes if you ask for dried beans, you also get turkey necks and then you can make a soup but only if you ask for the beans, otherwise they won't tell you about the meat, then later somebody will come back and ask them for turkey necks and they'll say, "Only with the dried beans," and then that same somebody will go, "You never told me the beans come with the turkey necks," but that's the thing, there are rules, secret little rules known only to the pantry ladies, like the calculations for who gets how much of what, which supposedly have to do with how many portions are listed on the food labels but how is it that one week I end up with three cartons of milk and the next only two, and how is it that when the fresh tomatoes were handed out I didn't get one, even though half of them were split down the middle and weeping and the woman who always asks for substitutions was so disgusted with hers she gave it back without even trying to exchange it for anything? I've been watching them for months now and I'm beginning to suspect that the pantry ladies make the rules up as they go.

The food I'm collecting isn't for me, it's for my friend Glen, and I have to keep track of all the different rules and stay in line with them because I want to be sure he gets everything he can. Glen used to come here for his own food, then I came with him and now, since his amputation, I collect it for him. Glen is a diabetic and he's not my boyfriend. He's my very good neighbor and friend but he's not my boyfriend. That was the first thing the pantry ladies asked when I started picking his food up from them, "Is he your boyfriend? Are you living together?" and I hadn't even asked for any food for me. They wanted to catch me out but they couldn't because all I did was bring a note from Glen saying it was okay for me to pick up his food and I don't need food for myself because I'm on disability due to a certain psychiatric diagnosis that's between me and my doctors and I have a part-time job and I don't eat very much so I can get by without their help. As for me and Glen, well they are completely wrong and they had no business asking me my private business, which is we've been living in the same apartment building for nearly fifteen years and that's all. Glen did ask me on a date once and I said no and we never talked about it again and I know he thinks it's because he's sixty-one and I'm forty-four and because he's missing half of his left leg, but it's not, it's because I don't want a boyfriend, I don't want anyone. If I did, though, it would definitely be Glen because he's quiet, he lives quietly and he lets me be.

No matter how early I get to the pantry, I'm never first, which is all right, yes, really I don't mind, because the system for deciding who is first is more or less fair. There's a sign-in sheet. However, when I get down to the waiting room this time, there is no sign-in sheet, not on the table, not in anybody's hand. The man behind me also needs it, the scrawny, acne-scarred black man with the elastic-bottomed sweatpants and the liquor on his breath, and when he sees it's not there, he yells, "Ladies, we require the sign-in sheet." Naturally they hand it to him, the last down the stairs but the loudest. So I'm seventeenth on the list instead of sixteenth, but of course I don't argue. Besides, most of the names have already been crossed off.

I would wait if they weren't all crossed off. I would wait if there were thirty four people ahead of me because how could I go back to Glen who is missing half his leg and has to get around in a wheelchair and tell him I couldn't be bothered to wait for his food when he never asks me for anything and he says every week that he's sorry to trouble me and he could go by himself and give me a break some week just say the word Sandy? Of course I couldn't. So I wait. The place I wait is the food pantry in the basement of Gethsemene Episcopal Church. The pantry waiting room is a drafty hallway between the main pantry and the stockroom and it has a worn out green carpet and damp stains on the walls. The three fold-up metal chairs lined up in front of the used clothing rail are always taken by the time I get there and the rest of us have to stand. We stand and we wait and we listen, or we don't listen. It's our turn and we're supposed to be listening for our food choices and instead we're yelling across the room at one of the guys who just came in, *we* being the old lady with the soft white hair and the cataracts sitting at the wrinkled-men's-shirts end of the clothing rail.

"Where's Jimmy these days?"

"He's in the hospital. Upstate."

"Mrs. Brady? Macaroni and cheese or plain macaroni?"

"Kidney disease. How's Uncle Ken?"

"Just as miserable as ever. You got clam chowder? I'll take that. Kidney disease. That's terrible."

I never have conversations with people because it annoys the ladies and it holds everyone else up and when the ladies get annoyed they tend to forget things, not the important things but the little extra things like cookies and hot chocolate or tea and when you ask for something, even politely, they'll suddenly have a rule for why you can't have it so it's best not to get into conversations with other people, even when it's not your turn since it could be your turn any minute despite your keeping track, because the person ahead of you might get sick of waiting and leave or just plain disappear or be disqualified suddenly due to coming here twice already this month when the rule is you can't, you can only get food once in a month because it's supposed to be emergency food.

It is emergency food and it isn't, just like it is five days' worth of food and it isn't, it's more like three. Mostly I see the same people every month and so they are technically having an emergency every month, usually the last week of the month when they've run out of money and they're waiting for, say, their next disability check. Glen always is and it's not because he wastes money on lottery tickets and scratch off cards or alcohol or cigarettes like everyone always says about poor people; he doesn't do any of that stuff, not that I would blame him if he did because God knows we all need something to get us through this life, like with me it's cleaning products, but no, Glen doesn't waste money on himself, he sends it to his daughter Mel who has a lot of mental problems and can't manage her money.

Glen is not selfish, which is another reason I would be with him if I could be with anyone, which I can't, due to my own psychiatric problems, which do not involve me being wasteful with money. The opposite is true in fact; I am very very careful with money. I'm very careful with everything, which is my problem according to my social worker, my doctors and also sometimes Glen except that Glen doesn't make me feel bad about being careful the way my social worker and my doctors do and that is another reason I would be with him if I could.

"Hello? Excuse me?"

The loudmouth who stole my spot this morning is standing in front of the trestle table stretching out his back and balancing on his toes so he can look down on the pantry ladies as he yells at them.

"Where's the list? I need to look at the list." I'm not scared yet because he's not yelling at me and anyway, I already know what I'll do if he starts yelling at me, what I'll do if he starts to say anything bad to me is I'll just point to my headphones and pretend I can't hear him. My headphones aren't attached to anything but I feel safer when I wear them. When I twirl the wire leading from my headphones deep into my jacket pocket around and around and around the fingers of my right hand, I know nobody can reach me because I'm gone, I'm smiling and I'm pointing to my headphones and I'm out of trouble's reach, so sorry I can't hear you, so sorry.

"Ladies, could we hurry it along, please?" the loudmouth says. There's a small shower of sparks coming off him. "Ladies," he says again, "we have appointments elsewhere, places to be."

I don't have an elsewhere appointment until next Tuesday afternoon at one o'clock, when I have to start steaming clothes again at the Boulevard, at the Boulevard Salvation Army, and today is Friday. I work two afternoons a week, always Tuesday and always Thursday, and I get paid fifty cents more per hour than the New York State minimum wage because I'm extremely thorough and yes, it's true I see the good stuff before it goes out on the racks and I can put dibs on it if I want but this is only fair. Last week I found an Extra-Large Eddie Bauer shirt that was fleece and lined with quilting and still had the original sales tag on and I put it by for Glen and with my staff discount it was only seventy-five cents so I got it to thank him for the dream catcher he made for me in his art therapy class.

The pantry ladies ignore the loudmouth. Mae and Lynnelle are discussing their last sorority reunion, Alma is pulling our cards using the sign-in sheet and Ann is counting out teabags into sandwich bags. They are all volunteers, all retired from well-paying jobs, and they all think we should get down on our knees in gratitude for them being here. Ann is white like me; Alma, Mae and Lynnelle are black. Anyway, nobody is listening to the loudmouth, which is not deliberate or if it is it's not obvious; they're just busy, each one thinking the other is taking care of the next client in line and nobody seeing the sparks come off of his head. Oh Lord, watch out ladies, I warn them silently.

"The 'Js' disappeared," says Alma.

"How many times have we been meeting there and they run out of chicken?" Lynelle says to Mae.

"My carrots were ice cold."

"Mae, did you take the 'Js' out?" Alma asks.

"Stone cold."

"Oh, no, here they are. Somebody stuck them in with the 'Is.'"

"As much as we pay them . . ."

"Mr. Jones, when were you here last?"

"It's been a while, Miss."

"Months or years?"

"More like years." Mr. Jones is a very old black gentleman dressed in a wool jacket and pants and holding a felt fedora to his chest. Alma explains to him that she can't find his card and he'll have to fill out his paperwork again but he just smiles, showing her the four teeth he has left in this world, and right there I can tell he will be getting a lot of optional extras.

Optional extras depend on pity or nerve or luck. The pantry ladies will pity you if you are frail and very humble and polite or if you are worn down and have too many children, also if you are foreign and very humble and frail, otherwise you have to be nervy or hope for the best. Nerve is pointing to anything you can see past the trestle table that looks good, like a jug of iced tea or washing detergent, and not caring if one of the ladies snaps at you, tells you it's for a large family only, then closes the door so you can't look any more. I have to depend on luck because I have no nerve and no children and I'm mostly healthy and have all of my teeth and I'm too afraid of talking to most people to manage being humble.

Glen would probably make out way better than me on the optional extras because of his missing-half-a-leg issue but he can't stand to be pitied, which is another reason I come here instead of him although I'd never tell him that. What I do tell him is that my doctors want me to get out and meet people and stay busy instead of locking myself in my apartment night and day scouring the baseboards with an end-tuft toothbrush.

"Who's next?" the loudmouth shouts. The old man, Mr. Jones, has gone back to his seat to start filling out his new paperwork. "Which one of you is next?" The loudmouth motions to Alma. "Could we *have* the sign-in sheet, ma'am?"

Alma's looking through her index cards for the next person on the list and she puts her manicured hand up to quiet him.

"Oh no, oh no," he says under his breath, "not that, uh-uh. Like you better than me?" He turns on his heel, stomps up the stairs to the church lobby then comes back down again, stopping at the table. Sparks are coming off of his feet now and his clenched fists. Still Alma is going through the cards.

"Who's next, Alma?" Lynelle asks. Lynelle is the pantry boss.

"Elissa Torres."

"Ladies, I asked a question."

"How many in her family?"

"Just her."

"Elissa Torres?" Lynelle calls.

Elissa Torres puts her hand up then sort of ducks behind it. Her left hand is bandaged, badly, like she did it herself and when the loudmouth thumps the table, she flinches and holds it tight to her waist. Lynelle storms up to the loudmouth, arm fat wobbling like the 49 cent jello she gives us at Thanksgiving and Christmas.

"Sir, I don't have time to be handing you back the sign-in sheet every two minutes so you can check where you are on the list. We'll see you in turn. Now could you please let Miss Torres come forward so we can take her order because the quicker we do hers, the quicker we can all get out of here, okay?"

"No." The loudmouth folds his arms and squints at Lynelle.

"Excuse me?"

"I ain't movin' unless you tell me where I am on the list."

"What's your name?"

"Hah," he says. "Sweet, Raymond."

"Well, Mr. Raymond, I just explained why I don't have time for all that. We're using it right now and when we're done with it, we'll put it right back on the table there."

One, two, three . . . Ann's mouth stops counting out tea bags and she lets the last two drop right to the floor in front of her. Elissa Torres looks over at me asking me with her eyes if I can see what she can see and I nod *yes I can, I can see the sparks,* but I have to look away when her expression changes because I can't help her any more than I can help me. All I can do is put on my invisible shield and this is what she should do too, she should try to be invisible and not look at the sparks. That's what Amy always says to do, Amy my social worker who also has a bachelor's degree in psychology. She says, "Sandy, try not to look at them. Put on your invisibility shield until they go away, like in Star Trek." Glen says Amy is a fruit loop.

"What is wrong with you woman?" Raymond Sweet says to Lynelle. "Are you ignorant? Are you stupid?"

"Who're you calling stupid? You're the ignorant one. You think I'm going to hand out food to you while you stand there and insult me, you're the fool. I should call the police and tell them you've been threatening me. I've got witnesses."

I am one of the witnesses but how will I explain to the police what happened to this man while he was being yelled at by Lynelle, the boss of the food pantry? How will I explain how he turned the color of hot coals and grew so high his head hit the ceiling and so huge that all he'd have to do to send all of us flying is give one tiny puff? How will I explain that the walls closed in and the exit door slammed and the ceiling started to crack all the way from Raymond Sweet's head to the four corners of the room and all of us in the waiting room, me and the girl with the bad hand and the old man with hardly any teeth, we all shrank down to church mouse size and started to quiver? I guess I won't. I guess I'll probably keep my mouth shut and I won't tell Amy and I also won't tell Glen or he'll finally realize that I am the fruit loop, not her, and that's why I can't be with anyone, not even someone quiet and kind like him.

Alma moves toward Lynelle, puts her arm around her shoulders, while the girl with the bad hand gets up suddenly and rushes upstairs.

"Don't you go, honey," Lynelle calls. "You don't need to leave. You stay and keep your place." But she's gone.

I watch Raymond Sweet shrink back down to normal size and color. The smile on his face says, *I'm going to win this*, but I can still see sparks zipping off of his head and I close my eyes for a second and try to breathe slow, wondering if he has a knife. It's doubtful. He's the kind of man who if he had a knife, he'd have to pawn it. He swallows and his Adam's apple shivers up his long neck.

"I believe I was next after her," he says. "Isn't that right? Any of you want to argue with that?"

Nobody wants to argue with that except Lynelle.

"Sir, you need to leave," she says, stabbing at the table with her finger. "Nowhere in the rules does it say I have to put up with being insulted and yelled at so you need to leave."

Mr. Jones looks over in my direction and shakes his head. People like Lynelle don't ever back down. Why is that? Like it would have hurt her just to tell him where he was on the list and shut him up so we could all have some peace but no, she had to drag us all down with her. What does the man have to lose, being yelled at like a first-grader by a woman hardly older than he is, down here with the rest of us in the bottom of this raggedy old church? All he has is his voice and his sparks and his fists. I smile back at Mr. Jones because he's old and friendly and not scary even though he practices poor dental hygiene. I smile and I roll my eyes real quick to tell him I agree with him and to secretly thank him for not saying anything to me but I don't do it quickly enough because something bad happens. Raymond Sweet sees me. I glance back to check on him and there he is staring at me and now I have to do something to make him look away without saying anything to me and I can't pretend I haven't been paying attention, can't pretend there's music in my headphones because he knows I've seen everything and worse, he knows I have an opinion about it because of the eye-rolling and smiling at old Mr. Jones, so I do what I do when I can't think of anything else, which is I pretend to sneeze. I pretend to sneeze three times. Each time I sneeze, Mr. Jones and Raymond Sweet and Lynelle and Alma say *bless you* and each and every time they say *bless you*, I whisper *thank you*. It works. It always works. I don't know why it always works but it does.

"All right, ladies," Raymond Sweet says. "I'll just sit down here and wait my turn. I'm sorry if I offended you, my dear."

Alma steps forward and almost pushes Lynelle out of her way. "That's okay, sir. All we're asking for is a little patience. Now I think you were right behind Mr. Jones, weren't you?"

"Yes, ma'am, I believe you're right."

ThankyouAlmaThankyouAlmaThankyouAlmaThankyouAlmaThankyouRaymond Sweeteven. This, nobody hears but God so I thank him as well.

"Mr. Jones, are you ready with your form?" The old man goes up to Alma at the desk and in a low voice says to her, "I got time to wait. Why don't you see to him first?"

She nods and whispers, "Thank you." Yes, thank you too, Mr. Jones.

"Sir, why don't you come forward? Mr. Jones doesn't have all his paperwork in order yet."

"Yes ma'am."

It doesn't take her two minutes to write down his order and give him his food, but I notice that she only gives him the cheap plastic bags that always break, not the usual sturdy paper bags inside the superior quality plastic bags and I think, Oh Alma, I'm beginning to warm up to you.

"You put the turkey necks in?"

"Uh huh," says Alma.

"Good girl."

Alma gives him a long hard stare.

"Thank you, ladies," he says as he leaves. "Have a blessed day."

When he's gone, Alma calls Mr. Jones forward and laughs as she thanks him but her eyes are wet.

"If he was here another minute," she says, "I would have wrung his turkey neck, I swear."

"Oh, that knucklehead, honey, wouldn't be worth your time." The old man grins.

Alma puts her hand to one side of her mouth and whispers, "Half the time he's in here drunk. Isn't that right, Lynelle?"

"Well, let's get started, Mr. Jones," Alma says. "What kind of meat do you want?"

~

"Way to go, Sand, got the good bags," Glen says when I drop off his food.

These aren't just the heavy paper sacks inside the good plastic; these are the cloth reusables they sell at the store for ninety-nine cents and up.

"Yep," I tell him, "and that's not all. You should see what's in them. I got a whole roasting chicken, and dressing and cornbread mix, and gravy, I got cookies and pudding mix and mayo, and turkey necks for your beans and even detergent and I didn't have to ask for any of it."

"You hold the place up at gunpoint?"

I shake my head and laugh. I don't tell him about all the trouble with Raymond Sweet because I don't want him to feel guiltier than he already does about me going to get his food.

"Let's see what you got," I tell him and I plonk myself down on his sofa and start sorting through it. "I'll put it up for you in a minute. I just want to make sure you got everything."

"Three bags instead of two," he says, "I think we're good."

I keep going anyway because what I really want is for him to *see* how much I got for him. It was hard this time, much harder than usual and even though I can't tell him what I had to go through, I can still show him what I achieved.

Juice. Family-Size, Brand-name Fruit Punch. I wave it in the air, which isn't easy since it's extra heavy but the surprise on Glen's face is worth it. Usually he gets an aluminum can of orange or apple but Lynelle was waiting on me. I dread having Lynelle waiting on me, even when she's in a pleasant mood and here she was taking my order five minutes after yelling at that loudmouth trouble-maker Raymond Sweet. When she called out Glen's name (nobody there ever has asked me what *my* name is) I almost ran out of the place like the lady with the banged up arm.

"You got your note, honey?" she asked.

I passed it to her and she wandered off to file it and for at least five minutes she didn't come back. Instead she got into a conversation with Alma. This was not all right but after standing near the table waiting for the first minute I realized that it could end up being all right because when Lynelle took my note she was still mad about Raymond Sweet and she was mad at Alma too, I guess, for not backing her up and so maybe if Alma could work things out with Lynelle, she'd come back to take my order and not be mad anymore and that could only be a good thing, for me and Glen. So, instead of worrying over it not being all right to be kept waiting, I watched the two of them as closely as I could, watched Alma put her hand on Lynelle's arm, watched the two of them get into their working-things-out huddle, watched Alma put her arms out for a hug and Lynelle get all stiff and straight, watched Alma hug her anyway, watched Lynelle's shoulders sag at last.

"I'm not going to put up with that nonsense," Lynelle said. "I'd rather get shot and you know it, Alma. I don't care."

"I know it." Alma said. "But you need to be careful."

Lynelle said something I couldn't hear and Alma laughed and Lynelle did too and then I knew that it was definitely all right that I'd been kept waiting for over five minutes on top of all the trouble and waiting I'd already suffered. It was all right except that almost immediately after they laughed, something not all right happened and that was, Lynelle came up to me and asked me, again, if I had a note for Glen. I felt the floor shudder beneath me and the tips of my fingers sting from the heat of the sparks shooting out from them.

"I just . . . I . . . gave it to you," I whispered.

"That's right, you did," Lynelle said. "Now where did I put it?" Off she went to search for the note. I was the only one left and I was certain, as I stood there trembling still, that the ladies would decide they wanted to close up early, that it wasn't worth the trouble of waiting on me, so I shut my eyes tight tight and breathed as deeply as I could and tried with my mind to make Lynelle see where she'd left the note.

"Here it is," she said after nearly another minute. "Now let me get the order sheet."

I opened my eyes and the floor dropped beneath me a fraction so I lost my balance, had to hold on to the table but the table was so light I nearly pushed it over.

"You all right, honey?" Lynelle said, laughing at me, coming at me with the sheet, filling up the doorway between the pantry and the waiting room. The sparks from my eyes got her straight in the heart but she didn't collapse or explode, she only shrank back down to normal size.

"Let's see," she said. "What type of juice? Orange, Apple, grapefruit . . . hold on . . . how about some fruit punch?"

That is the one good thing about being in the waiting room close to the end of opening hours, the ladies want to get rid of all the stuff they should have given out earlier but refused to give out earlier because of whatever rules they were following then. That's how I got all that extra stuff for Glen. Not because I was patient, not because I was polite and quiet. I got it because of good timing and because Lynelle made up with Alma and her mood took a turn for the better. I got it because of stupid luck.

"Sandy?" Glen says. I'm still sorting through my haul.

"Hang on," I tell him. Something's not all right. "I thought they put coffee in here."

"Are you okay?" No, I am not okay. I am not, I am not, I am not okay.

"Damn it! She said they had bags of coffee and she was going to put one in for you to have with the cookies."

I start tossing stuff out of the bag, the boxed macaroni, the powdered milk, the cans of pork and beans and carrots and ravioli and still there's no sign of the coffee and there's not even the usual baggy of tea, so why would she say that? Why would Lynelle promise a thing like coffee if she wasn't going to put it in? Why would she make me imagine it sitting snug in the good shopping bag waiting to be taken and measured out so carefully into one of the paper filters left over from the last time Glen had coffee at home, which was over a year ago, and brewing just two cups of it so as not to waste any, and sitting down on the sofa next to Glen's recliner with the smell of it filling our nostrils, filling the whole apartment which normally smells of stale cat litter, cradling the hot mugs in our hands and letting the steam waft up our noses and make them run and taking that first sip and then chasing it with a bite of cookie, of fudge cookie that wasn't even past it's use-by date? Why? All the times I've seen them open packs of cookies for themselves and take stuff for themselves that was supposed to be for us and I've never complained. All the times I've seen them give extra stuff to the people they like, stuff they didn't even have to use up, stuff like detergent and sanitary pads and special frozen vegetables instead of cans and

"Sandy?"

"What?"

"What are you doing?"

I look around me and see everything spilled out over the floor and Glen's cat Tip is staring at me and Glen's staring at me and somehow I've gotten from the sofa to the floor on my knees and there's pieces of fudge cookie broken up all around me on the carpet.

"I'll fix it later," I tell him, pulling myself up from the floor, and I can feel myself smiling at him because I know that I can fix it and I will fix it and I go right over to him and kiss him on the cheek which I've never done before and it feels all right, even though he hasn't shaved in days, not romantic but just right, and then I tell him I'll be back.

I'm running now, running down the stairs, fourth floor, third floor, second, first, and out and down to the front gate and out and down the hill to the first corner and across the road, almost getting hit by a motorcyclist but not, got to make it before noon, so up the next block to the church, blessedly open, and down the stairs and I can already smell the damp and now I'm in the waiting room but there's no trestle table and the door's closed and the light's off but I can hear voices, they're still there I know it and I knock, I don't care, I knock and knock with the side of my fist and I'm breathing so hard I can hardly talk when Lynelle opens the door.

"We're closed," she says and then, "Oh, it's you again."

I tell her, "You forgot my coffee, Glen's coffee."

"Who's Glen?" she says.

"My friend Glen, the one I collect for."

"Oh, yes, I remember him. He's blind, isn't he?"

"No, Ma'am," I say, "He's an amputee."

"Well, you're lucky you caught us," she says. I can see old Mae puttering around behind her but there's no sign of the other two. "Two more minutes and we'd have locked up. What'd you say I forgot?"

"Coffee," I tell her, "And cookies. You said you'd give him a bag of coffee and some cookies but when I dropped off his food I couldn't find them and I went through his stuff twice."

"Oh God," she says and disappears behind the pantry door and I'm beginning to worry that she'll remember she already gave me cookies when she reappears with a shiny white bag in her hand and a box under her arm.

"Sorry you had to make the extra trip, honey," she says, setting both on the table in front of me.

I grab them before she changes her mind not feeling a shred of guilt about lying. I told Glen I'd fix it and *it* includes the cookies I broke all over his carpet. But I can't leave yet. I've spotted something on the shelf behind Lynelle, something I want for myself.

I stand up straight, clear my throat and point. "Ma'am," I say. "Is that furniture polish?"

She turns to follow my gaze. "Where?"

"The bottom shelf there, at the front."

A spark hits the brown bottle and turns it gold.

"Oh, I see. Yes, it's polish." She looks at it for a moment then she turns back to me.

"You want it?" she asks.

"Yes," I say.

As she bends to retrieve it from the shelf, she looks positively tiny. I reach out to take the polish from her, and for a fraction of a second, my hand is the hand of a giant.

The American House

Bram Takefman

Ichiro Oku returned to Japan after two weeks of visiting friends and customers in the United States. Every weekday evening at his favorite drinking club, not too far from his factory, he would regale his drinking buddies with tales of the things he saw and did in America. He enjoyed his role of storyteller and the incredulity of his companions, although when he described the homes he had visited, they grumbled that his talents for embellishment had passed all acceptable limits.

"No, it is all true," he would insist. "They really do have a room called a 'living room' just for entertaining guests and another one called a 'family room' just for entertaining themselves. They also have a room for the morning meal, which they call a 'breakfast room,' and for the evening meal a 'dining room'; I never did find out what they do for the midday meal—eat out, I suppose. These areas just for eating and entertaining are as big as my entire house—and their bathrooms, why, they are not mere rooms but splendid temples of marble dedicated to the gods of urination and defecation. These shrines are numerous in most of the homes I visited, never more than thirty paces from where one is when the divine call comes. I still wonder whether Americans really are a pious people or simply a race with small bladders and short colons."

From the telling of the stories began a dream that soon became a compulsion; he would build an American-style home for himself and his family. He asked for my help in obtaining back issues of the major architectural and home design magazines, which I was to send to Osaka—to his office, not his home, for he had to keep the dream secret. Mrs. Oku would surely not approve.

Mr. Oku thought back to the terrible months of suffering he had endured so many years ago when he told his wife that they were to leave the family farm and seek a new life in the big city. He was right at the time, for his elder brother was the heir to the land, and while the younger siblings would be secure, they would always be subordinate. He knew that he had not handled the matter well and recalled, with unease, his wife's clenched teeth and pursed lips when he told her of his decision. He remembered the months where his normally chatty wife was silent and the tea was served cold with dinners that no longer included any of his favorite dishes. *Unagi*, sweet, smoky-tasting, grilled eel, became only a memory, and his most favorite, *tonkatsu*, stalwart pork cutlets, were banished, gone, it seemed, forever. The move proved to have been the right thing to do, for he now exceeded his elder brother in wealth and status, but this time he would handle his wife more carefully and would put to use the skills he had mastered in the world of commerce.

And so Mr. Oku nurtured his dream in secret, sketching in his few available moments variations of the wondrous, exotic things he saw illustrated in the magazines. He met clandestinely with real-estate brokers in search of the perfect property and he located a local architect who had actually studied for the profession in California and who could explain the functions of the unusual rooms. Finally he decided to commence discussions with his wife, but to do it in two parts. The first part, the easy one, was to convince her to sell their present home and move to an area more appropriate to their current economic status. The second, the more difficult part, would be to convince his wife that they should build, to phrase it benignly, a nontraditional abode.

~

Three months after returning from America, he initiated the first gambit. From his office he phoned Mrs. Oku: "*Tsuma* (my wife), I am thinking of coming home for dinner tonight—could you prepare some of your wonderful dishes so we may eat together?" He was a man of few words when talking to his wife.

"But Ichiro-san, this is not the weekend. Is there something wrong? Why will you not be going out as usual to carry out your business obligations?"

"Is there something wrong with a man wishing to dine with his wife? If you have made other plans, just tell me."

"No, I am happy that you will be coming home to eat—only a little surprised."

~

Dinner was a pleasant affair, and Mr. Oku was lavish in his praise. In fact, he found that giving up an evening drinking and dining with his staff and buddies was not such a burden. "Wife, I forgot how good a cook you are and how poor the food is in the miserable restaurants that I must endure for the sake of the business. We should do this more often. We have talked a few times about moving to a bigger, more comfortable home. I have been busy with my growing business, but now it may be time to start harvesting that for which we have toiled so long and so hard. Do you recall me telling you of how American men stay at home so much with their wives and children? It may be that their homes are more comfortable than ours. A more pleasant home to come back to would encourage me not to stay out every night."

Mrs. Oku was surprised. "When the Tanakas moved to a better district and finer home last summer, you seemed to disapprove. What has changed?"

Mr. Oku shifted uncomfortably on the *tatami*, rearranged his kimono, and cleared his throat. "When I was in America three months ago, I saw that there was more to life than work. You are in charge of all our savings and investments, so tell me if we have enough money to buy a new house. It should be in a good, high-class area so that the wife of my elder brother will not continue to slight you." He was pleased with that last improvisation.

This was all bewildering to Mrs. Oku, but she tentatively replied: "We could probably afford a new home, for we have more money than I ever dreamed possible. In fact, at the last meeting of our ladies' investment club, the guest speaker spoke of how well investments in real estate have been doing."

"So it's settled. I'll get listings of available places and together we will view them."

~

The first part of the plan had gone better than expected, but that was the easy part. Now Mr. Oku began to come home for dinner more regularly. After dinner he would suggest that they watch a movie on TV. Soon it became a custom and Mr. Oku always volunteered to pick up a video on his way home. It usually was an American film and, more often than not, featured the wealthy, showing them in lavish, elegant homes. After each viewing, Mr. Oku brought the conversation around to the lifestyle of the Americans. When he believed his wife to be completely indoctrinated, Mr. Oku casually produced his twelve-inch-high pile of architectural magazines. He showed her his favorites, some going back for one or more generations, and made his pitch.

Mrs. Oku's reaction was immediate; she clenched her teeth and pursed her lips. "So this is what the past weeks have been all about. Husband, I always knew you were devious, but this is beyond anything I could have imagined. I will not live in this thing you call a split-level, neo-Spanish, California ranch-style house with or without what you say is a 'Florida breezeway.' We are considering land in the best area of Osaka. Many of the mansions there date back to the Meiji period. Do you really believe that our new neighbors would be happy to have what you call an 'alternative lifestyle' home in their community? Even if I did agree, we would be ostracized. Why, the kitchen has no walls, and that big hole in the living room that you call a conversation pit would seat people too shocked or laughing too hard to make any conversation at all."

"Wife, you are wrong. If I could prove that all our neighbors would welcome the new addition to their 'traditional' community, would you then agree?"

It was unseemly to debate with one's husband without some attempt at compromise, even if he was being foolish, so Mrs. Oku took the safe but sure way out. She agreed they would build an American-style house provided all the neighbors approved, but if any disapproved, they would then build a conventional home. They bought the land, had an architect make sketches of the "nonconventional house," and Mr. Oku had a scale model with a removable roof made.

~

When building a house in Japan it was the custom to visit your new neighbors to introduce yourself, present gifts, and apologize for the coming disruption of their tranquility. Mr. and Mrs. Oku followed these traditions, but in addition Mr. Oku invited all to a meeting the following week to view his plans and the preliminary model and also to help in planning and designing the new home. As he later told me, he hoped to preempt the critics.

The open kitchen startled all and Mr. Oku explained that the kitchens in America were social centers and that many of the men there enjoyed doing the cooking. This intrigued the local women but shocked their husbands. A few of the men began talking about ancestral values and the possible drop in the neighborhood real-estate prices; about the big hole in the living room floor and how shameless it was for men to do the cooking.

Mrs. Oku suddenly became concerned; her husband was about to lose face. Besides, his eloquent presentation had convinced all the other women, most of the men, and even her. She was beginning to be excited about the new house. She was also angry at the narrow-mindedness of the man who disapproved of men cooking and who called it shameless. She decided to act in her husband's defense with irony and, assuming a guileless demeanor, she spoke: "I suppose the square hole in the living room that they call a conversation pit is where American men and women sit and exchange favorite recipes—and then discuss how the shameless male cooks of America won the war against Japan." There was a shocked silence and then roars of laughter. Her risky quip had herded the stray ducks back into line.

That night Mr. Oku gravely told his wife that she had done well. She bowed in acknowledgment, slowly, to hide the warm flush of pleasure and pride she felt and then, with appropriate modesty, she replied: "I did what had to be done to muzzle that terrible Mr. Sakai, who was the barking dog that would set the whole street barking." The following day Mr. Oku proudly told all his buddies how his own wife was wiser and wittier than any of the hostesses in their drinking club.

~

The split-level, neo-Spanish, California ranch-style house was built, but without the Florida breezeway, which the architect insisted would destroy the integrity and cohesion of the other three styles. The conversation pit was yielded in a tactical retreat before the combined forces of Mrs. Oku and reality.

~

After Mr. Oku completed the house, his visits to his favorite drinking club ceased, then began again, occasionally at first but gaining in regularity. Now every weekday evening, at his club, not far from his factory, he again regaled his drinking buddies with the tales he told so well. When he told them he would be coming regularly, they welcomed him with unbridled emotion—each a deep bow. One of his friends was curious: "Ichiro-san, it is good to have you back, but it seems that you will spend little time in your new home. Is it not what you had hoped for?" Mr. Oku answered enigmatically that it was beyond anything he had anticipated.

Sometime later I too asked Mr. Oku about his American home. He told me the story I have just recounted. As I was a co-conspirator in the original planning, he added a personal note to the tale: "When I built my house, I was eager to see the changes it would bring to me and my family." Mr. Oku paused, and then continued ruefully, "It was to be as a pebble tossed into calm waters, causing gentle, ever-expanding ripples. I now know it was a large rock I tossed, and my wife, who was so reluctant at first, is being carried high on its waves. It began with tours of our home by the Architectural Society, which led to her becoming a member of that organization, which led to her joining their board, which led to her being active in the American Cultural Association. The waves continued, ever expanding; English lessons, TV appearances, and now one of the liberal parties is trying to get her to run for public office." He again paused and then ended the saga of the American house on a poignant note: "Now even eating a simple meal at home is like trying to dine in a celebrated restaurant—I must make reservations well in advance."

The Witness of High Hats

Lockie Hunter

    At 22, I slept with my childhood teddy bear and my musician boyfriend in a 400 square foot studio in the TenderNob district of San Francisco. With one tattoo parlor, two fortunetellers and a sad hotel, the TenderNob is positioned between affluent Nob Hill and the transvestite-hooker district of the Tenderloin. Moving west from Tennessee, I was to be Mary Tyler Moore, hat high in the air, pleats twirling. I did toss the hat once, and a horizontal wind hosting the ever-present fog carried it down Jones Street, and it was run over by a taxi. My boyfriend cautioned against tossing the hat. "You toss it, and it will land in hooker pee or Gray Man will snatch it in the air and claim custody."

    Gray Man lives on my stoop. He is not part of my chosen landscape, my attempt at Mary-Tyler-Mooreishness. He is pale with purple veins on his neck, face and arms. He wears a gray coat and has a beard, but perhaps he does not. Now, thirty years later, it is like squinting at too-brightly colored Polaroids, trying to recall the names of those that were once vital.

    Gray Man spare-changes me. His upper lip is crusted with something yellow. He smells like the Mission Street garage, like an unclear threat. I give him whatever silver and copper is knocking in my pockets until one night when I dump on the stoop beside him and explain that this is my home. "*My home*," I yell, as if being homeless also makes him hard of hearing. "*I'm making a real home. Fresh flowers, hat rack.*" My vivid dream of home, (cat-books-hats-tea-pjs-plants) is jostled into dusty reality each time Gray Man panhandles, so we work a deal. Paid monthly, Gray Man is to stop spare-changing me. He then takes an ancillary step. Friends are shocked that I have a doorman in *this* neighborhood, on Jones? He winks at me each time he opens the door— and I smile. We have an agreement.

Gray Man peeks inside my shopping bags. I share my apples and grapes. He does not whistle when my skirt is too short, though the boys on the street do. When he sleeps, slumped against the railing, his head swallowed by his coat, he resembles a bundle, a care package left for me at my new home. He safeguards my lies. "I can't go to church. I'm sick," I tell my mother when she arrives at my stoop. Minutes later I emerge, dressed for brunch, and take a cautious step outside. Gray raises his eyebrows then winks. He understands. He opens doors for me.

Gray Man has seen me like few others have: checking on lipstick in the side view mirror of a cab, picking my nose, weepy drunk and fumbling for keys, flirting with my neighbor, struggling with my boyfriend, belligerent to a meter maid, bogarting a joint, lying to my mother about my job, arms loaded with laundry, dressed in church clothes, in vinyl and boots, blue jeans and t-shirt, hat in the air, hat in the gutter.

The day before the explosion, I bought a large T.V. I remember loving the look of it, the sleekness. The modernity of its flat gray face would bring the news, sitcoms, trashy miniseries to my TenderNob home.

June, 1990, and I am scaling salmon. Rice is boiling, the TV blaring, and I've had too much homegrown to be properly wielding a knife. I hear the honk-honk blare of a fire truck on the TV and the urgent sound of a news reporter. I even smell smoke, and I think it is because I am high, a stoned writer creating her own story, packed with sensory details. But now I hear the sirens in stereo, coming from the TV in front of me as well as the door behind me. "An explosion on Jones Street has turned into a blaze," the announcer says as if concerned. "Police believe the explosion was caused by crack cocaine production and is coming through the manhole...residents are advised..."

Who can say why we're drawn to one object or one person? I have a tattoo of a Picasso on my right hip, so in love with the acuity of line that I wanted it to be a part of me, etched into my skin. In memories of my TenderNob apartment I walk past my winking doorman into the lobby, then through the burlwood door, past the steaming clawfoot tub and stroke the poetry books on the shelves. A multi-colored afghan, grandma-knitted, is smoothed on the bed. Small red circles spot the white bedstand, evidence of evenings of wine. A flokati rug with curly white high pile fibers is littered with takeout boxes. A 45 of my boyfriend's new single sits next to the old record player.

As the smell of smoke and sound of sirens surges, every piece of furniture, every book, is prized. I take all my arms can carry: seven books, the stuffed bear, a potted plant, a trophy from softball, the afghan.

Gray Man is waiting on the stoop, eyes wild. "Out!" he says, leading me across the street, away from exploding manholes and shattering glass. Though it is not cold, I offer him my afghan, and he wraps himself in it completely, like a woman in a burka. I am wild. Gray is calm. I am molten. Gray is solid. I coil up from the curb then sit down then rise up again until he makes a disapproving noise. I sit. His profile is dark for a second then glows red then blue then red with the sirens. My flamboyant afghan looks strange on him and I smile to see him so dressed up, so full of color. We wait together for the red trucks.

The next day he is not there. The stoop looks blank, incomplete. "Did the blaze scare old Gray off?" asks my boyfriend. I wait. He doesn't return. I still wait. I want to be ushered inside again; the home that awaits is framed by this ritual. He never returns. I realize I had been pretending that Gray Man fit into my landscape, my home. And, in pretending he was something he was not, we both became more valuable. He became a guard, while I became less guarded.

My vivid dream of home (cat-books-hats-tea-pjs-plants-doorman) is again altered. I enter the building—day after day, tired and energized, formal and funky, clean and stinky, crying and giggling—with no one to observe my arrival, no one to note my departure, and no one to witness my hat—high in the air.

Digging In

Colin Rafferty

There's a part in Tony Horowitz's *Confederates in the Attic* where he talks with Civil War re-enactors about what it's like to "die" on the field. No one wants to die, they complain. The first volley of shots from the other side, and it's like everyone's got bulletproof vests. Once you die, you're dead, they say, and that means you can't move, that you have to lie there on the field while everyone else continues to fight.

For once, I'll admit that the re-enactors are right; no one wants to be the dead body. It's the part of the war that all of us think about in the most abstract of ways: noble sacrifices and glorious valor and all that. Lines on a map and numerals on a page don't reveal the reality of corpses on the battlefield, or the fact that something has to happen to those bodies, that they have to be buried, one by one.

I don't know if you've ever dug a grave, but it's difficult work. You know how in crime shows and Lifetime Network movies, a small woman will dig a grave large enough to hold a full-grown abusive husband, not to mention fill it back up? No fucking way. All I had to do was dig a 2x2x1 grave—four cubic feet of dirt—and it took me an hour and a half, tore up my hands, and left me sore for days.

~

The emergency veterinarian had told my wife and me that we had three options for the body. We could take her home in a cardboard casket, or we could have her cremated singly, or we could have her mass cremated. I was horrified by the idea of the third, and something rankled me about the second—the waiting, maybe, or the cost—so I asked for the cardboard casket for my dead cat.

They brought Olive out to us in a white cardboard casket, a few strips of tape circling it. It had blue lines on it, which made me think about the Priority Mail boxes at the post office. We took Olive home, and I put her in the basement. I made sure we had a shovel, and then we buried her in the backyard, in a space that she could have seen from the window, but as an indoor-only cat, never gone to.

It felt futile, digging that grave, like it was labor without reward, but I realized that it was the last protective thing I could do for Olive, to dig the grave deep enough to keep her body safe from scavengers.

I was about halfway through the process—just reaching a point when the hole I'd dug was big enough to let the edge of the pile of sandy soil removed begin to fall back in—when I thought about the cemeteries in Fredericksburg. The biggest one—just a mile from our house, at the bottom of the ridgeline that we live on—is the National Cemetery, part of the Fredericksburg and Spotsylvania National Military Park complex. It's where the Union soldiers are buried. The rebels are buried at the Confederate Cemetery, another mile in another direction away from our house. Within a mile radius of my home, 19,000 bodies, most of them unidentified, lie in graves.

It's unsettling to think about, but the graves make the town. Along with the battlefields themselves, the cemeteries are the greenest spaces here. They draw in tourists year-round, especially during the anniversaries and most noticeably on Memorial Day, when the local Boy Scouts and Girl Scouts set luminaria out on the graves of the National Cemetery, lining the path along the Sunken Road. On the same day at the Confederate Cemetery, re-enactors in grey uniforms and hoop skirts plant flags—the Stars and Bars—on the graves of the Southern dead.

I don't know what it means to live in a town that's surrounded by death, that's defined by death. For the most part, it's something we walk past on our way downtown, something we're slightly embarrassed about when the re-enactors invade in the winter and spring. But it points to the thing we rarely consider: every one of those graves is filled with at least one person (and usually more; most of them are mass graves, two or three or four bodies filling a grave, marked only with a number).

~

A few years ago, before I'd moved to Fredericksburg, I visited Auschwitz. I stuck around for a few days, longer than the average daytripper. One evening, walking back from the little neighborhood grocery near the camp, I came upon a park. In the middle of its greenery, a low wall stood, outlining a rectangle, with a plaque that marked the site of a mass grave holding about 700 people who'd been killed or had died in the final days of the camp or just after its liberation by the Soviet Army. It was a lovely evening, the last rays of sunlight bouncing off the apartment buildings, kids playing soccer on a nearby field. And here was that grave, grown lush and green and with 700 skeletons in it.

I remember thinking at the time that it must have been impossible to reside in a place like that, that there was no way people could live with that historical weight on them. Now I know differently; you *can* live there, easily. You can go to school and work, you can shop for groceries and postcards, you can stroll with your dog down the Sunken Road, behind which Confederate infantry opened fire on the Union soldiers. And after a while, you never think about it, unless something happens to make you think of it, to make you understand a detail that had always been vague before you started to dig.

~

The night we buried the cat, I woke to a thunderstorm. I could hear the rain splashing off the leaves I never bothered to dig out of the gutter, the occasional rumble in the sky. Although I normally fall asleep quickly and stay that way, I lay awake all night; I could see the grave crumbling, the Hammer Films-like idea of the earth rending open to reveal the casket. I stared at the ceiling, feeling something like fear at the base of my spine. *Not deep enough*, I thought, over and over. *Not deep enough*.

Early the next morning, I went to the backyard and picked my way through the wet grass to the grave. The paving stone we'd bought at Lowe's to cover the grave was undisturbed, the dirt around it soaked, but there was no indentation in the ground, nothing even close to a collapse. A mile away, the sun dried the rain off thousands of Union graves. A mile away, the squirrels ran in the trees over the Confederate dead. And Fredericksburg woke up to another day with the city and its dead.

The Drive from Morgantown to Baltimore

Stephen J. West

I walk out to the street with coffee in hand, climb into the car and turn the ignition. My wife quickly buckles her seatbelt and tunes the radio. It's 5:33 am. We're leaving three minutes late. As we make our way through the empty streets of Morgantown to the entrance ramp of 68 East, I think about how difficult it is to see in twilight, how each streetlamp is a stage prop spotlighting things we color with emotion. I think about the drive ahead, and the reason we have to make it.

We accelerate onto the highway and begin to carve our way across the rugged geography of Appalachia. No words pass between us. There's no need; we're accustomed to the drama of this landscape, to its weary mountains in various states of recovery, like the people who huddle among them. We speed through a collage of the backwater and ramshackle; of faded and tattered billboards bolted to rock outcroppings; of rusted automobiles and smoldering tires; of sagging gas stations and their announcements for *cigarettes, beer, ammo, bait*; of boarded windows that don't necessarily connote abandonment, and so many other vignettes that remind us what people think when we tell them where we come from. Together, my wife and I can see past all of this to how we really feel: content as outliers, connected by what we divine in these dismissed expanses.

Today we're driving with purpose, anxiously watching as the mountains slide toward sea level and dissolve into the industrial flats of the Eastern seaboard. We're driving to the Wilmer Eye Institute in Baltimore because my wife has a detached retina in her left eye. This is her second detachment in as many years. The first occurred in her right eye, and a botched surgery left it with a field of vision that's half daguerreotype, half darkness: a world in permanent twilight. Neuropathy. No explanation from her surgeon in West Virginia other than "bad things happen to good people." My wife can still see with her left eye, and we're driving today to find the best doctors we can, anyone at all that might offer more than cliché to help us believe it will always remain that way, to swaddle us and hush away the word that threatens to erode the world we share: *blindness*.

    I've heard that scientists can grow human ears on mice and clone sheep named Dolly; I've read of stem cells, of the blind seeing again and other stories that systems of faith could use as proof for their beliefs. And I want to believe in all of them. I need to believe my wife will see. She's only 29, and I'm only 29, and I want a life where we can look at each other. I want to share in the momentary reflections on mountain reservoirs and listen to her describe the density of chimney smoke spewing from hillside cabins; I want us to look warily at rusty trestle bridges on back roads and find relief in our eye contact when we reach the other side; I want to agree on the acquired taste of dilapidated red brick buildings and read the faded names painted on them aloud to each other, have her say they look like tattoos on an aging sailor; I want her to steal a glance at me and smirk when someone dismisses us because of where we live; and I need to reach out for her hand and always find it reaching for mine when, on the drive from Morgantown to Baltimore, we see the sun appear on the horizon and watch as it sets fire to the world where the continents once collided, where vision and emotion align, and know there's no need to describe it with words.

Human Resources

Michelle Valois

My father's hands were blue from the molds he made in the machine shop where he worked. My father's hands were strong. My father's hands struck out, sometimes; sometimes they repaired what was broken around the house. Usually, his hands held cups of coffee, cans of beer, or shots of Jack Daniels. On Saturdays, if there was no overtime, his hands cocked a gun. On Sundays, they were folded in prayer; later in the day they shuffled a deck of dog-eared cards as we and grandparents and sometimes aunts and uncles huddled around the dining room table to play Pitch. When we were infants, his hands cradled us, after my mother had bathed and powdered our tiny bodies but before she put us to bed. I could not remember his hands like this.

Last week, in my daily paper, I saw a help wanted ad for a job at the local university. The Physics Department was seeking a tool and die maker, someone to run the department's machine shop, someone who could assist professors and graduate students with the *instruments and tools needed in the fabrication of the scientific equipment used in sponsored research.*

My father met every requirement, except for a high school diploma, but I could see him fast-talking his way into an interview and into the job, offering to fix the diesel engine on the department chair's 475-horse-powered boat and then being invited to go deep sea fishing. He would smoke with the maintenance men, 100 feet from the nearest building; check lottery numbers with the department secretaries; and tease the academic dean, a bespectacled man in awe of my father's unwavering ability to operate and fix every machine in the university's shop (which would be cleaner and better ventilated than anything my father had ever worked in before).

My father would wear a white, buttoned-down shirt, ironed, but which would not stay clean and pressed long. I would visit him often at work. He would introduce me to his graduate students, young men who, when they looked at him, wished their own fathers could handle tools like that. He would make a point of walking by the offices of the department's faculty and introducing me as one of them. *My daughter, the professor*, he would boast, and add, almost apologetically, *English*, and then, because he could never help himself, *We always thought she spoke good enough*, which is what he started saying the year I left for college.

I want to pen a letter, on his behalf, to the department of human resources:

Dear Sir or Madam:

Enclosed please find the resume of a man who, with half a century of experience as a tool and die maker and extensive knowledge of manufactured materials, most notably plastics; three years of active duty during the second world war; a surprisingly gentle fathering ability; not to mention overall likeability and unquestionable collegiality; meets nearly every one of your desired qualifications.

At his wake, twenty-five years before such a job was ever advertised or maybe even existed, I was struck by how white my father's hands were, folded upon his chest—not the white of pressed dress shirts, not the white of an empty sheet of paper, or the white of a baby tooth or cream. He liked his coffee black.

Lettuce and Rabbits

Seth Sawyers

At the Cresaptown house, we had a garden as big as a basketball court. Jake was thirteen. I was eight, and Ryan was seven. In the winter, we rode sleds down the big hill, past the crabapple tree. When it was warm, we hurled a baseball until our skinny forearms throbbed. But in the spring, Dad planted. We watched as tomato seedlings shot up, as the cucumbers and zucchini spread, as the banana peppers came in as tiny and hard as Christmas lights.

But before all that, it was the lettuce that came up first. Dad sprinkled the seeds along the edges. I watched the lettuce. We all watched it. It was the first green we'd seen in months, since the snows, and it came up like little explosions, two leaves, then four, each set so green as to be almost illuminated from within. For weeks, we watched the leaves widening, thickening, that early green deepening.

The rabbits came. They sat in our front yard, serene, scattering when startled by headlights. At first, they nibbled only the white-green strawberries, but they were still too bitter. Then they found the lettuce and after that, rabbits were a different thing. We shouted at them from the garage, waved our arms from the big picture window, threw baseballs and clumps of brown that I thought were dirt but which turned out to be petrified dog turds. The rabbits shot off like scared rockets, and it felt good to see them run. But there were many of them, and they were skinny, and the green of the lettuce was very green. In the mornings, before school, I'd check on the garden. Some leaves were nibbled, some were chewed down to the tough stalks, some were gone.

"Might have to make a trip to the A&P after all," Mom said.

I began to think of rabbits as having sharp, yellow teeth, hooked dagger-claws, inflamed eyes. We watched their soft brownness from the breakfast table, us eating our cereal, the rabbits eating our lettuce. One morning, dressed for work, Dad came into the kitchen holding a coffee mug in one hand and his bow and a single arrow in the other. The bow, a simple recurve, was taller than me. I could not draw it, though I'd tried many times. We followed him onto the porch. A rabbit, a young one, nibbled at the lettuce, chewed, nibbled and chewed. We grew quiet. We held our breath. Dad drew on the bow, held it like that for five, six seconds. I thought he couldn't hold it any longer, but then he let fly. The arrow flew straight but fell, harmlessly, among the tomatoes. The rabbit froze, darted toward the Orndorfs' back yard, and vanished.

"Bastard," Dad said.

For a week, every morning, he shot off a single arrow. "Bastard," he said, every time.

The sun was high and strong on the seventh day, the kind of April day that finally turns everything green, that makes your forehead sweat, that fills your skinny muscles with warm honey. Dad got home from work and found us in the living room, watching cartoons. He was still wearing his corduroys and striped button-down shirt, but he held the bow in one hand and an arrow in the other. We followed. The sun was low in the sky, the warm afternoon light turning the garden green-golden-brown. A scrawny, nervous rabbit sat just on the edge of the garden, chewing. Dad drew back, said, "Hold it, you bastard," and let go.

That night, there was no lettuce for a salad. But we had Caporale's white bread with butter. We had some rice. And we had rabbit, which was chewy and dark, and of which there was just enough.

Improvement

Emily Roller

I think we can both agree that you have some room for improvement.

Nadu P. Ono did not agree. Dr. Alfred Paterson did not notice, though. He looked over his glasses at Nadu's forehead, handed over the paper and pretended to read a memo. He pretended so long that he forgot he was pretending and actually did read the memo. When he looked up, Nadu was still there.

Is there a problem, Dr. Paterson wanted to know.

Where? asked Nadu.

Where? asked Dr. Paterson.

Nadu waited for an answer that wasn't a question. He stared patiently at the nameplate on Dr. Paterson's desk. Alfred Paterson, PhD. Communications.

Young man, said Dr. Paterson. Do you have a question?

Nadu had only questions; it was answers he lacked.

Is there a problem? Dr. Paterson asked.

I don't know, said Nadu.

Well, do you have a question? Why are you still here?

Where? asked Nadu again.

In this room. Why are you still in this room, young man? This is my office. Can't you see that I've got other things to do now?

This is your room?

Of course it is. See the diploma? Dr. Paterson pointed to a framed diploma on the wall beside his desk. Whose name is on that diploma?

University of Phoenix.

Under that.

Alfred Patterson.

That's me. This is obviously my room.

Where is my room, then?

Dr. Paterson looked over his glasses at Nadu's forehead. He frowned. Your room, young man? Why would I know where your room is?

You said I had some room.

I said this is my room. I said nothing about your room.

For improvement. I want to know where.

Oh, said Dr. Paterson, understanding. I didn't mean you have a *room* for improvement.

I have no room for improvement?

I didn't mean that! Of course you do.

Nadu sat back in his chair and looked at the way Dr. Paterson's hair almost covered his head—like a threadbare baby blanket.

Here, Dr. Paterson pointed to the paper. You have room for improvement in your paper. I just mean you can make it better. You have a little room for improvement—that's all.

Nadu sat back in the chair and thought about it all.

Well, said Dr. Paterson. Anything else?

Nadu thought very carefully.

I think, he said, we can both agree that you have more room for improvement.

Room Theme Contest Winner – 1st Place

Come In, Come In

Jen Murvin Edwards

    I never thought anyone would answer my Craigslist ad, but you were the fifth lady who called. I changed the headline to "House Cleaning Professional," was that what made the difference for you? Well, maybe for some of the others. Don't think I was lying, because really there's no formal school for it, and I have been doing it for twenty years, so I'm about as professional as you can get. No false advertising. You have an interesting front door, and what is that little metal bar? Mezuzah? Sounds like Medusa. No, you're right, cultural symbols are important. I just never knew anyone who was Jewish where I come from. But one of my father's childhood friends was Jewish and he—my father—always said a bar mitzvah was better than any party he'd ever go to, even his own wedding. My mama passed just a month ago, so she won't mind me telling you that, even though she tried real hard and always told the story about how she made her own wedding dress out of her mother's silk tablecloth. That's why I'm taking on more houses you see, since she died. After she died, I mean, and because she died. Both together.

    Right, this room looks just fine, I should be able to clean it real nice for you. You have some nice things, where'd you get that couch from? I always wanted a white couch, never knew people actually put them in their houses on account of cats and kids and everything. No kids? Well, don't worry. Of course you're not worried, no, that would be silly. I'm sorry, I just never met anyone with a white couch before. Did you paint these pictures yourself? Oh, now that I think about it of course I've heard of him, yes, I should have recognized the style. I always thought paintings of naked people were so classy. Women in those paintings look more like real women, you know, with stomach rolls and soft hips, and their faces are rounder, like big peaches. They're always on couches or holding pitchers of water, why is that? You'd never call these women girls.

Would you like me to do the dishes for you? I'm a wonderful scrubber. Is that a basil plant? You probably cook a lot, don't you? No, I understand, being a bank manager would definitely keep you pretty busy, of course. My mama always told me a good wife cooked her husband breakfast and dinner and brought him coffee in bed, but I never had a chance to do that because my fiancé died before I got a chance to bring him coffee or anything else in bed, if you know what I mean. It's alright, it wasn't your fault. My mama warned him about that two lane highway so late at night but she couldn't have known, she wouldn't have wished it on anyone, I know that, even though she hated that he went to movies without me. I had to feed her through a feeding tube, in the end. But I didn't mind, you know. I mean him going to the movies.

You must get a wonderful workout going up all these stairs, it's probably why you are so thin and beautiful! You are! Your bedroom furniture is lovely, all the same design. Imagine, bed and nightstands and desk all matching, isn't that beautiful. Maple? Cherry, of course, I should have known. I'll get those little nooks and crannies, I have a special duster I designed myself, and I use Q-tips, that's a little trick of mine, I do a real nice job, you'll see. Nothing under the bed! I keep a suitcase under mine and a lot of cat hair, of course, like most people. You're right, a lot of people are allergic to cats. I'll separate the whites and the darks, no white shirts turning pink on my watch. Did I see you had a special hanger just for your bras?

Don't go in that room? Alright, I'll make a note, a mental note. I'd ask why not, but like I should have said before, I don't look, I don't ask, I'm not a curious kind of person. I had a room like that, too, for a while, where I put all my fiancé's clothes— remember he died, I told you—and his books and his little collection of figurines. It used to be my guestroom, but I didn't have any guests for a long long time and I kept it closed. He liked collecting these figurines and these little spoons from everywhere he went, and he had these wooden racks of spoons from places like Carpentaria, California and Minnetonka, Minnesota, and he even let his little nephew use the one from Poughkeepsie because he liked the name and wanted to lick up his ice cream with it. The nephew, not my fiancé. I had that room and I'd go in there and I'd just sit, right on the floor there, in the middle of his windbreakers and his spoons and his stupid little figurines. A grown man! There was one of a squirrel in a logger's cap and he told me once they reminded him to wonder. Wonder about what, I asked him, and he just looked at me. I didn't understand his eyes, eyes like my grandfather's when he told the story from the war about how he watched this young guy who had been a car mechanic get eaten by a shark in the South Pacific. He told that story all the time, at every party, even though we begged him to stop because we knew how much it upset him. I still think about that, you know, when I swim. Wonder about what, I asked my fiancé, and he never did tell me.

Can I tell you something? You seem like a nice lady and you won't be shocked, and it just hit me right here, right in front of your closed room where I can't go in, that maybe I loved him more after he died. Like maybe the way we remember our childhoods. Thank you for holding my elbow there for a moment, I think I'm recovered now, so sorry about that. You're so nice to say it's alright, it wasn't for a long time but it is now, the guest room, and I only kept the spoon from Old Santa Barbara, because the top of it is shaped like a mission, with the windows and everything, and you imagine that maybe in Santa Barbara there aren't any sharks.

I don't use bleach, that stuff will kill you. Vinegar does just fine, even though it'll stink for a little bit, but mostly on my hands.

What a wonderful tub. I just love blue tile, it's probably named something like "Sky" or "Serene." Like a magazine. You must soak in here every night. Well, of course, it's easy to just fall into bed, don't I know it, after a long day. And all these nice soaps shaped like seashells.

Your husband's bedroom? Of course, much more practical, as you say, and what more does a woman want than a closet all to herself. Does he snore? Well, that's good, I hear snoring could be a sign of sleep apnea. Yes, I'll keep his dry cleaning separate, and isn't the bedspread such a nice masculine color? Grey is so classy, I've always thought. No, no, it's only natural to keep a bottle of Scotch by the bed, no need to pick it up, that's my job anyway, a-ha! I read somewhere that a glass of alcohol can help you to sleep, and didn't my fiancé have a glass of red wine every night with dinner, or sometimes whiskey when one of the kids didn't make it. Did I tell you he was an orderly in the kids' unit at the hospital? Sometimes he'd take some little figurines to work with him. I always said a little prayer when the whiskey came out, still can't really smell it, you know, without getting heavy in the stomach. Would you like some water? Yes, there's something going around, and of course you're tired, so busy at the bank. Here, let me. What a lovely faucet, and I always loved those sinks that look like bowls sitting on the counter, what a creative idea. Drink this, there you go. There you go.

    These stairs again, my, it'll be like a job and a trip to the gym at the same time. You're so thin! I've always been a bit rounder, pear-shaped. But maybe that's a good thing, right? Like something people used to paint.

    Did you forget something? Of course, I'll come back up with you. Huff and puff like that children's story. What beautiful pictures, did you use a level to line them up so perfectly? They're of you, I see you there, but they look like they could be in a magazine. Isn't he handsome, the way he has his arm around your whole waist, like a safety belt.

    What are you doing? This door? Like I said, I don't ask questions, and I won't go in. I promise, I won't go in.

    Oh my, I see. What a beautiful nursery. You did such a wonderful job, pink like cotton candy or the inside of a shell. Winnie the Pooh is perfect, I always thought he was so gentle with that high voice. Twenty weeks? Oh, my. I never had children myself, no, but that seems pretty far along, doesn't it. Old enough that it's more than an idea. I'll use a Q-tip, there, for the little picture frame with the shells all around the edges, and for the little carousel up there on the shelf. Those aren't horses on that carousel, but I see an elephant, and a wolf, and is that a mushroom cap? How creative, like someone thought about all the different ways they'd like to ride around the world. Sometimes I wonder how people imagine these things. Now let's sit down in our usual spots, there you go in the rocking chair, and I told you I always went right here, on the floor, right in the middle of it all. There's a word for this. Yes, that's the one I was trying to remember. *Shiva.* What a lovely word, like a whisper. It's only natural for us to cry, it's a loss, isn't it, and that's how the body responds. We lose blood, we cry, we lose skin, we cry. Isn't it natural, the most natural reaction in the world. No, it's easy for me here, I can just reach right out, I'm really quite flexible, and it's not far anyway, is it. Your hand is so soft, you must use lotion all the time. I'm sorry mine are so rough. Yes, you're right. From all the cleaning. I like it, you know, cleaning houses. A space says something about a person, what they let in, how they surround themselves, and maybe I'm part of it somehow. I kept my fiancé's figurines, you know, in the end. They say don't be materialistic, but sometimes we keep something to remind us what's been taken away. Hold on, I'll be right back.

    I never liked the taste, I told you about the smell, but it just seems right, doesn't it? I knew you'd think so. Maybe there's something to it, maybe it's been there all along. Here, down like fire, isn't that what they say. So warm, I can feel it already. Like fire, down our throats, into our blood, into our hearts, our hearts.

Room Theme Contest Winner – 2nd Place

On Maimeó

Heather Martin

My paternal grandmother Maimeó was not of the usual sort. I remember her best sitting at her kitchen table, smoking cigarettes and singing Irish folk songs. Not sugary lullabies—no "Toora, Loora, Loora"—but thumping, raucous ditties. Songs of sailors, pints, martyrs and revolution. She sang with joy and grief, with swinging elbows and knotted fists. She sang without invitation or regard for neighbors or visitors, humiliating her husband and son—a sin for which, I'm certain my father never forgave her. Born in Manhattan at the dawn of the *Roaring 20s*, my grandmother was, among other things, a housewife a storyteller, and an alcoholic.

Through the years, she serenaded my grandfather with "Mullaghdoo" in his early-morning flurries out the door to work, and warbled "Dublin Lady" in the evenings as my father arm-yanked frightened dates out the front door, all the while cursing his mother to an early grave. My father despised her, my grandfather beat her, but nothing could stop the singing.

When I was a child, and my father spent entire nights in his office, Maimeó looked after my brother and me. He amused himself as boys do, but I wanted only to be near her. She'd sing for hours alone, smoking. I hid beneath the kitchen table, watching the soles of her feet roll from heel to toe. I was her invisible audience of one.

And as I listened, I learned that she intended the songs not for her family, her neighbors, or even me. And her design was not to embarrass or anger them as she did. It was something much simpler, I think.

Her songs were an overture. They set the stage, called out ghost players to rehearse a distant history from some other place and time.

Maimeó sang and the company shuffled in with choreographed precision, changing the backdrop, elbowing aside her troubled reality. The walls around us flimsied and peeled away like heavy curtains. The scene opened. Maimeó sang, and I heard the accompanying fiddles and pipes, flutes and accordions. The air slowly warmed with the sounds of breathy chit chat and good-natured *craic*. Maimeó glowed in the light of this grand fantasy. She led this chorus of voices in song. She lifted her glass to outstretched arms, exchanged knowing nods with other time-worn faces. The rhythmic thumps of her calloused feet were joined in perfect unison by dusty brogans and Shillelagh walking sticks. It was glorious, and it was happy.

But there was no script. And there was no plot.

It was a scene stuck on loop, playing over and over. Her glass emptied and refilled, emptied and refilled. When she grew tired, dropped the tune and her head to the table, the players froze for a moment and then fell away completely. I was alone then in her kitchen; the lazy clicking of the clock's second hand hollow in the void. When she died, it was a relief to my father and grandfather. Her song had finally ended.

In recent years, I have found myself thinking of her more and more. The lyrics and melodies of those songs are mostly disappeared from my head. I so wish to remember them. But in their place, I find something else: a story. I didn't remember it at first, but then it was there, as if it had always been, carefully tucked away, preserved somewhere in the recesses of my memory. A strange and haunting story, it was—a far cry from the breezy days of Dick and Jane—and surely not meant for the ears of a child as young as I was. Madmen and beasts, loved ones cast out and abandoned, murdered and resurrected, only to seek revenge on those who had wronged them—setting fires, taking children. I remember the intensity of her gaze, the way she called me *darlin'* and implored me to come from beneath the table for the telling; but, most of all, I remember her whisper. Perhaps she whispered for effect, or to keep the pagan tales below the ears of her God, or maybe even out of habit to escape the waves of criticism from husband and son. It could be any or all of those things. But as I think of it now, I believe that it was because the story was a sacred and secret thing that was told to *her* in hushed female voices. It held warnings, wishes, instructions, and truths. She was telling me something, instructing me—one who saw meaning through beer and whiskey spiked utterance, through blighted speech, through loosed grey bun. And I listened.

Room Theme Contest Winner – 3rd Place

The New Victorians

Linda Barnhart

Bulldozers are voracious, violent pieces of equipment, capable of gouging and tearing up great swathes of earth, a breed of mechanical T-Rex, their form and function an extension of my older brother, John's personality. Rugby player, resident of the mosh pit in his younger days, he runs our excavating business. Me, I do the books and handle the human resources—the sensitive side of things.

Our father and founder, Rufus Applegate, was married at seventeen and bought his first dozer at twenty-five, a Caterpillar D6. Today we have seven of these monsters all equipped with GPS not to mention excavators, graders, compacters and a convoy of dump trucks. By the time Dad was forty, those machines were moving more cash than dirt as cornfields gave way to houses and the bumper crop of shopping malls, schools and water treatment plants required to keep up with them. He asked that a sketch of that original D6 be engraved on his tombstone when he died. And it was. What he'd originally wanted was an immense hunk of marble carved into a bulldozer, but the cemetery board unanimously rejected the design. Our mother, bless her heart, will be buried in Florida. She never wanted to be one of his hunting trophies.

When he wasn't digging, he was shooting, out west, Canada, even Africa. A few of his big game mounts are the extent of my inheritance other than my stake in the business. This interest is about all we had in common. He and John were inseparable, a secret society of two. When he passed, letting go of him wasn't as difficult as giving up on the idea that someday we'd understand each other, that we'd be friends.

So now behind the green velvet sofa in my living room, I have Dad's bighorn sheep, a record three hundred and nine pounds, hauled out of the Rockies in 1970. Over the mantle in my kitchen is the head of the wild boar he shot in Arkansas. The boar's death lunge spooked my father's horse, which dragged him through the Ozarks and nearly killed him. For the rest of his life, he had three pins in his right leg. The difference between my father and me is that I don't kill anything myself. In fact the majority of my collection is much older, 19th century, purchased at auctions, on-line and from dealers around the world. I'm what is known these days in the style sections of dying newspapers as a new Victorian or a young antiquarian. Even as a child I had my own natural history museum in my room, tables adorned with sea shells, the skulls of small critters found in the woods behind our house, butterflies and the vacated nests of birds and hornets.

Later today I'm stopping by an estate sale at an old mansion in the city. The guy on the phone said there are quite a few English birds—herons and ducks primarily, not songbirds, a baby hippo (too large) and some unusual examples of Victorian preserved pets. I don't think he really knows what he has. He just wants to get rid of the stuff from what I could gather. That means there should be some real bargains, which is fine by me. Parsimony is no sin these days, especially with business being more than a bit soft. Nobody's building houses. "Thank God for hospitals and nursing homes," John says, "or we might have lost the company."

~

The sky is as black as caviar. I slip my little car into a snug space between a Range Rover and a silver Lexus, not a good sign, at the Morganwyke mansion. An iron fence that looks as if it's made out of pikes from the Tower of London hems in all five acres of the property. I walk around the corner to the ornate gates bearing the letters G and M to find a sort of protest going on.

"Sir, will you sign our petition?" a girl asks, shoving a clipboard under my chin. "To save Morganwyke?"

"What do you mean, save it?"

"Don't you know? The bastard who bought it, he's going to tear it down and build a McMansion."

"Really? I didn't know." Her eyes are a chocolate brown.

"My great, great grandfather was a gardener here, and my grandmother a cook. They emigrated from Ireland."

"Well, you certainly have a personal connection then, don't you?"

"None of that matters to Scott Tanner. He made his fortune inventing a self-cleaning litter box, and now he's submitted plans for a bogus French chateau kind of thing. It's a nightmare, an absolute travesty!"

"Litter box?"

"Exactly. Morganwyke's an architectural treasure. We can't let this happen. Will you consider becoming a friend of Morganwyke? Just give us your e mail address and we'll send you updates."

I look down into a face not unlike my own, round with luminous skin and a heart-shaped mouth full of small, blunt teeth. As a child my brother John, senior by five years, called me Moonie. He still does once in a while. Her hair is loosely pinned up in a Gibson girl style, deliciously swirled on top of her head like soft serve ice cream. Could this be another new Victorian?

"I'll find you after I'm finished inside," I tell her.

"Inside?" her face falls. Not far off, thunder claps and lightning stabs the sky. "Are you a . . . friend of Mr. Tanner?"

"Never met the fellow. I'm here for the tag sale. I think I might very well sign that petition of yours when I leave." I squint up at the sky then head through the gates toward the front doors, briefly glancing over my shoulder at the young woman, hoping that the weather doesn't drive her away before I'm finished. I'd like to see her
again, perhaps get her number or if that's too forward, join her group. What was it Friends of Morganwyke?

I broke it off with my last girlfriend, Lily, over a year ago. She was a collector of beaded purses and chatelaines with every ounce of
the passion that I devote to my specimens. Armed with flashlights, we haunted many a flea market and yard sale before the crack of dawn. On summer Sundays, we'd picnic in John's rowboat on the liquid glass of Crystal Lake at the state park, me in my straw hat, Lily under her lace

parasol. But she was prone to melancholia, a trait either missed or ignored in the fog of the initial infatuation. Now I devote my energies to bringing home the plunder, the booty.

I just barely escape the deluge as I reach the porch, the veranda, the piazza, a grand sweep of deck, a veritable boardwalk that ushers me up and through a set of arched doors with crackled black paint, and into a cavernous hall where I can feel my heart thumping all the way up to my clavicle in anticipation of the hunt. And this is a hunt. Though the prey is already deceased, it is no less a struggle to secure that which I desire.

The first thing I see is the backs of my competitors, who are studying a collection of gilt framed oils hanging away from the wall on sturdy chains like the figureheads of ships. Everything is numbered, even an old fire bucket being used as a waste can. At the rear of the hallway, leaning against a marble table topped with a dried arrangement, is a man who appears to be in his late thirties and in charge. He's triangular in build, all shoulders, no hips, tanned and square jawed with slicked back blond hair. My brother John used to look like this before everything just sort of collapsed in the earthquake that is middle age. His attire is impeccable, double breasted navy jacket, custom shoes, not what I anticipated for the litter box tycoon.

"Welcome," he booms, approaching to crush my hand with his own, flashing me a broad grin, a solid block wall of smile, a salesman's smile. "I'm Scott Tanner, I bought this place, or should I say tomb." He lets out a deep horsey laugh. "There's wine and cheese in the dining room. Help yourself. Everything's numbered and there are corresponding price lists in each room. Anything in particular you're interested in?"

"Taxidermy."

"Taxidermy. Well you've come to the right place. Do we have taxidermy? I'll show you taxidermy," he says, pressing a big mitt to my back and steering me into the study, a room adjacent to the 1950s era kitchen. "I'm sorry if you were after the baby hippo. He's gone. A health club bought him."

One wall is lined with cases holding leather bound volumes, works by Carlyle and Scott, the Romantic poets. The other three are covered with wallpaper that simulates cut stone. In the center of the space are several round tables displaying a menagerie of stuffed birds and a few rodents—rabbits and squirrels. There's even a Pekinese dog. "Beloved Bolo," the brass plate on the base reads.

"Most of it's English," Scott tells me. "That grey heron's pretty nice." He points to a case with wavy glass and a magnificent creature that has to be close to three feet tall. "I thought about keeping it, but my wife would have a fit. The only birds she wants to see are Flamingos in Miami." I half nod in amusement, consulting the price list, not wanting to appear too eager.

"What's that?" I ask as something wedged into an upper shelf of one of the book cases catches my eye.

"Now that's a genuine curiosity," Scott chuckles. "It's a mermaid, can't you tell?" He wheels a ladder into position to retrieve it, catches my eye and winks.

Climbing down, he skips the final step, lands with a thud and whips around to deposit it between the heron and Bolo. What *it* is, is the head and torso of a monkey sewn onto the tail of a large fish and rather crudely at that. If that isn't bad enough, she's missing an ear and the moths have had their way with her. In spite of it all, I'm smitten. There are a lot of men out there, men disappointed by love, who would tell you that in a way all women are mermaids. They promise you something magical and then in the end, it's just an illusion.

"This little doozy's not European," Scott says. "There's a card with it that says Allen Morgan bought it from a saloon in Deadwood, South Dakota in 1928. I guess it was good enough to fool the cowboys and gunslingers after a few drinks."

~

I'm not leaving without the heron, Bolo and the mermaid. Scott has fetched me a glass of pinot grigio while I prepare a personal check. I take a sip of the washed out wine, noting nothing about it except the coldness at the back of my throat and the way it warms in my belly once down.

"Applegate?" Scott says as I hand him the payment. "Any relation to John Applegate?"

"He's my brother."

"Well, what do you know? He wants to quote the demolition too."

"He does?" I say, swallowing hard.

"Yeah, I suppose you noticed the hysterical preservationists outside?"

"I did," I answer, remembering the girl with the Gibson girl hair.

"You'd think they could find something better to worry about than this decrepit pile, this termite smorgasbord. Like maybe world hunger or AIDS or puppy mills. Yeah, how about those puppy mills? I don't get people. They're extremists, fanatics. I want to build something nice in the city and this is the thanks I get."

I make a brief inspection of the room before knocking back the rest of the wine and, though I admit I'm no structural engineer, I can't help but think that this joint is far from decrepit. Morganwyke was built in the early 1850's by George Morgan, third cousin twice removed to J. P. and a captain in his own right. Built in the Gothic Revival style, the house is a mountain range of arches, points and eaves, yet the stained glass gives it a serene and holy air.

~

The rain has stopped and I wonder if she's still out there, my little preservationist with her clipboard and petitions, because if she is, John or no John, I'm going to sign that damn thing.

She is and I do. And what's more, I offer her a peek inside.

"You can help me load up my purchases," I say. Her name is Alice, a lovely old fashioned name. Afterward, we walk to a gelateria operated by a crotchety Italian gentleman who once told me he left Tuscany to get away from Americans. I didn't get it at first. Alice has the strawberry, the fragola the Italian calls it, and I, the lemon ice.

"I just love old buildings," Alice gushes, sucking on her diminutive wooden spoon, "rough plaster, rickety windows and all. Can't remember when I didn't. My friends think I'm crackers. They watch these home makeover shows where they knock everything down with sledgehammers and start over. Not me," she giggles. "I say give me old or give me death! I'm sorry to be so silly," she adds, blushing.

"Crackers," I repeat, utterly charmed. No one uses that expression anymore except my mother.

"I grew up in a condo, single mom, two sisters, a birdhouse really. Actually, I've seen bigger birdhouses. We were constantly on top of each other. No detail, no substance, no atmosphere. Ouch," she cries suddenly. "I think I got a splinter in my mouth."

"What? Are you OK," I gasp, reaching across the table, my fingers grazing a downy cheek. Then I brush the hair from my forehead, feeling as if I've left some trace of her there, like pollen from the most fragrant of peonies. Exquisite.

"False alarm," she laughs. "I'm fine." She sighs. "Poor Morganwyke. It's a Downing design for God's sake. Downing! From his book The Architecture of Country Houses. He said a good house is a powerful means of civilization. Somebody should tell that to Mr. Scott Tanner." Poor Morganwyke, indeed. With all of its excess, it's like the top of an extravagant wedding cake frozen in time, and I recall the rain streaming down the red glass in its windows as if they were bleeding tears.

~

"Hey Moonie," brother John greets me between bites of a sausage sandwich and an oversized hash brown, as I stroll into the office with Alice still on my mind. I dab at the corner of my mouth to let him know he has a spot of catsup there, and he dabs at it with his index finger and licks it. That was one of our mother's attempts at gentility, the dabbing, not the licking, after our father had made his fortune.

"I've got a line on a nice job," John begins. "It's as good as ours. The guy who bought the mansion on the Avenue, he's taking it down. Good thing too if you ask me. That place is an eyesore and overgrown. It's like the freaking Black Forest over there."

"Yes. I met him."

"You did?" he says suspiciously.

"The estate sale. He had an estate sale. I bought a few pieces."

"Oh excellent, excellent." He chomps down the last bit of his sandwich.

"To tell you the truth, I didn't think that house was in bad shape. Seemed fairly solid to me."

"Really," he responds, raising an eyebrow appraisingly. "And tell me little brother, what do you know about construction? Stick with the stuffed ducks and tax deductions."

"I'm just saying, the walls were plumb."

"It doesn't matter. If the customer wants it gone, it's gone." He cracks his knuckles and dumps himself into his big leather chair, grabbing a desk ornament, a rugby ball used in the "99" World Cup and kneads it the way I imagine he does his wife Kathi's breasts. Not that Kathi doesn't get what she needs from John as well. Our mother used to say, "Kathi wasn't born to money, but she got used to it very quickly."

What I don't tell him is that I've been driving up and down the Avenue—Morganwyke's neighborhood, noticing things I've taken for granted my entire life. The Civil War Memorial, a larger than life statue of a local hero, Colonel Augustus Craig, who fought at Gettysburg, the terra cotta horse's head on an old carriage house converted to luxury apartments and the cemetery with its cast iron fence identical to Morganwyke's, full of avenging angels, lambs and obelisks—and I keep returning to the same question, *how will a faux French chateau fit with all of this?*

And so begins my double life. On our first real date—a walking tour of the cemetery—Alice asks what I do for a living. I tell her I work for the family business.

"And what might that be?"

"Excavating."

"You mean digging holes?"

"Yes."

"Like for swimming pools?"

"Yes, just like that." She smiles and then explains that she's a radiology technician.

"Primarily mammography, boobs, I work with boobs. Fried eggs to bed pillows, every shape and size and every last one of those women is scared to death." She exhales deeply and says somberly with a faraway look in her eyes, "I hate my job, enough of this."

~

Here in the basement of the Unitarian church, a low-ceilinged, blah beige space, Alice squeezes my hand as the Friends of Morganwyke meeting gets under way.

"Thanks for coming." She stands on her toes to whisper in my ear. Her breath smells of coffee, but still not bad.

"We have good news and we have terrible news," the speaker begins, calling the meeting to order. "First the bad. The demolition permit has been approved." The crowd issues a collective gasp. "But we have a court date tomorrow and I'm confident they'll affirm a public interest right and grant an injunction, a stay of execution—I mean demolition—for our marvelous Morganwyke." The din of applause fills the room before dying down, and they conclude their business, reviewing finances, upcoming events, etc. Afterward, there's a potluck dinner, heavily weighted toward bean and pasta salads, hummus and pita, vegetable and fruit trays.

It's obvious that Alice enjoys being the youngest member of this coalition of retired schoolteachers, architects, a few lawyers and housewives. She's floating around the room visiting each fading flower, not sure of their names, getting quite a few of them wrong while they all seem to remember hers. I catch a couple of the old men stealing glances at her backside.

Later, I take her back to the dreary duplex from the 1970s that she calls home and has done her best to spice up. There's a Moroccan theme, pierced brass lamps, bright blue pottery, exotic arches painted over doorways and gargantuan pillows tossed about. The scent of Mediterranean fig candles chases the ghost of fried fish or chicken.

I'm hoping to get lucky tonight, as my brother habitually refers to it. "Get lucky this weekend, Moonie?" he'll mumble, bleary eyed from behind the rim of his coffee cup on a Monday morning. But the tension and anticipation seem to be all one sided—mine. After a blitzkrieg of comments about the meeting, the members, and the counterattack to halt demolition, Alice yawns and passes out against an oversized pink pillow as abruptly as a narcoleptic—a book closing on the evening. The poor naïve kid. I don't think she has any idea how easy it is to knock down a house, even as substantial an edifice as Morganwyke. I don't have the heart to tell her that you just rip the roof off and push the walls into the basement and it's done.

~

A month has passed, and I have been dutifully attending the weekly meetings of the Friends. There has been a temporary victory; the court has issued a stay of demolition until further review. My relationship with Alice, however, has not progressed beyond comrade in arms. I had expected exactly the opposite reaction, informed perhaps by old war movies where members of the French resistance, in the face of insurmountable odds, throw themselves at each other because each day, or should I say night, may be their last.

I tell myself it doesn't matter. But it does matter. When I bow to kiss her, she clasps my arm and presents a cheek, not her sweet lips. I fear that like the ancient mariners, I have been bewitched. My Alice is no mermaid. She is only a dolphin or manatee and swimming away at that. But I can deal with this. What I can no longer stomach is the idea of Morganwyke existing only in memory and in photographs in the vault of the historical society. It is already its own repository of the tangible and intangible, the plaster walls packed with the hair of horses born before the Civil War; its hand-made bricks, course and uneven, bearing the fingerprints of the dead, and that musty smell—the breath of a thousand dress balls. *Of mermaids.*

Scott Tanner is a barbarian. My brother is a barbarian. Eager to sacrifice our city's history for vanity and personal gain. And now one of the barbarians, John, is waltzing into the office at ten of five after being a no show all afternoon when I needed him to sign a stack of checks that require both of our signatures. He's shadowed by Dickie, an equipment operator with us for decades, a stringy, sun-baked man whose pants always seem to be in danger of falling down.

"Ted's going to load the excavator," John tells him. "Go home get some supper, meet me back here around nine." Dickie nods, pulling a cigarette out of his shirt pocket and poking it through his cracked lips.

"What's going on?" I ask John.

"We're going in, that's what."

"In? In where?"

"Morganthyke or Morganlyke, whatever they call it. Scott's tired of dicking around with the city and he's willing to take the heat. We're knocking that bitch down tonight."

"What?" I shriek. "When were you going to tell me?"

"I'm telling you."

"Are you crazy? We can't do this."

"No, you listen to me little brother. You know as well as I do that we could use this job. Things are slow. Slow, who am I kidding? Business is horrible. Most of the contractors I know would be happy to build a dog house."

"We don't need it this badly. Not like this! Consider our reputation. Dad didn't build this company up over forty years to have you tear it down in one night like that old house."

"Dad? Dad would have said it's a piece of shit and that you worry more than an old woman. He did say that about you on more than one occasion."

"I'm warning you, John. I'll call the cops on you myself if I have to. It's not worth it."

"You'll what?" he says, taking me by the sleeve, veins rising on his neck, his lower jaw jutting out like a bulldog's.

"I mean it. You're not going to push me around on this."

"Damn," he spits, releasing his grip.

"Thank you." I cough.

"You're right. I guess there's a first time for everything." He takes a deep breath and gets Tanner on the phone, holding the receiver away from his ear as a barrage of obscenities follows.

When John leaves, I revel in what I consider to be my finest hour, until the realization sets in that I can't tell Alice what a great good thing I've done. She'd never speak to me again if she knew I'd been this close to the men planning the obliteration of her beloved Morganwyke.

~

I sleep in on Sundays and as usual am still groggy when I pluck the paper from the pachysandra and tuck it under my arm to carry inside. Yawning, I unroll the Daily Express, see the headline, do a double take and stagger backwards into an armchair where a cup of espresso waits on the table next to me. MORGANWYKE BURNS – A COMPLETE LOSS. It's a scant ten days since I thwarted Scott and John's plot for a midnight tear-down.

Halfway through the article, there's a statement from Tanner. "I'm not surprised," he's quoted as saying. "It was a firetrap. Rats probably chewed through the wiring." The story concludes by mentioning that the blaze is under investigation. Then my cell phone rings, and it's Alice.

I race across town and into her arms—two pieces of a puzzle in a world with too many rough edges. She buries her face in my chest and sobs until I hardly recognize the raw red face beneath me.

"He did it, that bastard, that motherfucker. He torched it."

Raising my eyebrows and clearing my throat, I say, "If he did, they'll catch him. Believe me, the insurance company will have arson investigators all over that place."

~

When we parted that dreadful Sunday morning, after I fixed her a pot of herbal tea, she promised, "We'll get together soon, real soon." Then she added, "Thank God you were here for me. I don't know what I would have done." And then nothing—the black hole—no calls, no text messages, no lights on at night, no answer to the doorbell which played The Carnival of the Animals by Saint Saens, one of my favorite pieces of music. Finally I track her down at the radiology center.

She looks different, thinner, older, harder. She's cut off her gorgeous hair for a short spiked style that isn't flattering with her round, flat face. And when we slip out into the parking lot, she yanks a plank-sized chocolate bar from her cloth bag.

"Why didn't you return my calls, Alice?" She shrugs, ripping the wrapper from the candy and begins to gnaw feverishly on one end.

"I'm through with all that historical shit," she says between bites then reluctantly offers me a taste. I shake my head no.

"But what does that have to do with me? I thought we were friends?" She shrugs again, crumples the paper into her pocket and kicks a pebble toward the curb with her white nurse's shoe.

"Don't you get it?" she asks, staring up at me with her black rimmed eyes. "When I look at you I think of Morganwyke and all those other old people and their big ideas and then how they couldn't change anything anyhow."

"Other old people? Alice, I'm thirty-six."

"It doesn't matter. It's depressing. I want to move on. I'm volunteering at the battered women's shelter now, serving meals, helping with the kids. The kids are cute," she says. "I like it. I don't feel so sorry for myself anymore." She turns her back on me and gazes out over a zigzag of low-slung, nondescript professional buildings.

I take the long way home, out the Avenue, through the hollowed out downtown with its thrift shops and nail salons, a few fine restaurants hanging on for dear life, and finally out into the still respectable neighborhood of Stick-style row houses and hulking Second Empire semis, the neighborhood that Morganwyke once anchored. And I pull over in front of its massive iron gates unscathed by the fire's fury.

I get out of my car, walk over, and press my face between the bars. The trees closest to the house and singed by the blaze are dead or dying. It all smells, even on a dry day and weeks later, like one big drowned out campfire. And there it is—Morganwyke, like the crown of a dead queen, its jagged walls draped with yellow caution tape. For a brief spell, my hopes rise, pulled along as if on the end of the leash of a spirited dog. Maybe they'll throw Tanner in jail and some wealthy patron of preservation will ride into town and patch it back together again, raise it up brick by charred brick. Suddenly, I hear a loud flapping of wings and glance up to see a turkey buzzard take flight from what remains of the east chimney, breaking my trance.

Am I deluded? Morganwyke is done for, soon to be taken over, like Alice, by something cold and impervious with its own history to make.

2011 Short Fiction Competition – 1st Place

Spring 2012

IGP9448-1

Maureen Alsop and Joshua Gottlieb-Miller

Before the storm I stood tasting the wink
of leaves, moss winding
into my mouth, what I could not see. Flowers
embalmed incense; her face
in the mid-dusk. A wild-warrior green
thicket under the Hawthorne, gloam
snaking away from where I first found her.

The photographer had as his goal photographing everyone he had ever met. Which necessitated travel to see many people he didn't even remember he knew, also the influx of people on the way to these destinations. Polaroids helped, but sometimes he would see people at stoplights or in bars. Becoming a recluse didn't help. People heard about him and started traveling to meet him, of course he let them in, that's what the project was about all along. Desperately failing to capture everything.

I scratched a line into the horizon
line. I thought it best not to talk
of her. At the center of her lips,
a night long star flattened.

If he saw through awareness he would see the soul rehearsing its own destiny.

Crème de Kathleen

Jo Marie Darden-Obi

- *For Supreme Opera Diva, Kathleen Battle*

a victual of seemliness
lightly salted snow
sounds like a
wisdom- pressed mortar of divinity
sewn with cold wind
thinned with a pestle of honey

infused with still clear air
where bare is the pinnacle- icicle
blue brain dew goes all pink spectacle
hugs, lifts. a mountain top
high five with
God

if there were a wish,
a broth of sin and bliss
a tickle brushed madrigal
rushed from the lips to
itch itch itch in the pucker of the wrist
(how to aspire to music like this?) it would be you

a verbal nutation
a spinning gold dance on crystal
a witness
a manifestation
a conflagration of ice
an asphodel, a jacob's rod

if holy ghosts were sonant
they would intend themselves
to 14 metered pounds of flesh
blend themselves with milk-addled bray
lie awake and pray
to sound like you:

the gentle lifting of shoulders
the fizzling right now that pleads no contest
the sugar-child mama's arms stroke of i'm blessed
the honor of sonorous chocolate. the best
proof that God upended currency and paid with you,
the voice of His own money

Curtis

Jo Marie Darden-Obi

- *For Curtis Mayfield*

"diamond in the back/ sunroof top/ diggin' the scene with a gansta lean, oooh oooh"

that was more than a groove, dig?
dude was deep:
badass in glasses
masterful- hip.
professor curtis on that didactic tip
had the brown skin, knit cap, bell bottom, jean jacket trip
to a tee. he had me
in his pocket
sock it to me, now.
don't sleep.
y'all know curtis was deep.

creeped out from the leather trenches of '73,
when brothers stood on platforms
of ceremony that made no sense:

shovel snow, throw a pinch
seat a brother on the same whack bench
drop a dime kill some time
back behind a chain link fence
(same lie they told you from ever since)
what you gonna do besides hustle?
ain't no muscle in that.

somewhere over the rainbow of this came curtis
and the mayfield experience.
rattle came down like an african swill
ringing new church bells of twilight
highlife horns on a window sill of opportunity
whatcha got to do to beat obscurity?
answer is a call and response
in the trill of the swallow, hallow of a drum
ca coo coo cha, ca coo coo cha
popping off the tongues in the cheeks
wah, wah peddle guitar meets
chicago. hello! got to get mellow, now.

spitting all over the black keys
dude left a footnote on the corner of my history
repaved the walls
of acned, flesh,
bubbled over social unrest and danced
on down like a dashiki wiring my soul
with hcg, impregnating me with the boogie of
"life, more abundantly"

nah, wasn't just about a groove, y'all
dude said keep on pushin because we're a winner
spoke to the inner workings of a mind trap that panders to the grandeur of
something for nothing.
man, ain't nothing free
i learned that back in '73
so superfly types had nothing for me

but curtis? dude sanctified my youth
the music, the message-
curtis was truth.

A Love Supreme
- *John Coltrane*

Mary Morris

No coincidence that in Renaissance paintings
the angels are playing horns. They got that right.

It's about the deep choice, the passion
one comes into after so much suffering,

digging in and turning out
a hymn without words,

about the evolution of his song—the angelus,
acknowledgement (I have wronged),

how love turns itself on,
finding resolution in the greater Master,

the one who saves you from yourself,
about pursuance (of this earthly heaven),

passages in psalms—notes,
translated through a horn—

a deep flower,
blue throat of the Lord.

Homing

Christina Cook

Imagine the twisted white
summer-night-sweat sheets I stripped
off our bed the morning you left

were something so similar
to homing devices, geese threaded them through
the southbound sky

to patch a plan for their return.
Imagine summer's upturned barrel burning
as love is said to burn, rusty and hot

as the seat of the John Deere
still sitting where you let it run
out of gas the day your brother fell

through hoops to the silo floor.
Imagine my mind's corroded metal,
its gear-teeth biting but failing to catch

hold of a hope that the rye will ripen without you,
then picture the rhubarb growing so red
I had to make a wine of it

to return it to the earth. Picture our sheets
like prayer flags along the clothesline,
coupling with the wind.

Between the Lost and the Forgotten

Steven Pelcman

The night comes
And someone always goes with it
As he shuffles by
Dressed in only a diaper
Unsure of where the bedroom is.

His hands know the music
Of small things
As he walks, almost enchantingly,
On a pure white floor
Full of a wife's discipline.

He travels in circles thinking
That his is a little death
The dark will not grieve over
And tightens his face
As insects do to unknown sound.

He does not belong
To the silence yet
And goes on imagining
Where a straight line
Can take him.

Six Months

Shira Hereld

The grass has grown tall as a tornado around us.

Deep beneath it, my memory of you is a shy brown rabbit,
Nestled in its close dirt burrow

Because it is spring,
You whisper ever more loudly in my ears –

And I laugh alone at our jokes

I dream of the graveyard where you and I sat,
Feeling the rough tombstones slide between our naïve fingers

Or of when we walked under ladders,
Pretending to find shelter from the rain

Soon you will fade into a blurry smudge
Wearing a faded flannel shirt

But for now, my memory of you is
Sharp as cumin or paprika

You are a flannel fish swimming through my neurons,
More alive with every spark

The grass, coarse as gravestones,
Binds, gags, and suffocates us

Because now it is summer.

Now you are bones.

Persimmons

Harry Bauld

- *For D. Schiller*

I can't touch them, you said
at breakfast. *So vaginal.* This ripeness
is all and then some, too
organ-orange, too pistil. Once I heard
someone call female masturbation
painting the Georgia O'Keefe.
Here is what mornings come
down to, the play of old forms
upon us. No desire, no word,
no utensil or extremity dare touch
this calligraphic stem
or the split petal of spilled strokes
too sweet for anything but the weep
of their own holy spume.

On the Train After Leaving

Harry Bauld

> *The east, west, north, and the south of you*
>
> - Cole Porter

I am some other orient. I would like
to be blind with you, to feel
my way clear, but I have eyes
only for a north where heat
is a lonely contract. Give me
some lip, I want to be able
to take it. I am a slim fit
in this compass. You can slip
away and do, Schrodinger's Cat
on southern tour. At the next station
you might wipe my face,
but I'm trying to shed
that, afraid of almost everything:
this train window, the print of my pierced heart
on the glass, the fourth and fifth rails, getting out
of these clothes, the incense of twelve stations
to come. Your absence violates every codicil
and rider. Once, flying west into Chicago,
I watched a small cemetery near the end
of the runway pass under the wing.
Meet me there.

A Cold Migration

Shiah IrgangLaden

The black ballet plays out across bare branches
of skeletal oak, silhouetted against violet
clouds, with hundreds of razorblack wings.
Beneath the stage, a tired mother pushes
twins in a stroller, a homeless man finds
warmth under the exhaust vent behind a
pizza parlor, and an endless line of cars
putter clumsily down Charles Street.
The cold does something to the smell of
a city, something predacious and beautiful
and dark. Maybe that's not right, but I feel
like I should be hunting. A girl in red zips
past me on a bicycle and for an instant I
smell anger and sex and maybe love and
the crows must smell it too because they
scatter overhead and follow her half a block
before perching again.

My parents met when they were twenty-two,
and now I'm twenty-three, standing in this chill,
below lofty trees and all those black feathers.
I don't know for sure, but I think we got it wrong.
Maybe we were supposed to flock and never got it right.
Maybe hundreds of years ago, we looked up at the crows,
lonely and jealous and angry that it was so simple
for them, so we gave them dark names and made
them dark omens, because we couldn't understand
and that might be the end of it.

The Day Before the End of the World

Brandon Hartley

The house is almost empty, open rooms
tongued by what little light is left.

Suitcases swollen like clouds sit
barely zipped in the corner of the living room.

What does one pack for such a journey?
If not shoes, then perhaps a map

drawn on the soul, folded in quarters
like a favorite T-shirt.

We lie on the floor where our bed once sat,
our eyes cow-heavy, hands raw from cleaning.

Outside, the stars begin to burn in the lie
they've been telling us for years.

Descent

Andrew Purcell

"Under tactical conditions, the operational element
is completely rigged at the point of no return."
U.S. *Army Field Manual 31-19*

My father spent a considerable period of his youth
falling from the sky.

He set fire to objects, a behavior he passed on,
downward. He has said to me "I didn't start the fire."
But that may have been rhetorical. Lyrical.

Some people build houses and some people burn them down.
Some people build the objects that burn down the houses. Those people are
in between, maybe, or at a right angle, their axis begetting
a spatial dimension through which to drop like an iron bomb.

The longer one falls, the faster, to a point. That is, one falls to a point,
as my father fell.

On average, men spend far less time falling than my father.
Our understandings of the verb *to plummet* are only superficially similar.

My mother waited, gravid, while he dove through the night's long dive, literally
a falling man, primed as he was, the fields alight with flares, a streaking mass,
the angel's plunge, an altitude's perishing, the fire, the dagger, the halo.

Male Bonding

Andrew Purcell

In the woods we subsist on canned hash and pinto beans,
corn mash whiskey and what we can recollect of Tom Waits.
The drinks lay us down and the cold wakes us up.
We fill our canteens at a creek, wash our cooking pot with sand and silt.
Our clothes stink sour.
Rationed portions, the things that live in the water,
drinking on empty stomachs, our notebook of notes,
songs riddled with hate about years we have wasted
on people and places—whatever it is,
we are losing weight.

Evenings are paranoia in the red pines:
a massacre, a malfeasance, a moribundity,
no, a murder of crows.
Alone for miles, we are thinking about women in cities,
in Liverpool, in Florence, in Chiang Mai ;
we are thinking about women in Portland, in Lafayette.
He says: nothing comes of it.
He says: miasma and your asthma.
He says: we're the teeming candycorn that fills the great glass pumpkin.

Our stomachs shrink.
Breakfast is seven greasy cashews and the saliva that wells at the taste of salt,
and for three weeks we are happy like this, stewing in ourselves,
relishing our vague turpitude, resenting the world
that is not the woods.

Death Row

E.M. Schorb

In the Prison of the North,
in some Bismarck of winter,
the bars are ice, the walls
are iceberg tips, and the guards
steer past the cells on sleds of frozen water.
Whiteness at night, with shadows
behind each corner: thin cotton blankets
to teach us a lesson, another lesson,
one more than all the others.
But Death Row is not a place,
any more than Purgatory,
it's a waiting period, and we stand
naked in it until, frozen, we fall,
we fall and break, we shatter,
we grit the floor like rice.
Fire here is the touch of ice—
we light our mentholated cigarettes
with a touch of ice, with our own fingertips,
our lost and blackened and found-again toes.
We light our smokes with our frost-bitten,
blackened toes and watch white paper
burning back, turning black, and a red spark
with its dark smoke vanish in the winter light.
This is what we get for being what we are—
monsters with ice-water in our veins,
cold-blooded killers of love, runaways.
The prison of the North does not contain us,

we contain it, got it young, most of us,
got it and walk about with it freezing up
inside us, got it and can't find warmth,
don't remember how, and the worst
of it is that we cannot even touch

one another or we shatter. Do you hear
that creaking sound? One of us
has tried to touch another,
the oh-so-lonely one we call
The Refrigerator, has tried to find a friend,
the friend he tried to find we call The Freezer.

Straw Man

Luke Rolfes

The Mexicans at the jetty are stepping on black bass. The fish they catch do not meet regulation, so they stand on them, squeezing fin and scale between heel and rock, until the body extends. The fish transforms into a longer version of itself. *Flattened.* The woman is frantic as she explains this to me. I should arrest the Mexicans. I should prosecute. But I'm not a cop or a lawyer. The most I can do is call the police on my radio, but I don't do that either.

The woman's eyes fill with tears. She's early forties, glistening sweat through a plus-size pink cardigan. Like a nervous tic, her gaze flits back and forth between my face and the two boys with wheat-colored hair (her sons?) who yell and laugh as they play balance beam on the concrete dividers in the parking lot. I explain that a fish goes into shock when it comes out of water. Imagine if you ate a chicken sandwich, and an incredibly strong, invisible wire yanked you out of the atmosphere, into outer space. Think about how our sophisticated mind couldn't process that pain. Think about how stupid a fish brain is.

One of the boys says fuck you to his brother. He has fallen from the concrete divider, and a patch of blood stains his left knee. The woman flinches but makes no move to scold the children. Maybe they aren't hers after all. The hurt boy remains down for only a moment, then he remounts the divider, seemingly happy.

I turn my head to the shoulder radio. I call unit 4 to whoever is out there. Waterpatrol Craig comes back, and I ask if he will do a license check at the west side jetty. He says, ten-four. The woman seems satisfied by the official-sounding radio talk. Make sure and check the gills, she says. Mexicans stuff rocks in the gills.

~

Working for the DNR is my summer life. During the school year, I study graduate English at Central Iowa University—they even let me teach a section of freshman composition—but I spend May through August at the lake. This is my third year, and I've grown to like it. I ride a Dixie Chopper mower in the afternoon, and then patrol the grounds in the ranger's truck after four o' clock. Every now and then, I see disturbing things. A woman who hit her mouth on the windshield in a fender bender showed me a hornet's nest of cut lips and teeth. I shined a spotlight, once, on a naked couple in their 50's rolling in the sand and making animal noises. Another time I found a runner collapsed, face down, on the bike trail. I thought he was dead, but he had torn his ACL. It hurt too much to move.

My worst memory is of an old black fisherman. He waved my truck to his bench alongside the north Hampton bathroom. He had a thick mustache and strands of silver folded under a green Pioneer seed hat. His rock-hard belly ballooned into his lap. Did I hear the news, he wanted to know. I hadn't. "Young man," he said. "The end of this road is a terrible place."

I didn't understand what he meant, but the hair on the back of my neck stood and goose bumps peppered my forearms. The old man said I ought to turn around, he'd already phoned the police.

I expected the worst—a catastrophe beyond words. The reality was less exciting. A man in a pickup truck had shot himself in the cul-de-sac by the Inland Cat shelter. There wasn't anything dramatic like a blood covered windshield. He was just slumped, dead against the steering wheel. People say it looked like he passed out.

I never saw him, of course. When I told the old fisherman that it was my responsibility to drive to the end of the road, he stood in front of my truck with his hands on the hood. I was too young, he said. I was his son's age, and he would never let his son see a thing like he had seen. Wait for the police. The first officer on duty, Chad, is eighteen months younger than me.

~

The fat lady with the kids (or whatever they are to her) asks if I will watch them while she goes to the bathroom. I don't know what she expects of me, but I agree. First I'm her cop, and now I'm her babysitter. She yells something about minding manners to the two boys with dirty blonde hair, and then waddles off to the port-a-potty.

Almost on cue, the kids appear in front of me, breathing hard. They want to show off. "I have a trick bike at home," says the older one. "It's a Dyno."

"That's good," I say.

"If you really want to be gay in school," he continues, "you ride a Huffy."

The little brother bristles. "You're gay," he says.

This starts a momentary wrestling match, or something close to it. They lock wrist to wrist and attempt to kick each other's ankles. Probably a year or two separates them in age, but they appear to be the exact same strength. "Listen," I say, "I used to have a BMX, but I broke the handlebars jumping a ramp. I'll show you the scar."

"We do jumps all the time," the younger one says, no longer interested in fighting. "I could maybe jump over a car."

"I could jump a semi-truck," says the older.

I'm starting to wonder what is keeping their mother. I ask them how long they expect her to be.

The older one laughs. "That's Aunt Hen. She's so fat. We could jump her fat belly, but I think it would be impossible. She eats all the time."

The younger goes into hysterics. "Aunt Hen is probably trying to poop all that food."

Both children squawk crazy with laughter. Then they resume trying to kick each other in the ankle. They argue over which one is more gay. For a minute I feel that this woman has left me with these brats. Maybe she doubled back through the woods, and there was some big biker dude with a fantastic beard waiting to take her away.

It isn't too much longer before Aunt Hen emerges from the port-a-potty, her cheeks sunburned, her hair mussed. "Thank you so much," she says. "Did they sass you?"

"Absolutely."

~

I don't know what I did to deserve Travis. He is waiting for me at the shop, smiling in ragged jeans and cutoff Led Zeppelin t-shirt. He's short, with bleached hair and teeth that sometimes don't touch and sometimes overlap, skinny, a chin that juts out like he's being pulled by an invisible beard. He has one long eyebrow in the shape of an M. A boy like him exists in every American sophomore class, one who takes no greater joy from life other than cutting somebody with a cruel word or sharp joke. Teeth and talons. He'd accuse Aunt Hen of stealing food meant for orphans, or maybe even eating one of the orphans if she were hungry enough. Those two brat kids would worship the ground on which he walks.

If Travis speaks, he lies. He brags about what it smells like between the legs of girls in his high school. When I'm driving him around in the truck, he holds his fingers to his face and inhales. Then he offers me the scent of his hand. The other DNR guys have various Travis nicknames: Virgin, The Jew, Nutjob, Needledick. As he's explained to me, black guys, especially the one dating his sister, never leave the couch unless it's out to the mailbox to retrieve the check Obama sent. Don't get him started on rappers, either. They make decent music, sure, but he can't stand the way they talk—crunk this, crunk that—and he hates how they cruise around in their bright purple cars with the windows down, and those ridiculous, oversized spinning rims.

Two hundred hours of community service in six weeks. That's what he owes. Waterpatrol Craig thinks Travis got caught with a whole bunch of XTC, or busted in a school parking lot selling marijuana. Though technically a criminal, Travis isn't scary like some parolees under the DNR's watch. The thirty-something with huge, fat forearms, as an example, beat his next door neighbor within an inch of life. Fat-arms doesn't talk to you when you drive him around, just stares out the window, stewing pestilence. We also have one high school civics teacher who tries to pass her community service off as charity. She pays restitution for her DUI by picking up diapers and cigarette butts on the beach. A hat and broad sunglasses cover her face. She'd wear a mask, probably, if they'd let her.

It occurred to me a couple days ago that Travis likes me. I'm the youngest one of the crew, and really, the only one he talks to. For all intents and purposes, I am the surrogate older brother of a juvenile offender. I don't know how I feel about that.

"They sent me home," he says. He's referring to his landscaping job. "I broke a weedeater."

He climbs in the truck and immediately turns on rap music, the only station we ever listen to.

~

I drop Travis off on the dam with trash tweezers and a big sack.

"This takes at least an hour," I say. "Go down the shoreline. Pick up all the garbage. Don't slip and bust your brains on the rocks."

"Aye, aye, Cap'n."

"Try not to spend the whole hour jerking off," I add. I don't know why I say it, but the kid smiles. I shouldn't joke with him.

By the time I drive the truck halfway down the road, Travis is sitting on the riprap talking on his cell phone. As usual, he isn't going to do a Goddamn thing. After work and on his days off, he comes by and pretends to sweep or shovel or mow, and Sutton, the manager, signs his community service sheet. Sutton feels a duty to punish parolees. He assigns them awful tasks: organizing cans in the pole shed known as WaspLand USA, or running a pushmower along the disc golf fairways where poison ivy leaves outnumber blades of grass. Travis is afraid of Sutton. Sutton could call the parole officer. The parole officer could call the judge.

~

Waterpatrol Craig is waiting for me at the beach. Of all the black people I know, he's the only one who wants to be a country boy. Travis says he's the lone gang banger on the block drinking a forty ounce bottle of Pabst. He wears aviator sunglasses over his dark-skinned face; a Velcro, policeman belt holds his radio and flashlight. He likes chewing tobacco, big trucks, and farm girls in tight blue jeans. His lifelong dream is to join the ranks of the conservation officers—the biggest and baddest soldiers in the DNR army, who spend their year chasing whitetail poachers all over the state.

"Guys at the jetty had a couple expired licenses," he says. "Wrote em up."

I tell him about Aunt Hen and the mutilated fish.

"Heard they do that, but these Mexicans here no speak-y English," Craig says.

He spits Copenhagen juice, and then continues, "I take it you're stuck with the little drug addict. Kid's been stealing beer out of the confiscation fridge. Watch him close. If you catch the little fucker, call the cops. He's violating parole."

I nod, and we both stare out at the small crowd populating the sand—ninety people, maybe a hundred. Part of me really doesn't like Craig. The look in his eyes tells me that he will make the worst kind of officer: one who enjoys ordering people to lower their voices. It thrills him when the sight of his uniform catches a man's breath, when that man willingly allows him a look inside a locked door, a glove box, or a livewell. Nothing in the world could excite Craig more than the thought of asking a woman to prove she has nothing to hide underneath her clothes. The secret doesn't matter. What gets him off is turning the key. Law Enforcement majors in my classes are the same. Even before they serve a day on the force, they act like they've joined a brotherhood of sacrifice and privilege. They look at me with smug satisfaction, knowing that they're the ones I'll be calling if I hear the front door creak open in the middle of the night. I'll come running right to them.

But there are other times when Craig acts with more humanity. He and I participated, once, in the rescue of an injured horse. The owner, a hard-faced woman with rough skin and thick, braided hair, drove me around the park looking for her lost filly. She lived on a small hobby-farm several miles away, and though she was certain the filly was gone forever, she kept her eyes glued to the pastures on either side of the road. We spotted the horse standing at the edge of the woods between the fishermen's trail and Atlantic Shelter. I don't know if I've seen a sadder sight. The filly had broken its neck a month before she ran away. She still retained the ability to walk, run even, but she was hobbled by substantial nerve damage. She shook terribly, as if punch drunk by late-stage Parkinson's. Her neck curved in an unnatural way, causing her head to hang in crippled obedience. You could see the muscles inexorably twitch, her eyes water.

Waterpatrol Craig had already found her, and he was talking to the horse gently when we arrived at the scene. He stroked her snout, and she eased into his hand, like an oversized dog seeking affection. "It's alright," he said to her. "Everything's going to be okay." The filly, when she saw me, cowered in fear. She backpedaled in an effort to hide behind Craig. I couldn't take another step. To think that horse was in such pain that the simple presence of a human face was enough to shame it into retreat.

Craig talked in a different tone, then, when he helped the filly's owner load her stock into the trailer. "Promise you won't give up on her," he said placing his hand on the woman's sleeve. "She wants so badly to stay alive. "

~

Thirty minutes later, I check on Travis. The dam is empty, but I spot him two football fields down the shoreline hiding by a willow tree. In the sun's glare, he appears as a shadow perched at the water's edge. The lake continues to the northwest through the Lost Lake access channel, but the land we maintain ends here. There's a yellow stake driven into the earth twenty yards past where he sits on the riprap, texting. That's the DNR property boundary. If he were to get up and saunter ten steps to the left, he would no longer be my problem. On my way over, I pass a crumpled bag and the trash tweezers wedged between two rocks.

"You done already?"

"I can't go on," he says, not looking up from his phone. "I'm too thirsty."

"There's a lake right there to drink from."

He doesn't respond, shakes his head and grins at the buzzing phone before clicking more buttons.

"Who are you talking to?"

"This girl, you don't know her," he says. "You wish you knew her, though. Tits like buttercream, unbelievable."

I stand there, stupidly, hoping he will rise and start picking up trash, but he makes no effort to move from the rocks. August is nearly finished, but summer remains in full force, and my hand is slick with sweat after wiping my forehead. I take off my sunglasses, and clean the lenses on my uniform.

"Be back in a half hour," I say, finally, "Bossman should be rolling through any minute in the ranger truck."

"Okay," he says. "Grab me a Gatorade from the marina. I'll owe you a dollar."

~

It's funny how an unremarkable time sticks to memory. I remember riding in the back of a pickup truck: warm sun on my bare forearms; the rumble of a neglected muffler; the smell of cut, yellowed grass. We had just dumped a load of tree clippings by the 100th Street boat ramp, and it was a long, twenty-five mile an hour drive to retrieve the mowers at the beach.

It was odd to me, laying my head against the lip of the bed, that I could enjoy the back of a pickup truck, floating along, no choices to make, no responsibility to own. My troubles consisted of waiting out a shift's end, my itching legs, the uncomfortable shell of sunscreen dried to my face. That was me. And then there was the guy who shot himself by the Inland Cat shelter two months earlier. He sat in the front seat. At twenty-four years old, I didn't take much seriously. I didn't try to rationalize concepts like death, aging, or even fatherhood. Lack of responsibility felt safe. What would I say, for instance, when one day explaining to my children how a man could place a gun barrel inside his mouth? Would I bend the truth—tell them how the man suffered from a terminal illness, or that he couldn't live with the guilt of hitting his wife in the face with a broken bottle?

Maybe I would say that the man couldn't handle riding anymore. He wanted to drive, to feel the steering wheel between his knuckles and the rotation of tires responding to his every move. Bad choices became so real, I'd say, he could see them beckoning him forward like ghosts on the windshield.

But how could he do it? They'd want to know. How could he give away the only thing worth protecting?

You have to dare yourself, sweethearts. Don't think about the aftermath. Just pull. But promise me you'll never do that, no matter how much it hurts. Find me, first.

I want so badly to save you.

~

I walk the beach. Show some newlyweds how to keep their Alaskan Husky cool. Give directions to an old guy. A couple girls in yellow bikinis ask if they can bring liquor on the sand. As long as it's in a plastic cup, I don't care. An hour passes, maybe ninety minutes. The sun is high overhead before I remember to retrieve Travis.

When I hurry back to the dam, I don't like what I see. Waterpatrol Craig and Earl, another summer employee, are messing with him from the DNR boat. They have him wading in the water after a floating life jacket. It's a faded bubble of orange, half sunk, twenty feet from shore. Travis doesn't know what is going to happen. Fifteen feet north of the riprap, he'll step off a cliff. The water will go from his knees to well over his head. I've watched fishermen do it. They wade out in the warm mud only to find themselves plunging like a lead weight into an ocean of cold water.

By the time I remove the buzzing key from the truck ignition, I've already heard the yell. Travis has stepped into Craig and Earl's trap. He flounders in the dirty water. For a moment, he disappears. Then he resurfaces, gagging and coughing. He bobs up and down several times, a yellow bonnet of bleached hair plastered to his head. Finally, he snares the wasted life jacket and hugs it to his chest. In the boat, Waterpatrol Craig and Earl have a total cow.

"Fuck you," Travis says, "I can't swim."

I can hear his breathing from shore—short, uncontrolled bursts. He clings to the life jacket. I think he's crying, or trying very hard not to.

"Kick your legs," I say. "You don't have to swim. Three or four kicks and you're in the shallows."

I worry for a second that I will have to wade in after him, but he buries his yellow head into the blaze orange pillow and frogkicks toward shore.

"You okay?" I ask when he pulls himself onto the riprap.

"You're dead," he says. I imagine he's talking to the guys in the boat, but his back is turned. He marches down the shoreline to where he left his shoes and cell phone. He steps into his sneakers, then chucks the garbage bag and trash tweezers as far as he can into the lake. The bag floats, but the tweezers instantly sink and are gone. I don't think they are expensive, but I know what Craig will do even before he does it.

"Get Sutton on the radio," he says to Earl. He's no longer laughing. "This kid's going to prison."

"Take it easy," I say. "He couldn't swim."

I'm not ready for what happens next. From my vantage Travis bends over to tie his shoelaces, but he rises up with a handful of stones. Before I can say another word, the air is full of them. I see them floating in slow motion, lazy arcs over the water. The rocks make one or two backward rotations. I know right where they are going to land. I wish for one crazy moment that he threw them at me.

The guys had dropped anchor maybe thirty feet from shore. The first stone grazes Earl's shoulder. The next one dings the hull. A third puts a ten-inch spiderweb in the glass windscreen. It's not the worst thing a guy could do. It's not as if Travis pulled a semi-automatic weapon and unloaded it at them, but that is how Waterpatrol Craig reacts. He yells at the top of his lungs, and I'm sure he's using his cop lingo—assault and parole officer and felony and I don't know what. Travis reloads, barks back, and hurls more rocks. Earl guns the motor, trying to retreat to deep water, but the old outboard sputters and stalls. Earl says Goddamnit and pulls hard on the cord. Travis throws more rocks. An older couple shorefishing on the west bank hurries to reel in their lines. The seagulls hanging out on the dam go absolutely berserk.

    I don't hear any of it, not really. None of it registers. I crouch in the grass, eyes closed, hands pressed against the sides of my head—probably some reflex I never knew I had. Warmth fills my chest, spreading to my shoulders, eyebrows, and ears. My knees quiver.

    I'm trying to figure out why any of this is happening. How did I end up here, on the edge of a lake, stuck between a rock fight and a hard place? It doesn't help that Craig is black, and Travis spends all day hating on black people. It doesn't help that Craig would call the police on his firstborn son, or that Travis can't swim, or that I should have been back to get him thirty minutes ago. I don't care who's to blame. I just want it to be a month from now –it's mid-September and I'm back in the classroom. All of this seems like another life or another place. Travis is just a story. Craig is a device, and I am a metaphor.

    When I look up, the moment has passed. The patrol boat has retreated to the far shore, and the seagulls have calmed. The old couple's lines are back in the water. Travis has a strange expression on his face, and it takes a moment to realize what he's staring at.

    It's me.

~

    The road between the dam and the shop isn't two miles, but it feels like the longest highway in the Central Plains. Travis buzzes like a disturbed hornet. He unbuckles and re-buckles his seatbelt, rolls down the window, spits, and then rolls it up. Over and over, he talks me through the scenario, the way it all went down. He wants to know if I am on his side.

    "He's going to bury me, isn't he?" he says. He's talking about Sutton. "I can't be responsible for fighting back. They almost drowned me."

    "I don't know what he's going to say."

    "You were there. Tell 'em what happened."

"I don't know what he's going to say," I repeat. I do, though. I know exactly. Sutton doesn't put up with nonsense. He'll call the parole officer this afternoon.

Travis balls his fist. He cusses and pounds the dash. "Those guys said my mom can't afford groceries. She goes around sucking dicks for food stamps."

He's lying again. I say, "Why were they making you get the lifejacket?"

"Because."

"Don't mess around. Because why?"

"Because they said a couple beers magically disappeared from the fridge."

"Did you take them?"

Travis doesn't answer.

"I can't believe you took that beer. It's expired. We pick that stuff up from minors at the beach."

Travis looks out the window. His fingers flicker to the door handle, tap it lightly, then the window crank, and finally the lock bolt. He presses the bolt, but changes his mind and tries to pincer it back up. The lock won't budge. "It doesn't matter if I took the beer," he says.

I expect him to say more, but he, instead, picks up the sweating Gatorade in the cup holder between us, cracks it, and drinks deeply. After what seems like a never-ending drink, he wipes his mouth, breathing hard.

"I owe you a buck," he says, and then, almost like an afterthought, "Goddamn, check out that fatty."

I look to see where he's pointing. Coming up on the right side of the road, there's a large, shoulder-hunched woman plodding through the grass toward a parked station wagon. She's walking with a lawn chair tucked under an arm. I recognize her immediately: Aunt Hen. The two brats with shaggy, wheat-colored hair are not far behind, careening back and forth like inner-tubes hitched to a mammoth pontoon boat.

I ease off the gas and raise a hand in greeting. Aunt Hen doesn't notice. Clearly, the last several hours have drained all the perspiration from her body and the redness from her face. Her eyes stay forward, her steps purposeful. She doesn't acknowledge her two trailing burdens. Their day at the lake is over. She's on a mission: keys already out, one foot in front of the other. Nothing in the world can stand between her and the station wagon. The two boys are a different story. Both have melon-slice grins plastered to their faces. One is doing an impression of fat, old Aunt Hen, lumbering forth with puffed cheeks. His sleeves hang limp and armless. His hidden hands balloon a huge belly out of his shirt. Each bumbling step causes the younger brother to twist and contort with laughter.

    I give the boys a quick honk from the DNR truck, and they lose their minds. They bounce up and down and wave furiously—hummingbirds gorged on Mexican jumping beans. For a moment, I'm forgetting about everything. I'm shaking my head and smiling. Stupid little fuckers.

    Travis stares at me like I've gone crazy. He turns around in his seat and checks through the back window.

    "They're flipping us off," he announces. He sounds almost happy when he says it.

Habitable Space

Marc Hudson

Doyle wants to make a baby. Emily likens this urge to an illness. A mental illness. The onset came exactly one month after he was struck by a car while riding his bicycle to work. He stands at the mirror buttoning his shirt. "I was thinking of painting the spare room," he says.

Emily doesn't answer. The spare room. At least he hasn't begun calling it the nursery.

He wraps his arms around her. "You're beginning to crack," he tells her. "I can feel it." It was weeks before he could hold her without wincing. She'd almost forgotten what it felt like.

~

"It's all different," he says. He has said this many times now, staring at some point on a wall. "It was brutal and ridiculous. He beeped his horn. Beeped his horn while he plowed me into a mailbox!"

~

The idea for the book occurred to her a week before Doyle's accident. Driving home from the dentist she noticed a wooden cross in the grass just off the shoulder of Route 7. Memorials sometimes sprang up in the wake of collisions, erected Emily guesses, by bereaved family members. She thinks it might be interesting to photograph some of these tributes, learn a little bit about the victims, make a book out of it somehow. Possibly, the photos might merit a gallery exhibit. Emily is a graphic designer by trade, a photographer by avocation. She has postcards selling in some of the shops downtown. The postcards feature a pair of mannequins posing around the city; Artemis and Mazy, she calls them. Mazy has a tattoo on one ankle of a surly-looking bunny.

Doyle thinks the idea is morbid. "Who would buy a book like that?" He notes the timing of the project coming just as his baby-hunger has begun to overwhelm him, suspects that it's a retreat on her part, this "channeling of the dead," a heavy-handed countering of his sudden biological imperative. She tells him that the timing is coincidental, but Doyle isn't sold on the concept of inspiration striking out of the blue. He thinks the project is premeditated, a conscious decision, a rubbing together of sticks rather than a serendipitous spark.

~

That night, at dinner with friends, he announces that they are contemplating parenthood. The room is immediately filled with ahhhs, a little chorus of verbal back slapping. Most of their friends are baby-people. They shop out of box stores, speak in euphemisms. They wear sweatpants on weekends, look disheveled and sleepy. Their houses smell powdery and fecund.

"Once you start, you can't stop," says Melanie Boyd.

"Like dominos falling," says her husband, Ted.

Melanie and Ted inhabit a fourth floor walkup. Doyle was winded from the climb, had to recover himself before he let Emily knock. He doesn't like to talk about the accident, doesn't want anyone to know that it haunts him. He's gone back to riding his bike to work, but the routine has lost its allure. He no longer feels invincible, leaves the house an hour early to avoid traffic, is tense after the ride home. Tuesdays and Thursdays he drives to work to give himself a break. As soon as he was back on his feet he insisted they trade the Nissan for a Volvo. No matter that he was struck while riding his bicycle. Emily knows that Volvos are baby-cars, knows what he's up to.

Melanie Boyd continues her baby-praise, her voice an octave higher, wine glass swinging from her fingertips. Used to be they would sit around getting high, drinking margaritas, dancing and laughing. "For the first time in your lives you'll feel like you're a part of something that's bigger than you are."

Emily wants to poke Doyle in the ribs for bringing this up, wants to flick his scar with her finger. She resents this tactic; the use of their friends as a lever, as if the application of genial intimidation might make her understand how out of sync she is. She feels forced into playing along for fear of looking like the heretic in a room full of baby-people. Doyle is one of them now, granted acolyte status merely by expressing a desire to rear a child. Emily manages to smile, her upper lip sticking to her teeth. Doyle is leaning forward, hands on his knees looking from Ted to Melanie, grinning like a fool. When he looks up, he seems almost surprised to find her there. He changes the subject. "Has Em told you about her book?"

Once again the room fills with little bleats of surprise. "What about?" asks Angie Dill, a free spirit, a breeder of Pomeranians.

"Roadside memorials," says Emily.

They all gaze at her expectantly, trying to puzzle out what she has said.

Peter Gayle owns a bistro downtown. "Roadside what?"

"Memorials," Doyle says. Emily examines his mouth for traces of a smirk.

"You mean those crosses people put up at car crashes?"

"Crosses, wreaths, mementos." Emily sees them processing the details.

"Huh," says Angie.

"Hate those things," says Melanie.

"Who's your audience?" Ted asks.

"Morticians," quips Peter Gayle.

Emily doesn't expect them to understand. "It's not a coffee table book. It's art."

"Art?"

Melanie asks if it's supposed to be edgy.

Emily squints at her. "It's an examination of grief. Expressions of grief."

"But art?"

"You can't help but be moved, one way or another."

"It won't sell," Peter tells her.

"It isn't meant to," says Angie. "Is it?" She doesn't wait for Emily to answer. "It's the sort of thing that gets one noticed."

~

When Doyle is on top her Emily puts her hands on his hips and imagines she can feel the missing piece of bone at the edge of his pelvis, the small declivity under the base of her left thumb. He is gentler now, slower, tells her that it has nothing to do with pain, that what pain he has is almost an afterthought compared to what it was in the weeks after the accident. Their lovemaking is subdued. Doyle wants the moment to last, wants to stay connected, linger inside her for as long as he can. The scar on his chest is pink; an exclamation point, the mark of something momentary and brutal, something she cannot fully understand. Sometimes she just wants him to be rough, wants to grapple, clutch. But the urgency has gone out of him. He needs to feel protected, enveloped. He wants to make a baby.

~

She takes her camera and drives out to Route 7 looking for the cross. She parks the Volvo on the shoulder. Cars pass. It isn't a busy road, but Emily feels self-conscious, wonders what the other drivers think of her—the young woman with her camera poking along the side of the road. The memorial is unremarkable; a slender cross painted white, surrounded by a ragged carpet of witch grass and clover. The withered stalks of an old bouquet lie at the base, bound by a tattered ribbon. A coffee cup has settled nearby, flattened into an envelope, imprinted with tire tracks. Emily squats, takes a few pictures. She feels a bit like a thief. There is nothing on the cross, no inscription, or if there was, it has been claimed by the weather.

~

"What about names?" Doyle asks. This is another of his tricks, his baby-traps. He is trying to hit a fly with a section of newspaper, trying to spare its life, to stun it rather than kill it, so that he can release it outdoors. He wields the newspaper loosely, slapping at the air as the fly zips from one side of the room to the other. There is more gray in his hair since the accident. Emily notices the little slivers of white as he moves past the window.

She is curled on the sofa, a book in her hands, wanting not to play along. "How about Baby?"

"Ha." He stops what he's doing, squares his shoulders. "Nobody puts Baby in a corner."

She chuckles, in spite of herself.

"What if it's a boy?" he says.

"Everybody would call him Babe, like Babe Ruth."

"Babe Ruth had an actual name." Doyle swats at the fly as if he is conferring blessings.

~

She takes out classified ads in the newspapers asking people to email her with locations of roadside memorials. Emily makes up a story about an anthropological study on grief. Within a week she receives half a dozen emails. She takes the Volvo and goes hunting. The sites aren't easy to find; few of the directions are specific. Rather, the senders tend to give a town, a road name, a landmark near which the memorial is located. Doyle hates the idea of her going off in search of these things, parking in breakdown lanes and wandering around. "I'm not wandering," she tells him.

To Emily these places feel sacred and sad, public and bereft. There is nothing uplifting about a memorial at the edge of a road. Cemeteries at least have something communal about them. Only two of the markers that she photographs have names on them. One has a photo of a young woman taped in a plastic bag. She is smiling a wide squinty smile, two people on either side of her cropped away, only their severed shoulders visible, pressed against her. The name Amanda is written in cursive along the horizontal bar of the cross. A few of the markers have flowers planted around them, signs that the spot has been visited; grass trampled, cards left, moldering.

~

They go away for a weekend at the ocean, to Doyle's parents' cottage. It's late spring and the water is too cold for swimming. They have the beach to themselves. They lie on the sand. Doyle takes off his shirt and the scar is stark and pink against his skin. Gulls squeal. The waves toss brown foam on the shore. The cottage will be theirs when his parents are gone. This is yet another of the seeming epiphanies, another of the baby-reasons that Doyle has struck upon since the accident. It would be unjust, he reasons, not to share such a place with a child. The beach yields a carnival of discoveries: intricate shells, jewel-like nodules of glass, fingers of driftwood, bleached crustaceans—to say nothing of the myriad things that dwell beneath the waves. Emily concedes the argument. It may be that she is weakening, the carapace around her heart becoming brittle. Perhaps she's just tired. She fought off her own biological imperatives three years before, her body suddenly wracked with some subterranean need to yield a life. She thought she was going mad. Neither of them had desired children, but Emily had not been prepared to do battle with something so innate. Doyle had remained stalwart then, pulling her through, Emily channeling all of her energies into her work. Now it is Doyle yielding to imperatives, craving the fierce love that comes with the stewardship of something so small and helpless. "It's a conceit," he used to say of parenthood, "couples scratching around for legacies. It's the ultimate narcissism." Emily has never carried the argument to these lengths. She has three sisters with five children between them. Nieces and nephews have always seemed like enough.

"What flavor?" Doyle asks. "Boy or girl?"

"What flavor? Do they come in mochachino?"

"No, really."

They are on their way home, Doyle driving with an abundance of caution, hands at ten and two, extra space between their car and the car in front of them. He signals when he is about to change lanes, chastises drivers who drive too fast or pass on the right. Shades of her father, Emily thinks.

Doyle chews his lower lip. "I'd be totally happy either way. I really don't have a preference."

"That's very Zen." Emily is squinting. She has become adept at spotting memorials, like a bird watcher, one eye always tracing the roadside. "Pull over."

Doyle flinches, taps the brake pedal. "What's the matter?" He spots the marker only after he is half-way into the breakdown lane, a slender cross decked with flowers. His cheeks and nose are pink from the sun; a little mask out of which his eyes peer with a look somewhere between accusation and disappointment. "Oh, Jesus," he says, already committed to the shoulder, the traffic sailing past them. "Jesus Christ, Em."

She is leaning over the seat, digging for her camera in a pile of coats and blankets. "I'll only be a sec." Emily climbs from the Volvo, buffeted by a surge of air from a tractor trailer hurtling past. Tendrils of hair trail behind her. The cross is newer than the others she has photographed, draped with a garland of artificial roses and grape vine. There are votive candle holders seated at the base, glass cylinders blackened by spent flames. There are skid marks in the road, two faded dashes. A jagged swath of turf has been plowed up, the scar ending in a swale below. Emily takes her photographs and hurries back, reviews the pictures on the camera's display.

Doyle mumbles something, mashes the gas pedal and slips back into traffic.

Online she puts the pieces together, searching the archives of newspapers for accounts of the accidents. The names of victims appear on the screen: young and old, male, female, single, married. She looks at their obituaries, gets to know them, if only a little. The photographs she has taken are stark. There is nothing about them that smacks of sentiment. The memorials are a chronicle of loss erected amidst the detritus of a busy world. Emily wonders what they are meant to impart; if they are intended as cautionary tales, or, as she suspects, simply emotional dowsers. She phones a man named Peter Fitzgerald, head of the DOT, to find out what their policy is on roadside memorials. He explains that the state does not have a specific policy with regard to such things—that shrines and markers of that nature erected in the aftermath of a traffic fatality are technically speaking, litter. He clears his throat when he says this, tells her that highway crews are nonetheless sensitive to such things and will usually let them remain for a few months, provided they don't endanger the public.

~

She shows her photographs to the owner of one of the galleries downtown. Emily has had a couple of them matted and framed to give a sense of the finished work. The woman asks to see the black and whites. She prefers them to the color photos, feels that they have more impact, that the contrast gives them weight. She thinks the photos might work in a group show. The mannequins, Artemis and Mazy sit in the corner of Emily's studio, Mazy seated in Artemis' lap, one black high heel dangling from her toes in a way that is both carefree and weirdly sexual. Emily tries to imagine Artemis and Mazy lugging around a plastic child; Artemis with bags of diapers, Mazy with a stroller, stopping to breast feed—the infant's rigid mouth searching the hard smooth hillock of her breast for a nonexistent nipple. For Emily there is nothing cheeky or jaunty about the image. Three seems one too many. Every morning she places the pill on her tongue. After so many years the act feels innate. Brush teeth, swallow pill. So ingrained is the ritual that stopping would require some kind of fundamental rewiring. She tries to imagine how it might feel to leave off, quit. Vulnerable is the only word that comes to mind, like cliff diving. The thought of it leaves her palms damp. Doyle has eased off on the baby-talk. Emily suspects that this may be another of his tactics—that without the pressure of expectation, she will heed the falsetto call of motherhood. If anything, her work has hardened her, the proximity to death, to tragedy. Caring for Doyle too, has sapped her of a desire to nurture, sharpened a need for independence.

~

She goes about calling them, the families of the dead. The first person she reaches is a woman named Melinda Cruz. Her husband was killed in a crash on his way home from work. Emily examines the photograph of his memorial; a plastic Mary in a grotto, forlorn red geraniums planted in the ground, spitting fire. She goes to see Melinda Cruz at her home, a tidy place surrounded by chain link fence and a strip of lawn. Emily photographs her standing at the gate looking down the street as if she is waiting for her husband to come home. A couple of families don't want to talk. Another has a number that is no longer in service. Some who do speak, like Melinda Cruz, tell Emily that the memorials are a comfort to them, that it is better than driving by and seeing nothing, as if their loved ones had simply vanished, as if the spot on which their lives were lost had no significance at all. They understand that the memorials will be taken away. They tell her that they will make their peace with this when the day comes.

~

A few more emails come in, some with new information, others telling her of the places she has already been. The gallery owner tells Emily that she would like at least ten photographs for a group show. Emily has seven. She goes out to follow some of the new leads, considers the possibility of having to travel outside the state. One day Doyle hides her pills. When Emily confronts him he denies touching them. He stands in the bedroom doorway declaring his innocence. The look on his face is one of manufactured concern, as if Emily has lost her grasp on reality. She counters each of his denials with an emphatic "bullshit," until he finally comes clean, insisting she's become obsessed with death.

"Not me," she says, "you, ever since the accident."

"Not at all," he tells her, recounting for the umpteenth time the experience of being bull-ridden into a mailbox. By the end of this recitation his voice has risen nearly to a shout. "It's about life," he says.

It feels as if the ground is shifting beneath her. The argument is seismic, flies in the face of every significant conversation they've had over the last ten years. "You're talking about a job. A twenty four-seven, three hundred sixty five days a year job. And after a while, it stops being cute," says Emily. "Everyone stops cooing. They go back to their lives and we're left with the responsibility of raising a child. I don't want to be standing here in two years saying 'what the hell did we do,' just because you feel vulnerable."

Doyle's eyes are glassy. He licks his lips, seems ready either to burst into tears or bury a fist in the wall. "And I don't want to be sitting here in twenty years feeling like some part of my life went unlived. Fucking roadside memorials," he shouts. "Whatever happened to cd covers and business cards? Whatever happened to propping up Mazy and Artemis around town and taking their picture? I don't get what you're doing."

This was just the part of her that he had always liked—the part of her that he didn't get. It used to excite him. Now it frightens him.

"It isn't like you'd be sacrificing a career," he says.

Emily flinches. The invalidation is cruel. Even the delivery is cutting, the offhanded way with which the words are meted out, as if he is saying something obvious and agreed upon—a statement of fact and not a withering condemnation of everything that she has made of her life up to now. Doyle leaves, not for a breath of air, or a walk, but actually leaves, packs a suitcase and goes, a shirttail flapping from one corner of his luggage like an epileptic's hand.

She finds the tenth marker on a rural route an hour from the city. Emily almost gives up, drives past the site twice before spotting the cross in a copse of trees just beyond a hard curve in the road. The cross stands in the shadows, a heavy object, carved from a single block of wood with a chainsaw, the edges rough with feathers of heartwood. There is a scarf wrapped around the top—black with flecks of color scattered along the length of it, like sparks. A few beech leaves from the previous winter have settled in a hollow between the folds. The cross leans to one side as if the earth around it had jerked to a stop and its momentum had carried it forward. As she takes her photographs a pick-up truck passes. It slows and stops just beyond the Volvo. A young man gets out, tall, grim-looking. No one has ever stopped as she has gone about her work. The presence of the man throws Emily off, stifles a spark, interrupts a connection, not just to the plot of land, but to something broader and deeper. She can only snatch at moments, hunt for clues. There is a reverie that encapsulates her on these occasions, a channeling of sorts. She hasn't realized until now how invested she becomes during these visits.

The man slinks through the shadows thumbs in his pockets, watching her. "Help you?" he asks.

Emily conceals her disappointment behind a short smile. It may be that he thinks she has broken down, has stopped to offer assistance. She lifts her camera. "It's all right. I've just stopped to take some pictures." She goes on shooting.

He comes closer. "Who are you?"

"I'm sorry?"

His arms are at his sides, bowed a little at the elbows as if he might fling them into the air, send her running. "What's your business here?" He wears a denim jacket, frayed at the cuffs, faded, is handsome in a malicious way, everything about his face sharp and thin, as if his skin were stretched over some sort of alloy. His eyes have the green coolness of a late frost over tender leaves.

"Did you know this person?"

He makes a sound, a soft burst of air through his teeth, as if to suggest that the question is foolish. "You could say that." He straightens the cross, plunges a boot heel into the ground to shore it up. Robins forage in the leaf litter beneath the trees, making noises that belie the fragile architecture of their bodies.

Emily notices a tree at the extreme left of the copse with its bark torn off. The tree is not small, has been growing there for some time, its shaggy hide thick and plate-like. The pith is mauled, splinters rising up and out like quills. "I'm sorry," Emily says.

"What do you know about it?"

"Nothing. I just stopped to take a picture."

"What for?"

There's a canister of pepper spray in the glove box of the Volvo. It was a gift of sorts from Doyle, another of his attempts to insulate himself after the accident, to swaddle the things he loved in an imaginary layer of bubble wrap. She wonders if she could beat the man to her car. "Did you put it up?"

He rolls his shoulders, squats down, takes a cigarette from the pocket of his jacket, lights it. "I made it," he says. The tone of his voice is neither prideful nor reflective.

Emily tries to sound casual, her heart beating fast. "Who was she?"

He squints at her through the smoke. "We were together."

"Married?"

"You writing a book?"

"Sort of. A book on grief—expressions of grief. A book of photographs."

He slaps the top of the cross with the flat of his hand, drags on the cigarette from one corner of his mouth, exhales from the other, never taking it from his lips. "She was hard of listening."

Emily doesn't ask him to elaborate. She is reminded of the fight with Doyle, the one in which he'd shouted at her, as if making a point was simply a matter volume. "I'm sorry," she says again.

He snakes his fingers through the tassels at the end of the scarf, gives it a little tug. He tilts his head back, gazes at her. His eyes are unblinking, watching and revealing nothing. "She liked to drive fast," he says. "Physics is a bitch when you take this corner at sixty miles an hour. Her parents went to pieces. I made it for them, the cross." The cigarette bobs in his lips. Bits of ash fall gray as dust.

"What was her name?"

"Shannon."

A car passes. And then another. Emily is aware of an exhalation of breath from her lungs, as if she has been holding it in the whole time. She asks the young man if he will stand beside the cross, and he rises, slowly. She takes his picture. He is something of a natural, unaffected as he is: sharp-boned and handsome.

It is her favorite of all the pictures, deceptively touching –the black and white image of the hard angled young man standing beside a cross, looking past her, pale eyes seemingly lit from behind, a pool of shadow in one cheek. At the gallery show it is the picture that is commented on the most, the one that people linger over, want to know more about.

After the show has had its run, Emily gathers the photographs and the notes she has taken. She removes the photos from their frames and together with the notes deposits them at the bottom of a file cabinet in her office. Buries them. She breathes easier. Doyle has taken an apartment across town. Emily is looking for something smaller. She cruises the city with Artemis and Mazy in the back of the Volvo, the mommy-car reduced to shuttling mannequins around the city in a quest for habitable space.

There Isn't Anyone Expecting Me Anywhere Tomorrow

Michael Kimball

After we were finished, we lay on our backs in the dark. She rolled up onto her side, put her hand on my chest, and traced her finger along one of my ribs. I reached out to touch the lower part of her stomach and it trembled against my fingertips. There was just enough light in the bedroom that I could only see parts of her.

She kissed me on the chest and the neck and the mouth. She crawled over me and sat down on the side of the bed with her back to me. I reached my hand out and touched her hair where it fell down between her shoulder blades and then I let my hand drag down her back as she stood up. I kept touching her for as long as I could.

She walked out of bedroom, down the hallway, and into the bathroom. Her body lit up when she turned the bathroom light on and the light reflected off of her skin as she closed the bathroom door.

She was away from me in another room and it made me miss her. I got out of bed and went to get us both a glass of water. I wondered how much ice she would want and if she were thinking about me too.

She didn't look up at me when I came back into the bedroom and that let me stare at her. I stood in the doorway holding our glasses of water and she lay naked on top of the bedcovers. She had her head propped up against the pillows and her legs turned open. She had the remote control for the television in one of her hands and had turned the television on. The light from the television screen had turned her skin kind of gray and blue. I wondered if she were sad. I wanted to make the color of her skin change to a different feeling.

I walked into the bedroom and turned the lamp on the bedside table on low. The light on her skin changed to a kind pale green tone and that made her look fresh and springy.

Me: You look pretty great naked.

Her: You can keep staring at me if you want.

She kept changing the television stations even though only the local stations came in. She held her other hand out for her glass of water and I handed it to her. She drank most of the water and then handed the glass back to me. She held her hand out again, but it was for me that time. I got back into bed with her and she turned to me.

Her: My main goal while I was growing up was to stay up past my bedtime. I was always afraid that something exciting was going to happen and I didn't want to miss it.

The talk shows were already over, but she left the television on a local station that was showing an all-night news program. Tornados had touched down in parts of the Midwest. A reporter was trying to explain what had happened as the television camera panned through an area where the houses had been destroyed. Roofs were missing and walls had collapsed on each other. There were places where only the concrete foundation remained and the rest of the house had been lifted up and then scattered around the surrounding area. Nearly everything had been pulled away from where it was and then set back down somewhere else. There were clothes hanging from telephone wires and a tricycle that had settled in upper branches of an oak tree. In one front yard, the furniture seemed to have been arranged into a family room setting, except there wasn't a television and all the cushions and all the people were missing.

The reporter interviewed a man who was picking through the debris where his house had been. The man said that they were still looking for their dog, that they couldn't find him before the tornado had touched down, that they just hoped he was hiding somewhere until he wasn't scared anymore. The man turned and gestured with his arm toward a woman who must have been his wife. She was off in the background with her back to the camera. She was holding her hands up to her mouth and seemed to be calling the dog's name into the distance.

Her: This is too difficult to watch.

She handed me the remote control and I kept thumbing the channel button, but all I could find were infomercials, static, or other all-night news programs. I pushed the mute button on the remote control and she thanked me for doing that. I set the remote control between us and we let the sports highlights run with the sound off.

Me: Isn't it amazing that human beings can do those things—run that fast, hit a ball that far, hit each other so hard and still stand back up.

Her: I had a dog named Princess when I was a little girl and I wish that she were still alive. She loved to play fetch in the backyard and she wouldn't stop running back and forth until I stopped throwing the balls. My arm always got tired before her legs did.

I wanted to say something to her, but I didn't know what. I wanted to do something for her, but I didn't know what.

Her: She wasn't like the rest of my family. She was always nice to me.

I reached out and touched her arm. I stroked her arm and squeezed her hand.

The serious news anchor came back on and the ticker flowing across the bottom of the television screen said there had just been another bombing somewhere in the Middle East. It was already morning there and the video footage showed medical personnel carrying bandaged people away on stretchers. The police and maybe also some army personnel were trying to keep the blast area contained, but too much had gone wrong. Some of the people were making gestures with their arms or their hands and others were waving flags. They showed close-ups of people who were crying or wailing, their mouths open, their hands on their heads or covering their faces. Nearly everything about their lives had just changed.

She reached out and touched my arm so I would look at her. Her face looked serious, worried.

Me: We should have an escape plan.

Her: Neither one of us has a car and I don't know how to steal one even though I've seen people do it in the movies. We probably couldn't drive out of Manhattan anyway. All the bridges and tunnels would be jammed with other people trying to do the same thing.

Me: Wait, what if we aren't together when it happens? We should have a meeting place.

Her: It can't be anywhere famous, no landmarks, no tourist attractions. It has to be somewhere other people won't think of. It has to be somewhere that probably won't get bombed or attacked, but where we can still find each other.

Me: We could just meet up right here. Then we could climb the fire escape up to the roof and try to see the best way to get off the island.

Her: We should buy some binoculars and maybe also gas masks and a good map.

She rolled up onto her side and into me. She pushed one of her arms under my shoulders, stretched her other arm around my chest, and pulled her body into mine. She smiled her relief, mushed the side of her face into my chest, and hugged me really hard. It hurt my ribs and I couldn't breathe, but I didn't want her to let go of me. Lying there naked with her made me feel brave. I thought I might be able to save us if anything happened.

She rolled back onto her back and picked the remote control back up. She turned the mute off and clicked all the way through the channels, but came back to the same local station and the same bombing in the Middle East. She handed me the remote and I turned the mute back on.

Her: I would be afraid to take any of the trains—subways, Amtrak, NJ Transit, Long Island Railroad—but I suppose we could just walk through one of the tunnels—the Lincoln Tunnel or the Holland Tunnel if we were escaping to New Jersey, the Queens Tunnel or the Brooklyn Battery Tunnel if we were escaping to Long Island. It seems like the rocky beach at the tip of Montauk would be safe. I stayed in a summer house out there once during the wintertime. There was only one taxi for the whole town and almost nobody else was out there. The sand and the water are beautiful when it's cold. But, no, what if the tunnels collapsed while we are under all that river water? Can you imagine how terrible it would be to drown in one of those tunnels—the water slowly rising until we were completely under water, the stupid fish swimming all around us?

The news program shifted to a reporter talking to a man who must have been somewhere near where the bomb went off. His hair was messed up and there were cuts and dirt on his face. His eyes were wild and he was leaning in over the reporter's microphone as he tried to explain what had happened.

Her: Maybe we could get away on one of the Staten Island ferries. But what if too many people had the same idea? It would just sink. How well can you swim? What if we bought an inflatable raft? Would that work out on the ocean? How far away do you think we could get?

Me: Maybe we could just take one of the houseboats docked along the East River. We could float across to New Jersey or maybe down the coast to Delaware or Maryland. Or if there isn't anyplace safe on land, then maybe we could just float out into the Atlantic Ocean. We could drop the anchor and live out there. We could listen to what is happening with the boat's shortwave radio and watch the beachfront with long-range binoculars. We could do that for as long as we have food that isn't rotten and water that isn't salty. We wouldn't have to come back to land until everything was safe again.

Her: We could go now. We could leave now and start over somewhere else. We could be different people.

I didn't know what to say. I really only wanted to be myself. I didn't know who that was, just that I needed to be somewhere else to be that person.

Me: I've had apocalyptic nightmares ever since I was a little boy and sometimes I still have them. I never know what has happened, just that it is something terrible, that it is always nighttime, that people are after me, and that nothing can save me unless I keep running away from wherever I am. There is always someplace safe, but it is never where I am. I have never gotten to that safe place. I always wake up first.

Somewhere outside, people started yelling and then we heard the sirens start up off in the distance. We looked toward the front of the apartment and listened to the sirens as they approached us. It was the kind of thing that happened every night all over the city, but these human emergencies are alarming when you hear them so close to where you live. I kept thinking that the emergency vehicles would stop somewhere else, but they just got louder and louder until we heard the fire trucks and the police cars and the ambulances turn onto the block where we were. We got out of bed and I went to the front door of my apartment, but my metal door was cool to the touch and I couldn't smell any smoke.

She walked up to the front of my apartment to look out the front windows and I followed her up there. We stood to the side of one of the front windows in the shadow cast by the streetlight. We watched the smoke rolling out of the windows of an apartment building that was across the street and up the block. A crowd of people stood out in the street and even more people poured out of the apartment building—out the front door, out the windows and down the fire escape.

The emergency personnel stepped out of their different vehicles. Some firemen hooked up hoses and then other firemen ran into the apartment building with all their gear. There were paramedics attending to people on the sidewalk. It looked like everybody who got outside was still alive, but we didn't know if there were other people trapped somewhere inside that apartment building.

I wrapped my arms around her waist and clasped my hands together over the lower part of her stomach. We looked out the window at a slant. She leaned back into me and I leaned back against the brick wall there. There was that momentary sensation of falling, but then we settled against each other. It felt safe to be inside with each other. It felt as if we could protect each other by holding on to each other.

We watched the people who were living in the apartment buildings on the other side of the street. Most of them were watching the fire and everything in the street below them too. They had come out onto their fire escapes or were leaning out their windows. But there were some other people who seemed to be leaving their homes with the important belongings they could carry with them—sleepy children in pajamas, cats in carriers and dogs on leashes, photo albums in their arms. Most of these people turned away from the fire, walked to their cars, and drove away from all the smoke. But one man carried a tall potted plant and we wondered if maybe he wanted it to feel more tropical wherever he was going. Another woman was wearing a nightgown and her running shoes. We watched her pull her hair back into a ponytail and then run away down the block and around the corner. For as long as we watched, she didn't come back.

    I thought about going out onto the fire escape, but we were both still naked and I could smell the smoke from the fire even though we kept the front windows closed. We kept watching all the people below us, though, and then we noticed that nearly everybody was looking up. There was an old man hanging out of the burning apartment building and waving his thin arms from one of the fourth floor windows.

    The old man couldn't reach the fire escape and it made me want to hold my arms out so that he could jump into them. I thought he would have to jump into one of those safety nets that firemen catch people in, but one of the firemen just climbed into a basket crane and we watched its two arms unfold until the fireman could reach out and pull the old man into the crane's basket. Everybody clapped their hands and cheered when he did it.

    We watched until we couldn't see any smoke or any fire anymore. The firemen hosed the apartment building down, so it must have still been smoldering, but most of the people who still had places to live were going back into their apartment buildings. Some of the ambulances and police cars were leaving the scene too.

    Watching the fire made my eyes feel scratchy and tired. She leaned her head back into my chest and looked up into my face. I tipped my face down to kiss her on her forehead. She reached up and patted my upper arms and I let go of her.

    Her: Let's go back to bed and hope that nothing else terrible has just happened in the world.

We turned away from the fire and walked back to the bedroom. The television station was still covering the same bombing in the Middle East, so I changed the channel to static. It gave off a strange light and made me realize how late we had gone into the night.

Me: Do you remember when television stations used to go off the air after the late shows? The national anthem would play and there would be the clip of the flag waving in the wind. There would be a little delay and then the television screen would go to static. I miss that.

Her: [ ]

Me: Do you think you will remember this part—us just lying here, the blankets pushed to the side of the bed, the sheets kicked off the end?

She laughed and spread her arms and legs out over as much of the bed as she could. She made a warm snow angel in the sheets and took up nearly all the space in the bed except for where I was. She pulled her arms and legs back together and then rolled over onto her side. She reached between my legs, cupped me in her hand, and lifted me up in the palm of her hand.

Her: It looks cute like that—tired, but cute.

She was playful and smiling, but I could see how tired she was too. Her eyes were still bright, but they were a little wild and she was fighting to keep her eyelids open.

I looked at the alarm clock that was on my bedside table and hated what time it was. I pulled the sheet up from the foot of the bed and we both slid down into the bed. I turned the television off and pulled the sheet up over us until its coolness covered most of us. I waited for my eyes to adjust until I could see the outline of her lying next to me in the bed. I closed my eyes and felt the sheet warm up where it touched my body.

God's Creatures

Jen Michalski

So many forest green Dodge minivans have been produced that they have become part of the North American landscape, as ubiquitous as shopping malls and Enterprise rent-a-cars and fast food restaurants. That's what Yuri is thinking when one turns off the thoroughfare and pulls to a stop on the sidewalk beside her and Dim-Sum, her Frenchie. She is not inclined to give the minivan, or its place in American automotive culture, a second thought, but then the driver's side door opens and the black man gets out.

"Excuse me." He is in his fifties, ample in a way that makes his black velvet sweat suit look like comfortable furniture. "Do you know of any dumpsters around here? We have some trash we want to throw out."

"There's a contractor right there—I'm sure they have a dumpster." Yuri points behind her, where one block over a house is being renovated. The neighborhood in which she and her fiancé rent is on the verge of gentrification, perfect for residents, close to the hospital, to the thoroughfare—at least that's what the rental agent had told them.

"Yeah, but they're a little weird about that," the man answers. The van is emptier than she would ever imagine a minivan to be—even when lacking in riders, they always seem to be cluttered with crushed juice boxes, cheerios, crayons, and indeterminate stains on the upholstery. The passenger door opens, and the white man, also in his fifties, although not as ample—perhaps a loveseat rather than couch—climbs out. He wears a pastel-striped Oxford shirt that accentuates his pink, Droopy Dog face, and a white t-shirt underneath. In the well of the front passenger seat Yuri spots the detritus of lunch from McDonald's—two collapsed white bags and waxy drink containers the size of liter bottles.

"What a beautiful dog." The man with the pastel shirt points at Dim-Sum. Dim-Sum, the color of butterscotch and wearing a pink collar made of hemp, is used to the attention. Yuri and her fiancé joke that she would probably let a burglar in and offer to fix him a drink.

"She's got some age on her." The driver, Black Velvet, has made his way around the van to them. Dim-Sum sniffs his outstretched hand, which seems as big as those rubber garden gloves she sees at the home improvement store, before losing interest. It is hot, spring hot, a warmth that feels safe but fleeting. Yuri can see every pebble, the size of oblong quarters, on the sidewalk.

"Is it a terrier? Pastel Shirt asks. He speaks in a halting/speedy pattern that she attributes to being from the South or perhaps developmental delay.

"A French bulldog," Yuri answers. Already she has been here too long. She feels her limbs shrinking inward as she recoils from their overbearing friendliness. At the hospital, they are all like this, the patients, offering details of their lives like so much clutter that she wades through to listen to their heart, take their pulse.

"There's a dog park in Hampden where I used to take my Rottweiler," Black Velvet says. Because of his girth, his arms arc away from his body like a gunslinger's. Alternately, he looks as if he might flap them and float away. Instead of this, he reaches toward his back pocket. "She died. Broke my heart. Sweet Lord, I never, *ever* cried so hard, I tell you what. It was like…human love, you know?"

"My Chihuahua died at three months," Pastel Shirt adds, nodding. Yuri wonders whether they are partners. They are too chummy for coworkers, too enamored of dogs. Too soft and harmless, neutered just like their beloved pets.

Black Velvet brings his hand around from behind his backside. It's holding an iPhone. "You gotta see some pictures of my baby."

His finger, the width of a sausage link, flicks over the photos. Dim-Sum begins to pant and pull away. Yuki decides to stay for only a second, a courtesy. She will only pretend to look.

"Can you see from there?" Black Velvet waves her closer to the van. "It's so sunny."

"I can see fine." It feels like hours since she has spoken, since she has been with these men and their ambiguous relationship. She wonders if passengers in other cars note their meeting, whether they note anything at all. Like the way Black Velvet is standing so close to Yuri now. He smells like exotic oils that her mother used to buy from Eastern Market. His breath is wet and audible as he holds up the phone.

"See now, here's my baby." He shoves it into Yuri's face. She is expecting pictures of a dog in the prime of its life, bounding in the muddy trenches of the dog park, chewing a bone by a sofa, or just looking regal, paw over paw, in the sun-bleached air. This Rottweiler lies on a steel veterinary table with a white sheet draped over half its body.

"I'm so sorry," she says. She means it. She has a picture on her iPhone of sweet Pooh right after the same injection. It is the last picture she has of their life together, and she can never look at it without crying. Most importantly, she knows how weird it is to keep it and therefore never shows it to anyone.

"And here's my Chow." He flicks through some more pictures. To her relief, the Chow is alive. "But I loved my Rottie. I don't know if I could ever, ever get another dog. Sometimes they just *touch* you. You know what I mean? They *steal* you, I swear. And that little part of me," he thumps his chest for emphasis, "is gone."

What kind of people, she thinks, turn off the thoroughfare just to throw away two McDonald's trash bags?

"Dogs are God's creatures," Pastel Shirt says. He wipes his hands on his hips, his grey sweatpants that remind her of soggy bread.

By her side, he hears Black Velvet's labored wheezing, like an oxygen machine at the hospital. The back door of the van is open. She doesn't remember anyone sliding it out. It is like a portal between the two men, the door to a castle, they the queen's entourage. The back seat is empty, a clean, soft green velour that holds the streaks of vacuum suction in sharp relief. The men smile at her. The way she smiles at a patient who she knows is going to die. Their eyes are the color of dead fish. Through them she sees herself from the thoroughfare: an Asian woman walking her designer dog, her hair pulled back, the white buds from an iPod in her ears. She hears their thoughts gnawing on her elbows and shoulders, tasting her skin, the whining stress of bones cracking. She feels bright and gaudy, like a diamond on the sidewalk. Cars punch by on the thoroughfare, each a small collision into her senses.

Her fiancé will be home from the hospital six hours from now, she thinks. So much will happen in the meantime.

"Jesus Christ, I told you I was coming."

Yuri and the men turn toward the sound of a lady talking on her phone. She is hard and old. She is denim and platinum. She walks up the sidewalk toward the thoroughfare, and for some reason, Yuri thinks the woman is with the men, that they have been waiting for her. She tightens the slack on Dim-Sum's leash as the woman rolls up on them, like the tide.

She passes. Yuri does not see where she goes. The sun is hot on her neck and cheeks. Her throat is dry. She coughs, taking a step, then a second step, away from the men, covering her mouth with her hand as if she is doing them a courtesy.

"You have lovely pets," she says. Dim-Sum begins to pull her away. "Thank you for sharing them with me. There's a liquor store a half block down—they're nice Koreans—and they usually keep a trash can outside the door."

"Thanks so much, ma'am," Pastel Shirt says. He and Black Velvet spring to life, as if released from a trance, and climb into the van. They become indistinct to her, as indistinct as the minivan. She could never point them out in a lineup. She could see them every day or never. They will slip into the landscape, into the unending pulse of things harmless and dangerous.

An Unwitting Accomplice

Beth Lefebvre

The 1988 blue Toyota Corolla is just one of four million to travel American highways since the model was introduced here in the 1960s. Its license plate, 3JFZ283, bears the carefree red script "California"—invoking sand and surf, perpetual playgrounds, Disneyland, and Hollywood.

The pristine tires emit a strong odor, half-sickening, half-sweet. Tiny tread hairs stick up like leafless trees on a barren, cracked wasteland. The interior is spotless, but only because a team has combed every inch of its fabric and plastic surfaces, excavating reams of documents, receipts, and personal letters.

And then there are the jarring details of abuse: a missing passenger headrest, a crack splitting its dashboard plastic from the windshield to the steering wheel, swatches of hood paint removed in a jagged pattern.

The car also sideswiped some unforgiving object, maybe another car, maybe a wall. White streaks slice the driver side. This wound was likely caused by the driver himself, via a simple, frantic shift of the steering wheel.

Despite its unique markings, the U.S. Government's 9/11 Commission report referred to this Corolla, VIN JT2AE92E9J3137546, as "older" and "non-descript."

But the car's purpose was not what the factory intended.

~

Nawaf al-Hazmi came to America to die. The 25-year-old had less than a year-and-a-half, and although he had traveled to Bosnia, Afghanistan, Yemen, and Chechnya, he was about to take his first steps on American soil. On January 15, 2000, he arrived from Bangkok, Thailand, walking off United Airlines Flight 2 into the Los Angeles International Airport's sunny terminal. He passed the sizzle of Burger

King and the sweet scents of Cinnabon. He bypassed the Last Stop News Shop.

He likely wasn't daunted by Los Angeles' jumble of bustle and noise. His hometown of Mecca, Saudi Arabia, swells each year to four times' Los Angeles' population during the Hajj pilgrimage, when more than 13 million Muslims visit Islam's holiest city.

Al-Hazmi barely knew English. His childhood friend, Khalid al-Mihdhar, who traveled with him, did not grasp the language either. But they wouldn't let that imperil their version of the American dream. They had overcome larger obstacles before, from fighting in Bosnia and Chechnya to attacking the Afghan Northern Alliance side-by-side with Taliban soldiers.

Money was not going to be an issue, thanks to financing from back home. Together, they applied for drivers' licenses and credit cards, traveled to San Diego, and rented Unit number 150 at the Parkwood Apartments, a compound of chunky light-colored stucco buildings with 175 units.

On February 25, 2000, they bought the 1988 blue Toyota Corolla for $2,300 and eventually registered it in al-Hazmi's name, federal investigators would later confirm. The Corolla was their vehicle to a better life: Al-Hazmi wanted to be a pilot. The Saudi grocer's son had even mail-ordered the training video "How an Airline Captain Should Look and Act." He had a few destinations in mind—perhaps New York City, maybe Washington, D.C.

Not much about this car—pre-February 25, 2000—would matter in 19 months. Not the fact that it once shone like a sapphire rolling off the factory floor, or that it probably was in desperate need of an oil change, or that an Australian auto report gave the 1988 model a worse-than-average safety rating while it received an "acceptable" rating in the United States.

Safety was no longer a priority.

~

The Toyota Corolla was nonetheless dependable, and it would take al-Hazmi and al-Mihdhar to play soccer in the park, to pray at the mosque, and to learn how to fly at two flight school classes in the spring of 2000. Still, the men couldn't break through the language barrier enough to continue training, so they signed up for English classes at the Language Instruction Centrum, across the inlet from Sea World, where the men had season passes.

The four-door Toyota took them to get carry-out at Papa John's Pizza, to shop at Old Navy, Wal-Mart, Macy's, and the Sunglass Hut, and to collect money wired from the Middle East to Bank of America branches in California.

Sometimes, al-Hazmi would linger in the complex's parking lot while the Toyota was idle, talking on his cell phone rather than using the phone in the apartment, according to federal documents.

A few months later, to save money, the pair used the compact car to move their sparse belongings to a cheaper rental home in Lemon Grove, California, a dusty hilltop dotted with palm trees and chain link fences. But al-Hazmi was becoming frustrated after flunking out of two flight schools in San Diego; the English lessons still weren't helping much, and time ticked toward a deadline.

So in December, the Toyota rumbled along the highway to Mesa, Arizona, to let al-Hazmi and al-Mihdhar try their luck at a different flight school. They moved into an apartment at the Indian Springs Village, just a few blocks north of the Fiesta Mall on Superstition Highway. It wasn't a great place to spend four of your last 10 months alive—residents often complained to police and on the Internet about the drug dealing, the roaches, and burglaries. It's likely that several of the Toyota's dings and scrapes were inflicted while it sat in the parking lot at night.

Still intent on flying, al-Hazmi drove the Toyota to Wide World of Maps to purchase charts: a National Geographic road atlas, two Unique Media maps—one of the United States and one of New York City—and a World aeronautical chart covering the entire northeastern United States.

Yet, for all his preparation, al-Hazmi just wasn't meant to fly. He couldn't even stay in a flight school class long enough to get the basics, let alone learn the intricate, difficult maneuvers required to navigate a Boeing 757, especially those needed to steer one into the Pentagon. Al-Mihdhar had gone back to the Middle East. For now, al-Hazmi was grounded, left only to be a "muscle" hijacker, subduing or killing uncooperative passengers.

He now depended on the Toyota, his unwitting accomplice, to help carry out preparations for mass murder.

~

Most drivers would not risk running a thirteen-year-old car across the country, but al-Hazmi—with his 154-pound, five-foot-five frame fitting easily in the compact car—would take it clear to the East Coast, with stops in Oklahoma, Florida, Virginia, Connecticut, New Jersey, and Maryland.

The trip included simple pit stops and ordinary outings. On March 10, 2001, with highs in the 50s and snow still on the ground, the Toyota wound through the Grand Canyon National Park after al-Hazmi paid the $20 entry fee, giving him a tour of what President Theodore Roosevelt said "every American should see."

In a cruel twist, on April Fools' Day, the Toyota, speeding along an Oklahoma highway, was pulled over by a state trooper who checked to see if the Corolla was stolen, looked up al-Hazmi's record, and issued a speeding ticket and summons for not wearing a seat belt. According to records, the police officer then sent the Toyota on its way.

On July 4, 2001, in the dusk hours before the fireworks began and after the parades had wrapped up, the Toyota steered into Newark Airport terminal B to drop off one of al-Hazmi's colleagues, someone who would die the same day: Mohamed Atta.

Atta had succeeded where al-Hazmi struggled, successfully learning how to fly. He now controlled their operation in America, and he would later take over the cockpit on American Airlines Flight 11 and steer it into the North Tower of the World Trade Center.

The two would meet over the course of several months to make plans, transfer money, and conduct surveillance flights—watching when cockpit doors would typically open, exploring weaknesses in boarding and airline procedures. They would take separate flights and meet in Las Vegas; al-Hazmi would travel back to Baltimore/Washington International Airport alone.

Al-Hazmi stayed in Laurel, Maryland, where he settled the Toyota at the Budget Host Valencia Motel on Washington Boulevard, which connects Baltimore to the nation's capital. The Toyota would come in handy to run al-Hazmi from Room 343 to places investigators found he was preparing for the attack: to a nearby Mailbox Etc., to public library computers to check his Yahoo e-mail account, to Gold's Gym to build up his muscles so he could overpower passengers, and to Target to purchase a Leatherman Wave box-cutter multi-tool. Sometimes he took the Toyota on longer drives, including several to Skyline Butcher in Falls Church, Virginia, a market that sells bulk meat. Days before the attack, he drove to a local Kinko's, where he surfed Travelocity's website and purchased a ticket for Flight 77—which would depart on September 11, 2001.

Al-Hazmi did occasionally abandon the Corolla in favor of a rental car – sometimes a cinnamon Chrysler Concorde, sometimes a Chrysler Sebring—but he would return to the Toyota when he needed it most.

The morning of September 11, 2001, al-Hazmi donned a blue shirt, khakis, and dress shoes. He shaved his mustache according to the rules for preparing the body for death. He drove the Toyota to the hourly parking lot in front of the glass-plated front of Dulles International Airport's main terminal at 7:25 a.m. He walked through security. Al-Mihdhar, back in the United States, would later join him on board. Video shows both men would set off metal detectors. Al-Hazmi set off two. A screener passed a wand over his body while another checked his luggage. They cleared him to board Flight 77, and he sat in first-class seat 5E. At 8:20 a.m., the airplane took off, bound for Los Angeles, the city where al-Hazmi took his first steps in America.

Twenty-seven minutes later, Atta plowed his aircraft into the North Tower of the World Trade Center in New York at more than 450 miles per hour. Sixteen minutes later, a second plane hit the South Tower. Meanwhile, Flight 77 took an unauthorized turn to the south.

At 9:37 a.m., al-Hazmi, al-Mihdhar, and three other terrorists took control of the plane. Several years of simple, incremental, planned movements culminated with a shift of the plane's yoke, which slammed the American Airlines jet into the Pentagon, killing 184 of the 2,753 people murdered in the largest terrorist attack in the United States.

~

Before September 11, 2001, Americans rarely considered the use of simple instruments of utility as means to this kind of end. By design, a box cutter helps unpack a crib for the new nursery. An airplane brings husbands safely back from business trips. A Toyota Corolla shuttles college students to dorm rooms and back home again.

Al-Hazmi and the other 9/11 hijackers changed the rules that govern our sense of safety at home, our trust in travel, and the way we search for clues to understand this new form of warfare—and defense.

By the morning of September 12, the Toyota had been sunning quietly for more than twenty-four hours in Row G of a lot meant for quick pick-ups and drop-offs. All across the country that day, airline flights were canceled. So a single car sitting in the hourly lot when there was no air traffic drew the suspicions of Dulles Airport Security personnel, who alerted the FBI. By 3:45 p.m., the Toyota was surrounded. Investigators wearing raid jackets with "FBI" in bright yellow letters swarmed the car, photographed it, towed it, and examined its most intimate areas—in the folds lining the trunk, in crevices between the seats.

All along, the Toyota had been collecting secrets. The small interior held more than fifty documents that detailed the seemingly benign preparations for September 11, 2001: packing slips, checkbooks, a Fry's Club VIP shoppers card, a library flyer, books in Arabic, ATM receipts, calling cards, four-color diagrams of a Boeing 757 instrument panel, a box cutter, store and restaurant receipts, a Flight 77 travel itinerary for al-Mihdhar, and a piece of paper with "Osama 5895316."

The car gave up a letter handwritten in Arabic, which federal investigators translated into English, with instructions for the hijackers' last night, the "second step," and the "third phase." It told the men to shave all excess hair, shower, and forget something called "this world." It asked the men to reflect: "Shouldn't we take advantage of these last hours to offer good deeds and obedience?"

They were told to bless their luggage, clothes, the knife. Al-Hazmi surely followed the instructions to "remember God constantly while in the car."

"Do not seem confused or show signs of nervous tension," the letter commanded. "Be happy, optimistic, calm because you are heading for a deed that God loves and will accept."

"Clench your teeth. ... Shout 'Allahu Akbar,' because it strikes fear in the hearts of the non-believers. ... Strike above the neck. Strike at all of their extremities. ... Take prisoners and kill them. ... Do not cause the discomfort of those you are killing. ... If everything goes well, every one of you should pat the other on the shoulder in confidence."

Then, the letter promises, they will all meet in the highest heaven.

~

For the Toyota, however, everything went dark. For nine years, it sat in an FBI warehouse of evidence, a forgotten player.

Then, a crane hoisted the Corolla into the second floor of the FBI headquarters in Washington, D.C., to be part of its 9/11 exhibit. Today, the car's taillights back up to an exterior wall. Its headlights stare at a column that bears a photo collage of more than fifty 9/11 victims, whose unsuspecting faces smile back at the Toyota.

The Nation's Capital, a repository of our country's sometimes violent history, features dozens of museums—from the Smithsonian to the United States Holocaust Memorial Museum—that showcase objects of war and tragedy, items easily identified as instruments of destruction or death: guns, knives, bomb casings, an embroidered Nazi swastika on a soldier's uniform.

But the Toyota shows us that it is not always easy to identify the enemy, especially one so familiar, so mundane, parked squarely in our midst. Within the 9/11 museum's wreckage—bits of concrete from the Pentagon, burnt metal shards of United Flight 175, a twisted New York

City lamp post—this "non-descript" Toyota Corolla is the clearest reminder of the simple driving forces of evil.

Gunslinging

Angela Morales

In the days before we could dial 9-1-1, I would have to speak with the operator and ask, "Can you give me the police department?" and the same woman, each time, would reply, "Certainly. I'll transfer you now," and I would be whispering hurry hurry hurry and listening for the thump of footsteps behind me, and I just knew that the operator must be taking her sweet time—fumbling absentmindedly with the cable, twirling in her chair, polishing her nails, and then finally, FINALLY, plugging the cable into the correct slot. A bored-sounding desk cop would then pick up, and I'd need to explain myself. How I despised my voice back then—so rehearsed and robotic. Those words made me ashamed of myself for failing at language, and at other things I couldn't name. I'd say, in my flat, ugly voice: My dad is beating up my mom.

The words, though true enough, were imprecise. "My" being a descriptor of "dad" never felt altogether accurate, even though, biologically-speaking, he was indeed my father, but he did not belong to me, in the way that some dads belong to their daughters or vice-versa. Another problem existed with the present participle verb "is beating up," which implied that he was, at that very moment, pummeling her with his fists over and over like Rocky Balboa slugging it out with Spider Rico after Spider had already crouched in surrender and was shielding his face with his gloves. "Beating up," although accurate to a degree, did not capture the subtlety of the day-after-day—the constant mind-numbing nature of the fight, the petty haranguing, the ebb and flow of the action itself: first escalation, followed by climax, and to use literary terms—a denouement— followed always by eerie silences and another surprise climax, no resolution in sight.

Furthermore, the object of the sentence—mom—was the passive vessel upon which the subject (dad) was acting. In addition, the verb "Beating up" implied that mom was further being acted upon and unable to fight back, which to an extent was certainly true, but did not adequately portray my mother as a three-dimensional human being with free will and an ability to make choices, both good and bad. (Consider: the Ex-Lax Hot Chocolate, a box of sugar in the gas tank, the dog-shit burrito). Of course I could not have articulated any of this at the time, though I am certain that this is how I felt.

Anyway, after I said that initial sentence, My dad is beating up my mom, the cop would say, "Stay on the line with me, okay?" and I'd say, "Um. I really can't." The cop, then, so as not reveal alarm, would say, "Listen, if you need to hang up, go right ahead and do that. We're on our way." Minutes later, as promised, two barrel-chested police officers would appear on our front porch, rapping on the front door with their billy clubs, their gorgeous badges gleaming in the sunlight. Police Officers! Open Up! One time my mother looked at me and sighed, disappointed that I'd called the police. She told me that, actually, I should have called my father's parents instead of the police. Her logic: at least his parents would feign disgust. They'd judge him and use words like shame and disgrace. Es la verguenza! The police, she reasoned, would only further infuriate my father. He'd get thrown into a jail cell; he'd call his brother Eddie; Eddie would bail him out; he'd return home, madder than ever. Also, my mother hated having to give a report to the police and then having to decide whether or not to press charges. She'd always be wearing nothing but a thin, clingy nightgown, no time to grab a robe much less put on some lipstick or drag a brush through the hair. Plus, they'd want to examine her bare arms, her neck. Plus, our neighbors on Country Club Drive seemed to enjoy standing on the sidewalk and staring at the police car and our house—children and adults alike. In our all-white neighborhood, they would gather with crossed arms, squinting beyond the sun's glare toward our front door, acting like they were one-hundred-percent entitled to stare, as if staring at my house and whatever emerged from it was no different than staring at elephants in the zoo. My mother said that they thought we were a bunch of dumb, dirty, low-class Mexicans. But I did not care. I liked the handcuffs, the starched black uniforms, the static of the radios clipped onto the shoulders, and the contrast between the supposed good guys and my father—in his threadbare Hanes t-shirt, polyester pants and work shoes, no socks—who always emerged from our house looking like an escapee from the local mental hospital as he was led to the back of the patrol car.

These police officers—always male—went out of their way to be nice to me. They talked in soft voices and asked for my side of the story. They sat with me on the couch, pens in hand, recording all my words onto little notepads. They said things like, Don't be afraid to tell the truth. I felt vindicated, then, even if only for a few minutes, knowing someone had listened to me and that someone could hear about the things I'd been seeing for years on the other side of our fat yellow roses and lush lawn.

But my mother was right. What good were those accounts, in the end? My words seemed to have evaporated into thin air. I didn't know what it meant to press charges or why the police did not lock up my father for more than a few hours at a time. Soon I learned that calling the police was useless, even more dangerous. And if my father always came right back home, faster than zombies in Dawn of the Dead, what was the point?

One day I called up the other set of grandparents—my mother's parents—and minutes later, Grandpa screeched up in his rattling, beat-up Ford pick-up truck. When my father opened the front door, Grandpa pointed his hunting rifle directly at my father's face. Grandpa's hands were shaking, and he said, "Son of a bitch." I stood there, frozen in place and dumb as a potted plant, half-hoping Grandpa would pull the trigger, fascinated by my father's rapt attention.

Not long after that, I pulled out the drawers of my father's built-in dresser, climbed up them like a ladder, and reached around in the highest cabinet until I felt cool gunmetal— his .22 pistol. I pulled it out and, balancing on the edge of a drawer, pointed the gun at my father's back as he held my mother by the hair. "Hey," I said, wanting to give him fair warning. (Never shoot a man in the back—I knew that much). When he turned around, he did a double take. His face went suddenly slack and pale, but he chuckled nervously and I, too, had earned his rapt attention, maybe for the first (and last) time in my life. Just like in all those Clint Eastwood and Charles Bronson movies that he had taken me to see (although I would have much preferred The Apple Dumpling Gang or The Shaggy D.A.), I said, "One move and I'll blow your goddamned head off." He said, "Ha ha, Angie, that's funny. Now put that thing down. That's not a toy. That thing's for real."

"No shit," I said, steady on the aim, just like I'd learned from Charles Bronson, right between the eyes. I felt that I'd been pushed to the edge of a cliff—I felt crazy from the aforementioned ebb and flow, like I wanted to live on dry land, no ebb, no flow. I did not really want to kill him. I just needed him, at that moment, to be erased from my life. From our lives. "Okay, not funny," he said. "Quit fooling around, now. I'm serious."

My finger grazed the trigger—a lovely, terrifying pulse—no tension, just a fraction-of-an-inch of freefall and then slight pressure—the threshold between one existence and another. Will it be curtain number one or curtain number two? Of course I did not know a thing about guns, whether they needed to be cocked or whether they came with some safety latch, but the expression on my father's face suggested that I was, indeed, on the right track. As I balanced on the edge of the drawer between two possibilities—my eyes on my father, my finger poised on the trigger—my mother appeared white and glowing in my peripheral vision. She glided closer, soft as a ghost, and said somewhere near my left ear in a low, gentle voice that made me look at her, for the certainty and conviction that I heard her words had startled me from my gun-slinging trance: "Listen to me," she said. "Do NOT ruin your life. He's not worth it. They'll take you away to Sybil Brand and I'll never see you again."

I knew Sybil Brand, alright. Sybil Brand, a maximum security prison for women, housed criminals like Susan Atkins, member of the Manson Family. We'd always driven by that massive hilltop structure en route to my paternal grandparents' house. Sometimes we'd see sixty-mile-per-hour flashes of orange-jumpsuit-clad women outside in the yard, many of them leaning against a barbed-wire fence, probably bragging about their crimes. I'd always feared that one day my mother would end up there, the syntactical structure being, She shot him, rather than He shot her—"she" being the actor—"he" being the acted upon. I was surprised, then, by my mother's warning, for I had not thought that I could end up in prison, too. Children must assume that because they are children, adults will protect them no matter what, even if they have killed someone. And perhaps I hadn't thought that this sort of killing was actually a crime; I had just thought of shooting my father as a practical solution to an ongoing problem. So in deciding whether or not to pull the trigger, I suddenly glimpsed myself—clear as a photograph—youngest girl in Sybil Brand—Eleven-Year-Old Girl Shoots Father. How quickly the brain weighs the pros and cons. Pros: he's gone. Cons: an explosion, blood splatter, sirens, police, child psychologists, a trial, traumatized siblings, a distraught mother. I'm led from the house in handcuffs, head bowed, neighbors watching. Like in those dreams when one person is at the same time another person, I would become my father, he would become me.

I remember how he stood there reaching for the gun and breathing heavily, his bloodshot eyes darting back and forth, his life one of take, take, take, a person as mysterious to me as any stranger. I knew then that I did not want his life—it would have to end some other way.

Rigor Mortis

William Arthur Delaney

I opened the door and called, "Ken?"

He always left it unlocked. He was too weak and past caring. Not that he had many visitors. In the short time he had lived in our building he had antagonized everybody. He thought he was better than they were. He had been an accomplished pianist and had consorted with famous people.

He did have a few callers—visiting nurses, social welfare workers, volunteers from Meals on Wheels, and a man from the pharmacy who brought medications Ken rarely took as directed. There were pills on the floor, pills on his bed, and unopened plastic vials all over. An old man's legacy: pills and bills.

I was his only regular visitor. In a building full of old people, we all needed at least one friend who would make sure we were still alive. Otherwise, a man or woman could lie dead until somebody complained about the smell in the hallway.

Once again I called, "Ken?"

I knew what I was going to see. I didn't want to see it, but now there was no turning back.

He was sitting on a wooden chair with one forearm on the dinette table. His chin was touching his chest. His face was drained of color. In his classic pose of total defeat he looked like Picasso's emaciated "Old Guitarist."

Ken had congestive heart failure, a condition which caused him to blank out whenever blood stopped pumping to his brain. He had lost consciousness and his heart had stopped pumping forever. When I tried to shake his shoulder, his whole body rocked back and forth. I felt the marble coldness halfway to my elbow.

A woman later asked me, "Weren't you scared?"

My feelings were far more complicated than that. I felt surprised. I felt a little uncanny. I felt guilty because I hadn't checked on him the day before. I felt relieved because he wasn't my responsibility anymore. I felt some pity for the old man who had nobody but me, a mere acquaintance, to pay this visit. I felt older and wiser. This was what death looked like.

I also admired him. After all, he was terminally ill. He knew it. The fact that he had gotten through it all by himself made him seem that much more courageous.

In addition to my other feelings, I envied the dead man. He had not only escaped from life but from these bone-white walls, thrift-store furniture, unpaid bills, unwashed dishes, and congealed leftovers in the refrigerator.

Lastly, it occurred to me that someday my daughter would have to empty my own little apartment, which wouldn't look too much different to her than this place did to me. What will she keep? What will she sell? What will she give away? What will she throw out? An old man's books and letters. An old man's bed. An old man's worn leather chair. An old man's clothes, all out of fashion, or never in fashion. An old man's personal possessions, most of them with meaning and value only for him. I would be sorry to leave my daughter with the problems--but I would be free of them forever.

I was talking to a man from Cuba when we saw three men in black wheeling a body bag past the laundry-room windows. The Cuban uttered something in Spanish, quickly turned away and made the sign of the cross on his forehead, chest and shoulders.

There was no other ceremony for the deceased.

CONTRIBUTORS

Maureen Alsop is the author of *Apparition Wren*. The collection was recently translated into Spanish by Mario Dominguez Parra from Tenerife, Spain. Collaborative poems with Joshua have appeared at *Switchback*, *Yemassee*, *Inertia*, and others. www.maureenalsop.com

Ned Balbo received the 2010 Donald Justice Prize, selected by A.E. Stallings, for *The Trials of Edgar Poe and Other Poems* (Story Line Press/WCU Poetry Center). His previous books include *Lives of the Sleepers* (U. of Notre Dame Press, Ernest Sandeen Prize and ForeWord Book of the Year gold medal) and *Galileo's Banquet* (WWPH, Towson University Prize). He is also the author of a chapbook, *Something Must Happen* (Finishing Line Press). He has received three Maryland Arts Council grants, the Robert Frost Foundation Poetry Award, and the John Guyon Literary Nonfiction Prize. He teaches at Loyola University Maryland.

Linda Barnhart is a native of Pennsylvania and a graduate of Albright College in Reading. She has published fiction in *Homestead Review*, *Columbia*, *Potomac Review*, *Pearl*, *Five Finger Reviews* and *Orchid A Literary Review*. In 2007 she was awarded second place in the Tonka Prize sponsored by the Minnetonka Review. In 2008 she was one of the Wordstock Ten—finalists for the Wordstock Short Fiction Competition. She and her husband are active in historic preservation efforts and reside in the historic village of Charming Forge.

Harry Bauld is from Medford, Massachusetts. He won the 2008 *New Millenium Writings* poetry prize, and his poems have appeared in *Nimrod*, *Southern Poetry Review*, *The Southeast Review*, *Verse Daily*, *Whiskey Island*, *The Binnacle*, and *Deliberately Thirsty* (Edinburgh), among others. He has taught and coached baseball, basketball and boxing at high schools in Vermont and New York and currently teaches in the Bronx.

Christina Cook is the author of *Lake Effect*, a chapbook of poems published by Finishing Line Press. Her work has appeared in *Prairie Schooner*, *New Ohio Review*, *Crab Orchard Review*, *Hayden's Ferry Review*, and *Cimarron Review*, among other journals. She holds an MFA from the Vermont College of Fine Arts and is a contributing editor for *Inertia Magazine* and *Cerise Press*. Christina is the senior writer for the president of Dartmouth College.

J. Marie Darden-Obi is an Assistant Professor of English at the Community College of Baltimore County, in Baltimore, MD, where she teaches Creative Writing, Composition, and Developmental Writing. She rekindled her love of poetry as part of a recent sabbatical project where she aimed to become either profound or succinct. The plan was not completely successful, as she still manages somehow to be long-winded and silly, but she was able to develop two chapbooks of poetry: *Remuneration for 1973* and *Psalms from her Volcano: God, Water Love*. A veteran fictionista in a newfound poet's blouse, Ms. Darden has two fiction novels in circulation, *Enemy Fields* and *Finding Dignity*, as well as several short stories published by Simon and Schuster's Strebor Books. Her poems are available or forthcoming in a few journals, including *Welter* Magazine. She holds an M.A. in English Education from The Johns Hopkins University.

William Arthur Delaney is a native Californian who graduated from UCLA. He has worked in insurance, advertising, real estate, and other fields while supporting a growing family and writing when he could find time. He has published hundreds of short pieces, including eighteen peer-reviewed literary essays in *The Explicator*. Now retired, he devotes his time to writing and has published in *The Christian Science Monitor*, *The Sun*, *South Dakota Review*, *Berkeley Fiction Review*, *The Writer*, *Writer's Digest*, *The Armchair Detective*, *Crime: Das Krimi Journal*, *The Iconoclast*, *L.A. West*, *Calliope*, *Neologisms*, and elsewhere.

Jen Murvin Edwards' stories have appeared or are forthcoming in *The MacGuffin*, *Palooka*, *Moon City Review*, and *Huizache* literary journals, and she was a Finalist in *Glimmer Train's* 2010 Very Short Fiction Contest. She has published in the comic book series *Chickasaw Adventures*, *Stories of the Saints*, and McGraw-Hill's *World History Ink*. A native of Southern California and alumnus of the Squaw Valley Community of Writers (2011), Jen currently teaches creative writing and graphic narrative at Missouri State University in Springfield, MO, where she resides with her husband and young son.

Joshua Gottlieb-Miller is the recipient of a 2012 Inprint Barthelme Prize in Poetry, awarded at the University of Houston. He has also received scholarships and fellowships from Sewanee Writers' Conference and the Bucknell Seminar for Younger Poets. His work has appeared or is forthcoming in *The Journal*, *The Birmingham Review*, *Linebreak* and elsewhere. His collaborative work with Maureen Alsop has appeared in *Switchback*, *Poetry Salzburg Review*, *Yemassee*, and elsewhere.

Nathan Gower holds a M.F.A. in Writing from Spalding University and currently serves as an Assistant Professor of English at Campbellsville University in Louisville, Kentucky. A writer of fiction, poetry, and critical essays, his work has appeared in various literary and academic journals, most recently including *The Birmingham Arts Journal*, *The Atrium*, *Paradigm*, and elsewhere. He lives with his wife and two daughters in Charlestown, Indiana.

Josh Green's work has appeared in *The Los Angeles Review*, *The MacGuffin*, *Atlanta* Magazine, *The Adirondack Review*, *New South*, *Lake Effect*, *The Midway Journal*, *Eclipse*, and elsewhere. By day, he's a freelance magazine writer and award-winning crime reporter with a metro Atlanta newspaper. By night, he's shopping his first collection of short fiction, a 2011 finalist for the St. Lawrence Book Award.

Brandon Hartley holds an M.F.A. from the University of Florida and was nominated for a Pushcart Prize. Once a high school English teacher, he currently lives and works as a freelance writer in Tampa, Florida.

Shira Hereld is a freshman at the George Washington University, majoring in Theater with a double minor in Political Science and Creative Writing. Her poetry has appeared in Choate Rosemary Hall's *The Lit*, in the print copy of *Teen Ink*, and has received an award from the National Council for Jewish Women.

Paul Hostovsky is the author of 3 books of poetry, *Bending the Notes*, *Dear Truth*, and *A Little in Love a Lot*. He has won a Pushcart Prize and been featured on *Poetry Daily*, *Verse Daily*, *The Writer's Almanac*, and *Best of the Net 2008* and *2009*. To read more of his work, visit his website: www.paulhostovsky.com

Marc Hudson's work has appeared in *The Seattle Review*, *Qarrtsiuni*, *Echo Ink Review* and *Hot Metal Bridge*. His story "Timo's Creations" was nominated for a Pushcart Prize. He writes and builds gardens for other people in southern New Hampshire.

Lockie Hunter is from a town in Appalachia where oral storytelling is vital to the community. She holds an M.F.A. in fiction from Emerson College in Boston and teaches creative writing at Warren Wilson College where she is the faculty advisor for the Swannanoa Journal weekly public radio program of the Environmental Leadership Center. Her nonfiction can be found in many publications including *The Christian Science Monitor*, *Brevity*, *Quarter After Eight*, *Opium*, *The Morning News*, *McSweeneys Internet Tendency* and others. Her poetry and fiction have been anthologized.

Shiah IrgangLaden is a nursery school teacher in Baltimore City. He studied creative writing at Goucher College and has a few pieces published around the Internet. In his work, he tries to grasp on to tiny moments in life that carry too much weight.

Tim Kahl [http://www.timkahl.com] is the author of *Possessing Yourself* (Word Tech, 2009) and *The Century of Travel* (Word Tech, 2012). His work has been published in *Prairie Schooner*, *Indiana Review*, *Ninth Letter*, *Notre Dame Review*, *The Journal*, *Parthenon West Review*, and many other journals in the U.S. He appears as Victor Schnickelfritz at the poetry and poetics blog *The Great American Pinup* (http://greatamericanpinup.wordpress.com/) and the poetry video blog *Linebreak Studios* [http://linebreakstudios.blogspot.com/]. He is also editor of Bald Trickster Press and Clade Song [http://www.cladesong.com]. He is the vice president and events coordinator of The Sacramento Poetry Center. He currently houses his father's literary estate—one volume: Robert Gerstmann's book of photos of Chile, 1932).

W. Todd Kaneko lives and writes in Grand Rapids, Michigan. His stories and poems can be seen in *Puerto Del Sol*, *Crab Creek Review*, *Fairy Tale Review*, *Los Angeles Review*, *Southeast Review*, *Blackbird*, and elsewhere. He has received fellowships from Kundiman and the Kenyon Review Writer's Workshop. He teaches at Grand Valley State University.

Michael Kimball is the author of four books, including *Dear Everybody* (which *The Believer* calls "a curatorial masterpiece") and, most recently, *Us* (which *Time Out Chicago* calls "a simply gorgeous and astonishing book"). His work has been on NPR's *All Things Considered* and in *Vice*, as well as *The Guardian*, *Bomb*, and *New York Tyrant*. His work has been translated into a dozen languages and he is also responsible for *Michael Kimball Writes Your Life Story (on a postcard)*. His new novel, *Big Ray*, will be published by Bloomsbury on September 18, 2012.

Peter Kispert is an undergraduate student currently living in New Hampshire, where he is Editor-in-Chief of *Aegis* and *Sandpaper*, the campus literary magazines. His work has appeared or is forthcoming in *South Dakota Review*, *PANK Magazine*, *Painted Bride Quarterly*, *Pear Noir!*, and others. He has worked with *The Adirondack Review*, *Mud Luscious Press*, *Monkeybicycle*, and *The Medulla Review*.

Dorianne Laux's most recent collections are *The Book of Men* and *Facts about the Moon*. A finalist for the National Book Critics Circle Award, and winner of the Oregon Book Award and The Roanoke-Chowan Award for Poetry, Laux is also author of *Awake*, *What We Carry*, and *Smoke* from BOA Editions, as well as a fine press edition, *The Book of Women*, from Red Dragonfly Press. She teaches poetry in the MFA Program at North Carolina State University and is founding faculty at Pacific University's Low Residency MFA Program.

David Dodd Lee has published six previous full-length books of poems, including *Orphan, Indiana* (Akron, 2010), *The Nervous Filaments* (Four Way Books, 2010), *Abrupt Rural* (New Issues, 2004) and *Arrow Pointing North* (Four Way, 2002). *Sky Booths in the Breath Somewhere*, *The Ashbery Erasure Poems* (BlazeVox, 2010) appeared as well in 2010.

Beth Lefebvre earned a M.A. in writing at Johns Hopkins University. She is a former newspaper reporter and editor, and her work has appeared in *Cobalt Review* and *Urbanite* magazine. She resides in Halethorpe, Maryland.

Christopher Lowe is the author of the short story collection *Those Like Us* (SFASU Press, 2011). His fiction and poetry have appeared widely in journals including *Third Coast*, *Bellevue Literary Review*, *Sport Literate*, and *War, Literature, and* *the Arts*. He serves as editor for *Trigger* and as an assistant fiction editor for *Fifth Wednesday Journal*.

Al Maginnes's most recent books are *Ghost Alphabet* (White Pine Press, 2008), winner of the 2007 White Pine Poetry Prize, and two chapbooks published in 2010, *Between States* (Main Street Rag) and *Greatest Hits 1987-2010* (Pudding House Publications). He has work appearing or forthcoming in *Brilliant Corners, Tar River Poetry, Platte Valley Review, Harpur Palate, Asheville Poetry Review, Verdad, Poem, Cimmaron Review*, and many others. He lives in Raleigh, North Carolina and teaches at Wake Technical Community College.

Heather Martin teaches at the University of Denver and co-curates the Gypsy House Reading Series. Her work has appeared in *Matter, Cold Mountain Review, DoubleRoom*, and *Electric Velocipede*. "On Maimeó" is an excerpt from a longer work concerned with female sexuality, obsession, and petrology.

Jen Michalski's novel *The Tide King* is forthcoming from Black Lawrence Press (2013; winner of the Big Moose Prize), and her collection of novellas is forthcoming from Dzanc (2013). She is the author of two collections of fiction, *Close Encounters* (So New, 2007) and *From Here* (Aqueous Books, 2013). Her work has been nominated for the Pushcart Prize. She also is the editor of the anthology *City Sages: Baltimore* (CityLit Press 2010), which won a 2010 "Best of Baltimore" award from *Baltimore Magazine*. Finally, she is the founding editor of the literary quarterly *jmww*, a co-host of the monthly reading series The 510 Readings and the biannual Lit Show in Baltimore, and interviews writers at *The Nervous Breakdown*.

Ryan Millbern is a copywriter at Richard Harrison Bailey/The Agency, a marketing firm in Indianapolis, Indiana. His stories and essays have appeared in *Notre Dame Magazine, Designer, Fogged Clarity, The Catalonian Review, Staccato Fiction* and *Thought Catalog*. He lives in Brownsburg, Indiana, with his wife, their two children and their yellow lab. You can follow him on Twitter @ryanmillbern.

Angela Morales' recent work has appeared in *The Southern Review, The Los Angeles Review, The Southwest Review, River Teeth*, and *Arts and Letters*. She teaches English at Glendale College and is working on an essay collection about growing up in Los Angeles. She lives with her husband and two children in Pasadena, California. Currently, she does not own a gun.

Mary Morris has won the Rita Dove Award and New Mexico Discovery Award. Her work has been published in *Quarterly West, Indiana Review, Blue Mesa Review, Gargoyle, Poet Lore*, and *Southern Humanities Review*. She has read her work at the Library of Congress, for the program, 'The Poet and the Poem.' Morris has lived most of her life in Santa Fe, NM where she can be contacted at Water400@aol.com

Devin Murphy's recent work appears in *The Cimarron Review*, *The Greensboro Review*, *The Michigan Quarterly Review*, *The Missouri Review*, and *Shenandoah* among others. He has recently completed his PhD at the University of Nebraska—Lincoln and is finishing a story collection and a novel.

Wendy Oleson is a Senior Fiction Reader for *Prairie Schooner*. Her recent work appears in *Copper Nickel*, *Fifth Wednesday Journal*, and *Rattle*.

Catherine Parnell teaches writing and literature at Suffolk University in Boston, as well as the occasional seminar at Grub Street in Boston. She's the fiction editor for *Salamander* and an associate editor for *Consequence Magazine*. Her non-fiction chapbook, *The Kingdom of His Will*, was published in 2007; recent and forthcoming publications include stories and reviews in *Post Road*, *Slush Pile*, *roger*, *Diverse Voices Quarterly*, *Fiction Daily*, *Dos Passos Review*, *Painted Bride Quarterly*, *Salamander*, *Stone's Throw Magazine*, *Consequence*, *The Poetry Dress Project 2011* and *Another Book*, as well as various newspapers and newsletters.

Steven Pelcman was born and resided in New York, then relocated to New Orleans, and on to Los Angeles before coming to Europe in 1997. He is a writer of poetry and short stories who has spent the past few years completing the novels titled *Riverbed* and *Spending Time* and books of poems titled, *Where the Leaves Darken* and *Like Water to Stone*. He has been published in a number of magazines including: *The Windsor Review*, *Paris/Atlantic*, *The Innisfree Poetry Journal*, *Voxhumana magazine*, *Nomad's Choir*, *Fourth River* magazine, *River Oak Review*, *Salzburg Poetry Review*, *Caffeine Magazine* and many others. He has been nominated for the 2012 Pushcart Prize. Steven has spent the last thirteen years residing in Germany where he teaches in academia and is a language communications trainer and consultant.

Andrew Purcell lives and works in Upstate New York, where he enjoys hiking, fishing, and working with Bruce Smith to complete his M.F.A. thesis at Syracuse University. His work has appeared in *Forge*, among other publications. He misses Baltimore's Inner Harbor, one of his earliest inspirations for writing, and he deeply admires the work of Bruce Smith, Tony Hoagland, Patrick Lawler, and Caki Wilkinson, a graduate of the Johns Hopkins MFA program.

Colin Rafferty teaches nonfiction writing at the University of Mary Washington in Fredericksburg, Virginia. Other recent essays can be read in *Utne Reader*, *South Loop Review*, and *Witness*. He is married to the poet Elizabeth Wade.

Luke Rolfes grew up in Polk City, IA and now teaches at Northwest Missouri State University. He is a fiction editor at *The Laurel Review*, and his stories appear in *Passages North*, *Bat City Review*, *Connecticut Review*, and many others magazines.

Emily Jean Roller graduated from Yale in 2007. She is completing an MA in Writing at Johns Hopkins. Her first novella, *Hookers, Flankers and Locks* will be coming out this winter from Bare Knuckles Press.

Seth Sawyers has had essays appear in *The Baltimore Sun,* online at The Morning News, and in the literary journals *River Teeth, Fourth Genre, Crab Orchard Review, Ninth Letter, Quarterly West, Fugue,* and elsewhere. He has recently completed a memoir, about growing up in the hills of western Maryland, and is at work on a novel about a ten-foot-tall temporary office worker. He lives in Baltimore and teaches writing classes at the University of Maryland Baltimore County. He has an M.F.A. from Old Dominion University.

E. M. Schorb's work has appeared in *The American Scholar, The Sewanee Review, Southwest Review, Poetry Salzburg Review, The Yale Review, The Iowa Review, The Virginia Quarterly Review, The Antioch Review, Stand* and *Agenda* (England), *The Notre Dame Review, New York Quarterly,* and *Shenandoah,* among others.

Edgar Gabriel Silex is the author of two poetry collections from Curbstone. He has received fellowships from the National Endowment for the Arts, the National Endowment for the Humanities, and the Maryland State Arts Council. He lives in Laurel, Maryland.

Bram Takefman is a retired international trade executive who has spent much of his adult life overseas, living in places like England, Japan, and Peru. Fascinated and inspired by these foreign cultures, he now writes about the experiences and customs he has learned in his travels. An ex-Canadian, he now lives in the United States, where he is an amused spectator and confused participant. His writing has appeared in *The ILR Journal* (Northwestern University), *The Review* (National-Louis University), and *The Front Porch Review.*

Catherine Thomas was born and raised in Wales and now lives in Syracuse, NY. She holds an MA in English from the University of Rochester and has benefited from workshops held at the Syracuse Downtown Writer's Center. Her short stories have appeared or are forthcoming in such journals as *The Denver Quarterly, Fourteen Hills,* and *The Broome Review.*

Angela Narciso Torres was born in Brooklyn and raised in Manila. Her poems are available or forthcoming in *Cimarron Review, Crab Orchard Review, Cream City Review, North American Review, Rattle,* and other publications. She holds an MFA from Warren Wilson College and co-edits *RHINO.* She lives in Chicago.

Michelle Valois lives in western Massachusetts with her partner and their three children. Her writing has appeared or is forthcoming in *TriQuarterly, Brevity, Fourth Genre, Moon Milk Review, Florida Review, North American Review, Tattoo*

Highway, *Pank*, and others. She teaches writing and humanities at a community college.

Ajay Vishwanathan has been nominated multiple times for Pushcart and Best of The Net Anthology and has work published or forthcoming in over ninety literary journals, including *The Baltimore Review*, *Smokelong Quarterly*, *The Minnesota Review*, *Raleigh Review*, and *The Potomac*. He is the Chief Editor of the *Foundling Review*.

John Walser, a founding member of the Foot of the Lake Poetry Collective, is currently working on a full-length manuscript, *Edgewood Orchard Galleries*, as well as two chapbooks of poetry, *19 Skies* and *Liable to Flooding*. John holds a doctorate in English and Creative Writing from the University of Wisconsin-Milwaukee and is an associate professor of English at Marian University, in Fond du Lac, Wisconsin. His poetry has appeared and is forthcoming in a number of journals, including *The Colorado North Review*, *Barrow Street*, *Verse Wisconsin* and *The Evansville Review*.

Stephen J. West lives, writes, and teaches in Morgantown, West Virginia. He is also a columnist and creative nonfiction editor for *THIS Literary Magazine*.

Gregory J. Wolos's fiction has recently appeared or is forthcoming in *The Los Angeles Review*, *PANK*, *A Cappella Zoo*, *Jersey Devil Press*, *Waccamaw Journal*, *FRiGG*, *Storyglossia*, *elimae*, *Apple Valley Review*, *Underground Voices*, the anthology *Surreal South*, and other many journals. In the last year his stories have earned recognition in several competitions, including a 2012 *Pushcart Prize* nomination. He lives and writes on the northern bank of the Mohawk River in upstate New York. His website is: www.gregorywolos.com.

Also included in the Winter and Spring 2012 online issues:

Visual art by Andrew Abbot, Roger Camp, Chandler Oliphant, Ali Wisch, Christopher Woods

Music video by Nemo Shaw